THADDEUS STEVENS

BY

SAMUEL W. McCALL

BOSTON AND NEW YORK
HOUGHTON, MIFFLIN AND COMPANY
The Riverside Press, Cambridge
1899

Copyright, 1899,
By SAMUEL W. McCALL.

All rights reserved.

𝔖𝔱𝔞𝔫𝔡𝔞𝔯𝔡 𝔏𝔦𝔟𝔯𝔞𝔯𝔶 𝔈𝔡𝔦𝔱𝔦𝔬𝔫

AMERICAN STATESMEN

EDITED BY

JOHN T. MORSE, JR.

IN THIRTY-TWO VOLUMES
VOL. XXXI.

THE CIVIL WAR

THADDEUS STEVENS

American Statesmen

STANDARD LIBRARY EDITION

The Home of Thaddeus Stevens

HOUGHTON MIFFLIN & CO.

PREFACE

THADDEUS STEVENS was the unquestioned leader of the House of Representatives from July 4, 1861, when it assembled at the call of Lincoln, until his death, which occurred in 1868. The legislative work of that period stands unapproached in difficulty and importance in the history of Congress, if not, indeed, of any parliamentary body in the world. Stevens was the chairman of the Committee on Ways and Means during the war, and afterwards of the Committees on Appropriations and Reconstruction. He was, therefore, especially identified with the financial measures of the war, including the legal tender acts, also with reconstruction, with the great constitutional amendments, and with the impeachment of President Johnson. I have dwelt very slightly upon his connection, during the later period of his congressional service, with other matters, which, although some of them would have been of great consequence in ordinary times, were dwarfed and robbed of interest by the stupendous events with which they were associated.

The fact that no extended biography of Stevens has ever been published would have very greatly augmented the difficulty of my work had it not been for the assistance which has been generously given me. I desire especially to acknowledge my obligation to Hon. Marriott Brosius, who has for many years represented Stevens's former district in Congress; to Professor C. F. Richardson, of Dartmouth College; to Mr. C. B. Tillinghast, of the Massachusetts State Library; to Mr. A. R. Spofford and Mr. J. Q. Howard, of the Library of Congress; and to those two venerable and distinguished statesmen, the Hon. Henry L. Dawes and Hon. George S. Boutwell, who served with Stevens in Congress during the war period, and were intimately associated with him in most of the important legislation of that era.

S. W. McCall.

Washington, D. C., January 19, 1899.

CONTENTS

CHAP.   PAGE

    I. YOUTH 1

   II. THE LAW 19

  III. ENTRANCE INTO PUBLIC LIFE—FREE SCHOOLS   28

  IV. CONSTITUTIONAL CONVENTION—THE "BUCK-
      SHOT WAR"—ELECTED TO CONGRESS . 46

   V. CONGRESS—ANTI-SLAVERY SPEECHES . 66

  VI. RESUMES LAW PRACTICE—AGAIN RETURNED
      TO CONGRESS—CAMPAIGN OF 1860 . . 89

 VII. SECESSION—CHARACTER OF SLAVERY AGITA-
      TION 115

VIII. LEADER OF THE HOUSE 136

  IX. THE LEGAL TENDER 152

   X. WAR REVENUE MEASURES 174

  XI. WAR LEGISLATION 182

 XII. EMANCIPATION 210

XIII. THE BEGINNING OF RECONSTRUCTION . 229

XIV. THE JOHNSON PLAN 244

 XV. THE RUPTURE WITH THE PRESIDENT . 256

XVI. RECONSTRUCTION LEGISLATION AND ITS RE-
      SULTS 285

XVII. WIT AND OTHER CHARACTERISTICS . . 309

XVIII. THE IMPEACHMENT 323

XIX. LAST DAYS 349

    INDEX 355

ILLUSTRATIONS

THADDEUS STEVENS . . . . *Frontispiece*
> From a photograph lent by John B. McPherson,
> Esq., Gettysburg, Pa.
>
> Autograph from a MS. in the possession of Mr. Mc-
> Pherson.
>
> The vignette of Mr. Stevens's home, Lancaster, Pa.,
> is from photographs and drawings kindly furnished
> by the Hon. Marriott Brosius, Lancaster, Pa.   Page

BENJAMIN F. WADE . . . . *facing* 246
> From a photograph by Brady in the Library of the
> State Department at Washington.
>
> Autograph from the Chamberlain collection, Bos-
> ton Public Library.

ANDREW JOHNSON . . . . *facing* 324
> From a photograph by Brady in the Library of the
> State Department at Washington.
>
> Autograph from the Chamberlain collection, Bos-
> ton Public Library.

REVERDY JOHNSON . . . . *facing* 346
> From a photograph by Daniel Bendann, Baltimore,
> Md.
>
> Autograph from the Chamberlain collection, Bos-
> ton Public Library.

THADDEUS STEVENS

CHAPTER I

YOUTH

THADDEUS STEVENS, the son of Joshua and Sally Stevens, was born in Danville, Vermont, April 4, 1792. Not much is known of his ancestors, although enough to enable us to determine the character of the stock, which was evidently Anglo-Saxon. His parents removed from Methuen, in Essex County, Massachusetts, to Danville, about the year 1786, with a small company of immigrants, mostly bearing the names of Harris and Morrill, the latter being the maiden name of his mother. The name of Joshua Stevens, or Stephens, as it was on that occasion, and often, written, makes a solitary appearance in the records of Haverhill, in 1712, before Methuen had been set off from that town. It is found with the names of eight others, all of whom lived in that part of the town which afterwards became Methuen, upon

a petition asking an abatement of their taxes for
the support of the ministry and the school "on
account of the great distance they lived from
the town and the difficulty they met with in
coming."[1]   If the signer of this petition was an
ancestor of our hero, this lonely circumstance,
coming from the distant past, stands somewhat
in contrast with the great speech with which
more than a century afterwards Thaddeus Stevens saved from repeal the free-school system of
Pennsylvania.

The father of Thaddeus does not appear to
have had the thrifty and enterprising qualities
necessary to achieve success in the wilderness,
although he was well versed in the science of
surveying, so useful to the pioneer, and which
in the settlement of this country has often
brought to its possessor not merely good wages,
but also large tracts of land gained by "surveying on the shares."   He re-surveyed the lines of
the town of Danville in 1790, and his measure-
ments are the legal ones to-day.   He was a shoemaker also, and his son Thaddeus learned enough
of the trade to enable him to make shoes for
the family.   He enjoyed a wide reputation as
an athlete, especially at wrestling, and was able,
like young Abraham Lincoln, to throw any man
in his neighborhood.   The accounts are uniform

[1] Chase, *History of Haverhill*, p. 237.

in attributing to him great poverty, although they disagree as to the method of his final escape from it. One version has it that he ran away from his family a few years after settling in Danville, and was never heard of again; another that he was killed in the war of 1812; while yet another has it that he died at home while his children were young. This much appears certain, that the mother was left in extreme penury with four children, all boys, to support and educate.

The location of Danville on the western edge of the valley which there takes its name from the Passumpsic, but a few miles further south merges into the Connecticut, is beautiful in the extreme. The land rises rapidly towards the west from St. Johnsbury, ten miles distant, and in general level it attains an altitude in Danville of about two thousand feet above the sea. The principal peaks of the White and Franconia mountains in New Hampshire are distinctly visible, and in the other direction the Green Mountains make a jagged horizon, with their summits uplifted against the sky. Pleasing as are the outlines of the mountains and the beauty of the valleys and lesser hills, they form by no means the most attractive features of the scenery. No verdure has a brighter green in the springtime, or a more brilliant variety of color-

ing in the autumn than the maple forests in that
portion of Vermont. One would not know
where to find a more gorgeous picture than can
be seen from one of the hills in that region upon
a clear September or October day. The maple-
trees afforded a more solid benefit than to color
the landscape; and when the supply of food was
almost exhausted at the close of a long winter,
they furnished that well-known, wholesome sugar
which helped to preserve the first immigrants
from starvation.[1] Not the least of the hardships
which those pioneers had to endure was the rigor
of the climate. At a point north of the 45th
parallel, and remote from the sea, the cold was
of course severe. The snow lay deep upon the
hillsides until late in the springtime and returned before the end of the autumn, but the
fertile soil yielded bountiful crops even in the
brief summer. In spite of these severities,
however, the settlement was soon firmly planted,
and, on the whole, with much less than the usual
suffering.

The start of Thaddeus Stevens in life was
lowly enough, but not on that account unpromising. It is true, as has been said, that his
family was even desperately poor; but the rude
state of the society about him presented slight
inequalities of condition, and interposed few

[1] *Vermont Historical Gazetteer*, vol. i. p. 313.

obstacles between him and nature, with whom he was invited to a struggle to win what she had to yield. The wild freedom of the life about him, the rigor of the climate, the great natural beauty of the surroundings, and the strong and law-abiding qualities of the community in which he lived, formed a series of happy circumstances. The social and political influences to which he was subjected were intensely democratic. The stirring events of the Revolution were fresh in the minds of men, and the heroes of that struggle, still in their prime, could be found in every considerable town. The system of government established by the Constitution had just gone into operation, and, while it imposed checks upon hasty popular action, it was admirably designed to secure, in the conditions then existing, the enactment into law of the sober second thought of the people, and was thus, in the best sense, a democratic government.

There were also special facts in the history of Vermont which powerfully tended to develop in a bright and studious boy the qualities of individuality and of a sturdy independence. The territory of that State had been claimed at the same time by Great Britain, New Hampshire, Massachusetts, and New York, and also by the government of the confederation. While her soldiers contributed greatly by their valor to win

the victory of the colonies over the common
enemy, the State, in the sounding language of
Ethan Allen, acknowledged no allegiance but to
the King of kings.[1]   For years she successfully
asserted her independence of all other powers,
maintained her own army, coined her own
money, and exercised such other attributes of
sovereignty as she chose to assume.   At length
she accomplished her desire, and was admitted
into the Union as an independent State upon
equal terms with New York, New Hampshire,
and Massachusetts, each of whom had previously
alleged ownership of her.

Among such a people and at such a time an
aristocracy of wealth and of birth stood little
chance of being developed.   The work to be
done required men, and the exacting difficulties
in the way of society uncovered merit and used
it wherever it might be found.   The possession
of property, of which indeed very little existed,
gave no unfair advantage, and the lack of it
caused no inconvenience, save the necessity for
more strenuous exertion.   If a settler did not
have a horse it was necessary for him to walk
and to carry his wood or other load upon his

[1] That the early settlers of Vermont did not consider themselves unequal to any task may be inferred from the resolution, passed by the Council of Public Safety during the revo-
lutionary period, that the laws of God and Connecticut be
adopted "until we have time to frame better."

back; and while the man with property might supply his wants with less labor, — for anything like real luxury was unknown, — he gained no social prestige over his poorer neighbor. The conditions with which Stevens was surrounded were thus admirably adapted to implant and powerfully strengthen the hatred of privilege and the idea of democratic equality, which so strongly characterized him in after years.

Stevens was most fortunate in his mother. All accounts agree that she was remarkable for character and strength of mind. She made a heroic struggle to overcome the disadvantages of poverty and to give her children a good education. Thaddeus was sickly in his youth, and his mother determined to send him to college. Her other boys, however, were by no means neglected, and each one of them afterwards achieved distinction in his chosen pursuit. The history of Stevens's boyhood is marked by few incidents except those which naturally grow out of a wild and stirring frontier life. When he was twelve years old his parents took him on a visit to Boston, which was then a small town, but by far the largest that Stevens had ever seen. The sight of it kindled his ambition, and he determined to become rich. Another incident of his early life is preserved, which shows the character of his mother. The year after his visit to Boston a

plague, known among the settlers as the "spotted
fever," broke out and raged violently throughout
Danville and the adjoining towns. So many
were stricken with the disease that it was impossible to procure proper attendance. Mrs.
Stevens was untiring in her care of the sick,
going from house to house, ministering to their
wants and alleviating their sufferings in every
way in her power. She frequently took Thaddeus with her upon these visits, and an impression was made upon him which he never forgot.
From whatever cause, his sympathy for suffering
was throughout his life one of the strongest
traits of his character.

He could never sufficiently acknowledge his
indebtedness to his mother. Long years after,
he said of her: "I really think the greatest
pleasure of my life resulted from my ability to
give my mother a farm of two hundred and fifty
acres, and a dairy of fourteen cows, and an oc-
casional bright gold piece, which she loved to
deposit in the contributor's box of the Baptist
Church which she attended. This always gave
her much pleasure and me much satisfaction.
My mother was a very extraordinary woman.
I have met very few women like her. My father
was not a well-to-do man, and the support and
education of the family depended upon my mother. She worked day and night to educate me.

I was feeble and lame in youth, and as I could not work on the farm, she concluded to give me an education. I tried to repay her afterwards, but the debt of a child to his mother, you know, is one of the debts we can never pay." He gratefully cherished her memory to the last, and by his will he established a fund, the income of which was forever to be used to plant each springtime "roses and other cheerful flowers" upon her grave.

The means of education at the disposal of young Stevens were not of so limited a character as might be supposed. That portion of Vermont had only just been settled at the time of his birth, and yet the tide of immigration set in so strongly that when he was a dozen years old his native town was nearly as populous as it is to-day. The first sounds of the axe had hardly broken the silence of the wilderness when, true to the instinct of the race from which they sprang, the settlers established a court for the peaceable settlement of their disputes, and a school for the education of their children. It was agreed that Danville should be the shire town and have the court-house, and that the academy should be established in the adjoining town of Peacham. A charter was obtained in 1795, and the academy now in existence in the latter town began its long and honorable career.

The academy possessed greater attraction for
Mrs. Stevens than the court-house, and accordingly she moved to Peacham, that she might
educate her boys. The school was a very humble institution both architecturally and in its
means of instruction. It had no large endow-
ment, no long list of learned teachers, and no
imposing buildings to strike the imagination;
but its rude halls were thronged with pupils
eager to acquire knowledge, and they made the
most of all the means at their command. In
fact, with the ardor of bright scholars, they
seemed willing to improve upon the ordinary
facilities of the school, and to introduce more
modern methods than the board of trustees were
willing to sanction. The rules provided that
there should be each year "an exhibition, in
which the male scholars shall be the only per-
formers, and that the pieces to be spoken shall
be selected by the preceptor and submitted to
the inspection of the prudential committee."
This rule apparently did not secure a sufficiently
sombre programme, and its defects were repaired
by two amendments, one of which provided
"that there be no performances by candle-light,"
and the other that the exhibition "be regulated
so as to exclude tragedies, comedies, and other
theatrical performances." [1]

[1] The Peacham Academy Centennial Address, by Hon. C. A.
Bunker, 1897.

At this point Thaddeus Stevens for the first time emerges into the full light of history, and in view of his subsequent anathemas against treason, it is remarkable that his first appearance should have been in the rôle of a rebel. However exemplary the course of Stevens at the academy may have been in other respects, his good deeds have eluded the vigilance of the historian of the school, and his open violation of both the rules I have cited is the one conspicuous circumstance that survives. He appears to have been stage-struck, and also to have preferred the glare of the candle to the daylight. Accordingly, on October 7, 1811, we find the trustees passing a vote, naming thirteen students, of whom Stevens was one, and resolving that their course, "in refusing on the day of publick exhibition, being the 4th day of September last, to proceed in their exhibition in the day time while the board were waiting to see their performance was conduct highly reprehensible. And that their proceeding to exhibit a tragedy in the evening of the said day, contrary to the known rules and orders of the school and the express prohibition of the preceptor, was a gross violation of the rules and by-laws of the institution, tending to subvert all order and subordination in said school, and to disturb the peace of the society, and that they be required

to subscribe the following submission, viz.:
We, the subscribers, students in the Academy at
Peacham, having been concerned in the exhibition of a tragedy on the evening of September
4, 1811, contrary to the known rules of the
board of trustees, on reflection are convinced
that we have done wrong in not paying a suit-
able respect to the authority of the board, and
hereby promise that, as long as we continue students at this Academy, we will observe such
rules as the board may prescribe." Mr. Bunker says that Stevens signed the paper with great
reluctance and because he could do nothing else,
and that he then completed his preparation for
college, but "never forgot his chagrin." He
may have signed the paper, but probably not for
the purpose of going back to the academy, for
his preparation was already finished, and he entered Dartmouth College during the fall of 1811
as a sophomore.

There is a lack of very definite information
as to his career in college. The commonly accepted version that he first entered the University of Vermont, and while a student there witnessed the battle of Lake Champlain, and that
afterwards he went to Dartmouth, is incorrect.
The battle occurred September 11, 1814, and he
graduated from Dartmouth in the summer of
that year. The records of the two colleges make

it clear that he took his entire college course at Dartmouth, excepting the latter part of the college year, 1812–1813.[1]

When Stevens entered Dartmouth more than forty years had elapsed since Eleazar Wheelock had planted it in the wilderness at Hanover. It remained for many years the only college in northern New England, and the rapid settlement of that region gave it great prosperity.[2] During Stevens's connection with the college its students usually numbered about one hundred and forty, and it had a faculty of eight instructors besides the president. Professor Moore, afterwards the president of Amherst and Williams colleges, and Professors Shurtleff and Adams were perhaps the most learned of the teachers. The president was Dr. John Wheelock, the son of the founder of the college. The quality of his influence may be determined in a measure from the portrait of him which survives in the journal of George Ticknor, who graduated from

[1] I am indebted to Professor C. F. Richardson, of Dartmouth, and to Professor J. E. Goodrich, of the University of Vermont, for the most important facts in connection with his college course.

[2] In 1791 it graduated to the degree of A. B. 49, while the number for the same year was 27 for each of the other leading colleges, Harvard, Yale, and Princeton; and for the decade 1790–1800 the number of graduates was: Harvard, 394; Dartmouth, 363; Yale, 295; Princeton, 240. Chase, *History of Dartmouth College*, p. 615.

the college four years before Stevens entered it. "Dr. Wheelock was stiff and stately. He read constantly, sat up late, and got up early. He talked very gravely and slow, with a falsetto voice. Mr. Webster [who graduated in 1801] could imitate him perfectly. He had been in England, he had had a finger in politics, and had been a lieutenant-colonel in the army of the Revolution, but there was not the least trace of either of these portions of his life in his manners or conversation at this time. He was one of the most formal men I ever knew." [1]

The course of study at Dartmouth College, in 1811, was very similar to that of the other colleges of that day. Timothy Dwight, who was at the time president of Yale College, has given in his ponderous volumes of travel in New York and New England an exact statement of the requirements for admission and the course of study at Yale, and he adds that the recital would be substantially true for all the New England colleges.[2] A candidate for the freshman class was examined in Virgil, Cicero and Sallust, in the Greek Testament, and in arithmetic. The course of study included a little Greek, a moderate amount of the higher mathematics, and considerable Latin.[3] But Paley and Locke were

[1] *Life, Letters, and Journal,* vol. i. p. 5.
[2] *Travels in New York and New England,* vol. i. p. 199.
[3] *Ibid.* vol. i. p. 208.

not neglected at a time when the professors were chosen quite as much for the soundness of their theological views as for their learning. The course contained no modern languages, which, indeed, appear to have been little in demand in this country at that time, for so late as 1813, and in Boston, when George Ticknor attempted to study German, he had great difficulty in procuring the requisite books.[1]

The course, then, of the New England college of that time was most meagre compared with the wealth of learning which the modern college affords; but it was full of strong discipline, and it was possible for the earnest student to acquire the rudiments of a sound education. The libraries were not large, but they contained the best books, which were doubtless read with great care by students who were willing to make such sacrifices to secure an education; and some of the scholars who were disciplined in those schools were able afterwards to contribute new models to the English tongue.

Very little is known of Stevens's life at Dartmouth to distinguish him from the mass of the students. There was nothing sensational about

---

[1] He succeeded in borrowing a grammar from Mr. Everett, a text-book from the Athenæum, where it had been deposited by J. Q. Adams on going abroad, and then he was forced to send to New Hampshire for a dictionary. *Journal*, vol. i. p. 11.

it, and, if we may draw an inference from his known industry, it was probably marked by patient and plodding labor. He was a hard student, was sensible of the sacrifice made by his mother, and there can be little doubt that he took away from those "cloisters of the hill-girt plain" all that they had to give. His style of speech shows the result of study in a degree of accuracy unusual among our public men. In the last years of his life, when he had attained the distinction of being one of the greatest parliamentary leaders in our history, he delighted in showing a contempt for literary form; but at the same time his own speech was faultless, and Mr. Blaine, who served in Congress with him, has borne witness that rarely did a sentence fall from his lips even in the most careless moment "that would not bear the test of grammatical and rhetorical criticism." [1]

Stevens did not pass the whole of the time from 1811 to 1814 in Dartmouth College, but for one term, and probably for two, he was a student in the University of Vermont. His name appears upon the president's list at Burlington for the second term of 1812–13, and also on the programme of the "exhibition" at the close of the third term on the afternoon preceding commencement day in the summer of 1813.

[1] Blaine, *Twenty Years of Congress*, vol. i. p. 325.

At this exhibition Stevens took part in an "English Forensic Disputation" on the question: "Ought the Gospel to be Supported by Law?" On the same day was presented "The Fall of Helvetic Liberty," a tragedy in three acts, written by Thaddeus Stevens. The "Fall" seems to have been a most imposing military performance, and to have recognized the desirability of having many officers and few privates. Of the fourteen characters in the play three were French and eight were Swiss generals. Stevens played one of the parts.

Stevens is cited as authority for a story, which is not wholly agreeable, of an affair which occurred while he was in the University of Vermont, and probably about the time when his play was presented. An obstinate resident of Burlington insisted upon pasturing his cow upon the college campus at commencement time, in spite of protests, and the dispute became so warm that one night the cow became the innocent victim of a somewhat practical joke, and was killed. Stevens, whose authorship of a tragedy had prepared him for the act, and another student, who had probably aided him in overturning Helvetic Liberty, were guilty of the offense, but circumstances pointed strongly to a student who was altogether innocent. The owner demanded satisfaction, and the suspected

student was about to be expelled from the college. Stevens and his college comrade were free from suspicion, but they could not escape punishment by keeping silent. They had the alternative of seeing an innocent boy bear the penalty for their misdeed, or of relieving him by making a confession. They promptly decided on the latter course, and made a clean breast of the matter to the owner of the cow. The man proved to be of a generous nature, even if obstinate. He refused to take pay for the cow, and exonerated the student under suspicion without exposing the real culprits. Many years afterwards Stevens, who never forgot a kindly act, sent him a draft for more than the value of the cow, and a gold watch and chain.

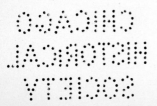

CHAPTER II

THE LAW

WHEN Stevens graduated from Dartmouth College he was twenty-two years old, well educated for those days, and wholly dependent upon his own resources. He determined to study law, a profession which, under the circumstances surrounding him, offered the shortest road to fame and to a livelihood, if not to fortune. In order to support himself while studying law, he taught school. His native State did not offer the opportunities which he desired, and the year after graduating he removed to Pennsylvania, where he secured a position as instructor in the academy which a few years previously had been established in the town of York. The place was the shire town of a large and flourishing county, and he was able to pursue his legal studies under favorable conditions. By this move from Vermont to Pennsylvania he gained a broader field for the pursuit of his profession. That, however, was the slightest consequence of the step. He exchanged a location near the northern frontier

of the country for one which was then very near
the centre of our civilization and upon the line
which, beginning at the Atlantic and stretching
to our western frontier, with a dip southward,
formed the line of battle along which was to be
fought the great contest for freedom. The
county of York and that of Adams, to which he
shortly removed, were bounded upon the south
by the slave territory of the State of Maryland.
He thus took his place, and doubtless without
any intention upon his part, in the thick of that
conflict in which he was destined to win the victory which has immortalized his name.

The struggle to change the location, at various points, of the line which separated the freeman and the slave was bitter enough, but it did
not compare in fierceness or in its influence in
bringing about the ultimate appeal to the sword
with the struggle over the degree of tribute
which the institution of slavery should receive
from free territory. The Constitution, which
nowhere used the term slave, provided that no
person held to service or labor in one State, escaping into another, should be discharged from
such service, but that he should be delivered
upon the claim of the owner. Did this mean
that the inhabitants of the free States were to
become slave hunters? Did it mean that a free
man might be claimed as a slave, and not have

the great question of his freedom passed upon by a jury? Stevens answered both these questions in the negative, and from the very moment when he settled upon the confines of the slave State he became an actor in a real tragedy which dwarfed the one spun from his imagination upon Helvetic Liberty. The sight of slaves, fleeing for their liberty and, after weeks of privation and suffering, gaining the doubtful protection afforded them by free soil, was to him a common occurrence. Fresh from the freedom and the untempered democracy of his northern Vermont home, he was peculiarly sensitive to the spectacle of men being claimed as property and remanded into slavery. Undoubtedly his hatred of that "institution" was thus made more intense and practical, and his eyes were opened to the fact that liberty possessed real benefits, and was not a mere abstraction.

It is certain that while in York he applied himself to his law studies with unceasing industry. Amos Gilbert, a famous Quaker teacher, was intimately associated with him at that time, and speaks of him as a very modest young man and a remarkably hard student. After he had read the scanty amount of law then required for admission to the bar, he crossed the line to Maryland, and took the examination in a court which was being held in a neighboring county of that State. The reason for this proceeding is somewhat obscure. According to one report, which rests upon doubtful authority, a special rule was made in York County to apply particularly to Stevens's case, requiring a certain time to be devoted wholly to the study of law. The rule itself was a reasonable one, and it may well be questioned whether personal hostility to Stevens was responsible for its existence, for at that time he was most retiring in his habits, wholly given up to his work as a teacher and student, and would not naturally have aroused animosity. But whatever was the provocation, it is evident that he took the examination in Maryland in order to obtain a more speedy admission to the Pennsylvania bar, which he could have as a matter of courtesy by virtue of his certificate of admission in another State.

He has left an amusing account of his brief connection with the Maryland bar. The examination took place in the evening before the judge and the bar committee. His Honor informed Stevens that there was one indispensable prerequisite to the examination. "There must be two bottles of Madeira on the table, and the applicant must order it in." Stevens complied with the condition, and, after the wine had been ordered and disposed of, one of the committee asked the applicant what books he had read.

He replied: "Blackstone, Coke upon Littleton, a work on Pleading, and Gilbert on Evidence," — a rather slender list, no doubt, but one which, if thoroughly mastered, would leave him not wholly at a disadvantage with the young practitioner of to-day, who is so often burdened with a multitude of cases that he loses, or never secures, a grasp upon the underlying principles. He was then asked two or three questions, the last of which related to the difference between executory devises and contingent remainders. A satisfactory answer to this question led his Honor again to intervene. "Gentlemen," said the judge, "you see the young man is all right. I will give him a certificate." But before the certificate was delivered, the candidate was informed that usage required that the ceremony should terminate in the way in which it had opened, and that two more bottles should be produced. Stevens very willingly complied with this requirement, was made a member of the bar, and was so elated at his success that he joined in a game of which he knew nothing, with the not unnatural consequence that his slender stock of money was soon exhausted. The next morning he was in the saddle early, with his certificate in his pocket, on his way to Pennsylvania. He finally reached his destination after narrowly escaping with his life in crossing the Susquehanna, and his brief career at the Maryland bar terminated as abruptly as it had been begun.

Uncertain in what county he should settle, Stevens visited Lancaster, returned to York, and finally decided to begin practice in Gettysburg, the capital of the adjacent county of Adams, and since made famous by one of the greatest and most dramatic of battles. He was favored with the usual amount of leisure which young lawyers have at their disposal, and doubtless employed it in supplementing his meagre preparation by further reading. His expenses were small, but his income was still smaller and his capital next to nothing. He had no acquaintance in the county, had had no opportunity of showing the stuff he was made of, and altogether found the prospect to be most discouraging. Yet he had not long to wait. Before many of the inhabitants of that quiet village had become aware of his existence, his opportunity came.

A murder was committed in the neighborhood, so horrible and so certain in point of proof that the older lawyers of the bar did not dare to risk their reputations by accepting the case of the accused man. Stevens had no reputation to lose, and, if he had enjoyed a great one, it is almost certain that it would not have

deterred him from defending one who was accused of crime and could secure no other counsel.
At any rate he accepted the case and proved by
the way in which he conducted it that, while it
might have destroyed some reputations, it could
create his own. He astonished everybody by his
skill, his eloquence, and the display of those
qualities which, according to a most distinguished
and by no means partial judge, made him before
he died the equal of any lawyer in America.

Very likely Stevens would not have gained
so much if he had won his case instead of losing
it. Success in desperate criminal cases not un-
frequently puts a lawyer in the apparent position of being an accomplice in crime, while a
vigorous and unsuccessful defense may establish
his reputation for courage and a patriotic willingness to demand the observance of all the
forms of law with whatever risk to himself. In
this particular case the proof was beyond controversy that the prisoner had committed the
act; but his counsel set up the plea of insanity,
which was a defense far less fashionable and
certainly less effective at that early day than it
has since become, and which was then regarded
as the last resort of the most hopelessly guilty
criminal. Stevens undoubtedly believed in the
soundness of the defense. Long afterwards, in
speaking of the case, he said that he had been

counsel for the prisoner in more than fifty murder cases, in all of which but one he had been
successful, but that every defendant had deserved
conviction except the one who was hanged.
That one, he said, was insane.

Stevens had thus at last established himself,
and not merely had received a very substantial
and welcome fee,[1] but had at once taken his
natural place at the head of the Gettysburg bar.
His fame soon extended into the adjoining counties, and he was employed upon one side or the
other of nearly every important cause tried in
the vicinity.   Doubtless these causes were of
slight consequence financially, if judged by the
modern standard.   Large combinations of capital and private corporations, which contribute
so much to the successful lawyer of to-day, were
almost unknown in the first quarter of this century.   But the principles involved were not less
important, their application was not so sordid,
and the work of Stevens at the bar was broaden-
ing in the extreme in its influence upon him.
He did much work gratuitously.   Many a colored man, claimed as a slave, gained his freedom
through the shrewdness and skill of Stevens,
who, when legal expedients failed, sometimes
paid the ransom out of his own pocket.   For

[1] Fifteen hundred dollars. Harris, *Biographical History of
Lancaster County*, p. 575.

fifteen years he devoted himself unremittingly to his profession, and gained in actual practice that knowledge of the law, which, joined with his natural qualities, made him a great lawyer.

CHAPTER III

IT was from necessity that Stevens had as yet refrained from gratifying his natural passion for politics. The Federalist party, to which he belonged, had disappeared, and there was no party for him to join excepting the one to whose principles he was opposed. In 1827 he was on the same side of a lawsuit with James Buchanan, then entering upon a political career destined to become distinguished. Buchanan advised him to support Jackson, but Stevens did not take the advice seriously, or at least he did not follow it. He did not believe in the political principles represented by Jackson, but, on the contrary, was ready to unite with any organization opposed to him which had any chance of success. With the exception of occasionally serving upon the Gettysburg town council he appears to have taken no part in politics in the early days of his practice.

Suddenly, however, a new issue forced itself upon the attention of the country, entirely disconnected with previous political questions, and which promised for the moment to overshadow all other issues. The abduction and probable murder of William Morgan by members of the Masonic order, and their subsequent trial, produced an intense feeling of indignation in many parts of the Union, and quickly forced into politics the question of the wisdom of secret societies, and particularly of the Freemasons. An anti-Masonic party at once appeared in New York, which mustered 33,000 votes, and at the following election increased its membership to 70,000. The effect of the Morgan incident was undoubtedly exaggerated, but it gave alarm to many good people. Stevens instinctively sympathized with the principles of the new party, and was one of the first men in Pennsylvania to declare his adhesion to it. The broad plane of American citizenship was none too broad for him. He denounced an institution whose members, he believed, were banded together by an oath to control a government whose blessings they shared, and to pervert the administration of justice in their own favor. He declared that Masonry was an *imperium in imperio*, and that republican institutions were endangered by its continuance. Largely through his leadership the opposition to the Democratic party in Pennsylvania was consolidated under the name of the anti-Masonic party, and it made an energetic but unsuccessful campaign in 1829, having Joseph Ritner as its candidate for governor.

For a time this issue promised to furnish a rallying cry for a great national party. A national convention was held in Baltimore in September, 1831, and placed William Wirt in nomination for the presidency. Stevens was one of the moving spirits of the convention, and among his colleagues were men no less conspicuous than Abner Phelps and Amasa Walker of Massachusetts, and William H. Seward of New York. The result of the campaign was disastrous, and showed the futility of attempting to construct a national party upon this single idea. Wirt received the electoral vote of only one State, and that the State in which Stevens was born. The truth underlying the new party was too narrow and too self-evident. Masonry itself languished, men quitted its ranks in great numbers, and many of its lodges were closed. But the American people declined to divide upon this particular question. Parties are evolved upon broader and more complex issues, and anti-Masonry stands as the first but by no means the last illustration in our history of attempting to produce a great political party to order upon a single question.

Stevens, however, did not at once give up

the fight. He doubtless perceived that the idea
was not without some elements of popularity, as
well as of justice, and popularity was not un-
grateful to him while he was in search of a permanent party with which he could ally himself.
The party of Jackson was then of overshadow-
ing importance; the Whig party was just coming into being, and he was very willing to
strengthen this nascent organization by whatever elements of attraction remained in anti-
Masonry.

In 1833 Stevens took his seat as a member
of the Pennsylvania House of Representatives
from Adams County.   He had reached the mature age of forty-one years without having borne
any part in parliamentary affairs.   But for fifteen years he had closely followed the practice
of his profession, and had acquired a thorough
knowledge of law as well as a readiness and
self-possession from the constant trial of causes
which gave him an admirable training for his
new work.   He very quickly took rank among
the leading members of his party by his trenchant and vigorous attacks upon Jackson and his
supporters.   Very early in the session he introduced a resolution aimed at Masonry.   It provided that an inquiry be made into the expediency of a law making Freemasonry a good
cause of peremptory challenge in all cases where

one of the parties was, and the other was not, a Mason; also in criminal cases in which the defendant was a Mason; and providing finally that a judge who was a member of the order should be disqualified from trying a case in which one of the parties was also a member. This resolution was defeated, but by a majority of only eleven votes.

On March 27, 1834, as the chairman of a committee appointed to investigate Masonry, he submitted a report which was a caustic attack upon the House itself for refusing to sanction the summoning of witnesses, and upon the Democratic governor and other Masons who held office. It could hardly be called a judicial document, but was an apt attempt at "playing politics."

"It was," says this report, "intended that the governor of this Commonwealth should become a witness, and have a full opportunity of explaining, under oath, the principles and practices of the order of which he is so conspicuous a member. It was thought that the papers in his possession might throw much light on the question how far Masonry secures political and executive favor. This inspection would have shown whether it be true that applications for office have been founded on Masonic writ and claimed as Masonic rights; whether in such applications the 'significant symbols' and mystic watchwords of Masonry have been used, and in how many cases such applications have been successful in securing executive patronage.   It might not have been unprofitable also to inquire how many converted felons, who have been pardoned by the recent governor, were brethren of the 'mystic tie.'   The committee might have deemed it necessary, in the faithful discharge of their duty, to have called before them some of the judges, who are Masons, to ascertain whether, in their official characters, the 'grand hailing sign' has ever been handed, sent, or thrown to them by either of the parties litigant, and if so, what has been the result of the trial."

During the same session Stevens secured, in the face of a determined opposition, the passage of a bill making a liberal appropriation for Pennsylvania College at Gettysburg.   His speech does not appear to have survived, but the editor of the "Harrisburg Telegraph" declared at the time that it "was one never excelled, if ever equaled in the hall."[1]   In grateful recognition of this event and of his other services in the cause of education, one of the finest buildings of the college was given the name of Stevens Hall.

Stevens was reëlected to the legislature in

[1] See *Pennsylvania School Journal*, February, 1891.

1834, and renewed the attack upon Masonry by
offering a bill to suppress it, but his party was
in a minority, and his bill was defeated by
twenty votes. It was during this session that
Stevens rendered his great service to the public
school system, and against great odds achieved
a victory which he regarded, even after he had
won his wide fame, as the greatest achievement
of his life. For many years the system had
prevailed in Pennsylvania of furnishing public
education, as of providing public subsistence,
only to self-confessed paupers. In order to get
his children educated at the public expense, it
was necessary for the father or guardian to
make it appear that he was not able to furnish
them the means of education, and in such a
case instruction would be doled out as bread or
meat would be doled out if he were unable to
buy food. The system was substantially that
illustrated by the Friends' Public School, established in 1697, — a system for the education
of "the rich at reasonable rates, the poor to be
maintained and schooled for nothing." During
the colonial times the church and local schools
were generally conducted upon this principle.[1]
The establishment of free institutions gave birth
to notions of equality which made it impossible
to continue a system under which a distinction

[1] Wickersham, *History of Education in Pennsylvania*, p. 294.

was maintained in the public schools between the children who paid and those who were regarded as public charges. "The class distinctions," says Wickersham, "that had been broken up in general society, could not be preserved in the school." Rather than permit poor children to be educated under conditions so fatal to their self-respect, their parents kept them at home.

The system was first cast aside in Philadelphia, which provided for free schools at the public expense. The agitation for the extension of the Philadelphia plan to the whole State finally bore fruit in the act of 1834, which, with many defects in details, recognized the grand principle of free public schools for all, and was passed with only a single dissenting vote. But like most noble things this principle involved some cost. There were the taxes, and there is no more certain method of stirring up the public opinion of a virtuous, thrifty and frugal people, such as then inhabited Pennsylvania, than by pricking their pocketbooks. They were willing to have reform, provided it did not come high or they were not compelled to pay for it. A violent reaction arose. Nearly half the districts in the State rejected the act or contemptuously ignored it. They were ready to do sweet charity and furnish schooling for the children of paupers, but they could not consent to a system which took by taxation the money of those who had no children and devoted it to the education of the children of the well-to-do. Thus it came to pass that the good Commonwealth, through all her rich valleys and across her noble mountains, was shaken from the Delaware to the Ohio, and a legislature of stern Spartans was sent to Harrisburg to wipe out the law.

The Senate made short work of it. That body summarily voted to repeal the essential parts of the act by a bill which bore the inspiring title, "An act making provision for the education of the poor *gratis*." This bill passed the Senate by a vote of nearly two to one, and among its supporters were found thirteen senators who had voted for free schools at the preceding session.[1]　It then went to the House.

Many members of the preceding legislature had lost their seats by their incautious vote for free education, and had given place to its pronounced opponents. The legislature was inundated by petitions for repeal. A committee favorable to the law reported that the number of signers was "deplorably large," and that 32,000 had petitioned for repeal, while only 2500 remonstrated against it. The Democratic members passed a vote at a caucus, requesting the Democratic governor, who was a friend of

[1] Wickersham, *History of Education in Pennsylvania*, p. 237.

the law, not to oppose its repeal, since a veto of
the bill, which seemed sure to pass, would defeat
him for reëlection.[1] During a considerable portion of the time while this tempest was raging,
Stevens was absent from Harrisburg. Upon his
return, his colleague from Adams County, who
was a warm friend of the law, informed him
that the bill repealing the act had passed the
Senate with only eight dissenting votes; that
the test vote of reference in the House showed
a majority of thirty in its favor, and that the
friends of the law had consulted together and
decided that it was useless to oppose the repeal.
He also advised him that they were bound to
vote for the repeal, as three quarters of their
constituents had petitioned for it.[2]

The situation was desperate, and the cause
of the law seemed lost. The Senate bill to repeal came up in the House on April 10 and 11,
1835. Up to that hour the popular excitement,
which is so often the precursor of an opposite
ultimate popular opinion, had gone on unchecked
and carried everything before it. One obstacle,
however, stood in the path of repeal. There
was one representative who would no more
pander to a popular passion, of which he believed the people would repent as soon as their

[1] Bates, *Martial Deeds of Pennsylvania*, p. 983.
[2] *Ibid.*, p. 984.

eyes were opened, than he would pander to a
mob. The people might reject him, but so long
as he was their representative he would follow
his convictions of duty. He braved the storm
when it was at its fiercest pitch, and boldly
moved to strike out all the Senate bill after the
enacting clause, and to substitute for it a bill
strengthening the law which it proposed to repeal. Upon that motion he made his speech,
which, even from the imperfect reports, must
be regarded as a powerful argument, and from
the uniform accounts of those who heard it must
rank with the great parliamentary speeches.
Certainly it produced an effect second to no
speech ever uttered in an American legislative
assembly.

The hall was packed to suffocation. Nearly
the entire Senate and most of the principal
state officers were present, as well as the members of the House. Stevens was in the prime
of manhood. His form had outgrown the slen-
derness of youth, and it was not bent with that
heavy weight of years which he dragged along
when, a generation later, he moved, a porten-
tous figure, across the stage of the national
House of Representatives. He was erect and
majestic. He may not indeed have had the appearance of "a descended god," as one of his
fellow members who has described the scene has

portrayed him, but we can well believe the
accounts of the wonderful beauty of those chis-
eled features which never lost their eagle look
even to his dying day.   It is fortunate that this
early portrait of him survives to remind us that
he was once young, and to enable us to trace
out the immortal lineaments of his beauty.
Otherwise he would have wandered forever
through history as the broken old man of more
than threescore and ten, such as he was at the
hour of his great fame and when the world first
knew him.

Many references to the speech, by those who
heard it, have been preserved, and they are uniformly of the most flattering character.   I will
refer to only two of them.   The venerable Dr.
George Smith, who had been a member of the
legislature of 1834, wrote, nearly fifty years
later, that "the House was electrified," and the
"school system was saved from ignominious
defeat."   The Harrisburg correspondent of the
"American Daily Advertiser" of Philadelphia
attempted to preserve the occasion by a report
which is all the more forcible because given in
the unsensational manner of that day.   After
crediting Stevens with preventing the repeal of
the law, he declared that "the speech of this gentleman was the ablest I have ever heard."   He
then endeavored to furnish a synopsis of the

speech, but he threw up the task in despair, and confessed that he was "unable to give even an outline of this most masterly production."

I know it is easy to give an undue effect to contemporary eulogy. Before the days of stenographers almost any orator could be great. Usually no printed record would survive for refutation, and it would only be necessary, a generation or a century later, for some writer of fine imaginative powers to dwell with particularity upon the pose, the gesture, the eye, the forefinger, — especially the forefinger, — the immaterial detail of language being omitted, and thus a possibly empty effort might be sent down to posterity as a great oration.

But when every allowance is made from the reports of the affair which have been handed down, the effect in this instance proved the working of a prodigious cause. The House immediately voted, when Stevens sat down; the victory so confidently anticipated by the friends of repeal was suddenly turned into defeat, and the motion of Stevens was carried by a nearly two-thirds vote. Most remarkable of all, the Senate, which but a short time before had so decisively voted for repeal, returned to its chamber, thrilled and delighted with the great effort, converted as no Senate had ever been converted before, and immediately concurred, with a few unim-

portant amendments, in the House substitute
bill.

Governor Wolf was a loyal friend of free
schools. Politically, he was opposed to Stevens.
But he immediately sent for him after his great
and unexpected triumph in the House, and,
throwing his arms about his neck, warmly
thanked him for the great service he had "rendered to our common humanity." [1] Some of
the enthusiastic friends of the system he had
saved had portions of the speech beautifully
printed on silk, and presented it to Stevens.

Although the speech itself was only imperfectly
reported, enough remains to show its wonderful
vigor and its condensed and weighty style. In
denouncing the former law, which afforded education at the public expense for those alone who
acknowledged that they were too poor to educate
themselves, he said: "Hereditary distinctions of
rank are sufficiently odious; but that which is
founded upon poverty is infinitely more so.
Such a law should be entitled 'An Act for
Branding and Marking the Poor.'"

He had said many sharp and bitter things
about Governor Wolf, who was a Democrat,
but that official was a friend of the system which
Stevens was advocating, and he was defended in

[1] Colonel J. W. Forney in *Washington Chronicle*. See the
Pennsylvania School Journal, vol. xxxix. p. 331.

one of the most effective passages of the speech. "I have seen the present chief magistrate of this Commonwealth violently assailed as the projector and father of this law. I am not the eulogist of that gentleman; he has been guilty of many deep political sins. But he deserves the undying gratitude of the people for the steady, untiring zeal which he has manifested in favor of common schools. I will not say that his exertions in that cause have covered all, but they have atoned for many of his errors. I trust that the people of this State will never be called upon to choose between a supporter and opposer of free schools. But if it should come to that — if that should be made the turning-point on which we are to cast our suffrages — if the opponent of education were my most intimate personal and political friend, and the free-school candidate my most obnoxious enemy, I should deem it my duty as a patriot, at this moment of our intellectual crisis, to forget all other considerations, and I should place myself unhesitatingly and cordially in the ranks of him whose banner streams in light."

He very ingeniously answered the argument that those who had no children and paid the tax received no benefit from it. It was directly for their benefit, "inasmuch as it perpetuates the government and insures the due administration of the laws under which they live, and by which their lives and property are protected." The industrious and wealthy farmer paid a heavy tax to support criminal courts and jails, but "he never gets the worth of his money, by being tried for a crime before the court, allowed the privilege of a jail on conviction, or receiving an equivalent from the sheriff or his hangmen officers. He cheerfully pays the tax which is necessary to support and punish convicts, but loudly complains of that which goes to prevent his fellow being from becoming a criminal, and to obviate the necessity of those humiliating institutions."

He regretted that any member should have consented to receive an election upon a platform of hostility to popular education. "If honest ambition were his object, he will erelong lament that he attempted to raise his monument of glory on so muddy a foundation." He would admit that the "war-club and battle-axe of savage ignorance" were dangerous to a public man in "the present state of feeling in Pennsylvania;" but he urged members not to cherish "the prejudice and errors" of their constituents, but to play the part of the philanthropist and the hero, even "if it be true, as you say, that popular vengeance follows close upon your footsteps."

He pointed out a glorious pathway for Pennsylvania, if her legislators should provide the means for polishing the "bright intellectual gems" of her children, and should learn to build her monuments not "of brass or marble, but to make them of ever-living mind." Neither fame nor honor could "long be perpetuated by mere matter." Of that Egypt furnished "melancholy proof." The pyramids which she had raised to her monarchs seemed "as durable as the everlasting hills, yet the deeds and the names they were intended to perpetuate are no longer known on earth. . . . Instead of doing deeds worthy to be recorded in history, their very names are unknown. . . . Who would not rather do one living deed than to have his ashes forever enshrined in ever-burnished gold? Sir, I trust that when we come to act on this question we shall take lofty ground — look beyond the narrow space which now circumscribes our vision — beyond the passing, fleeting point of time on which we stand — and so cast our votes that the blessing of education shall be conferred on every son of Pennsylvania — shall be carried home to the poorest child of the poorest inhabitant of the meanest hut of your mountains."

Speeches have sometimes changed the action of a legislative body when its mind had been

apparently made up. But a large majority of
the Pennsylvania House had been chosen with
reference to the educational issue and for the
purpose of repealing that portion of the law
which made schools free. The speech of Stevens
decisively turned them from that purpose. It is
doubtful if his achievement can be matched in
the history of legislative assemblies. Certainly
it at once established his position among the
very ablest men in Pennsylvania.

CHAPTER IV

CONSTITUTIONAL CONVENTION — THE "BUCK-SHOT WAR" — ELECTED TO CONGRESS

THE decisive victory upon the free-school question was acquiesced in by all parties, and the political campaign of 1835 was waged upon other issues. All the elements of opposition to Jackson were at last combined in the anti-Masonic party, which again nominated Ritner as its candidate for governor. The attitude of Jackson towards the national bank had alienated many of his friends in Pennsylvania, where that institution was popular. Ritner was elected, and his party also secured a majority of the members of the House of Representatives. Stevens was again chosen to membership in that body. He at once renewed the Masonic contest, and upon his motion a committee was appointed to investigate that and other secret societies. Wolf, the former governor, and many other prominent Masons, were summoned, but they declined to testify. The House refused to commit the witnesses for contempt, and the investigation resulted in nothing.

During this session of the legislature Stevens introduced a bill to confer a state charter upon the United States Bank, of which the national charter was about to expire by limitation. This action occasioned one of the most animated political contests of the session, and the charter finally passed both houses, and was approved by the governor. This step by Pennsylvania was met by hostile legislation in the States controlled by the Democrats, some of which enacted laws prohibiting within their limits any branch of the Pennsylvania United States Bank. The new institution purchased the assets of the defunct United States Bank, and after a brief and not glorious career, it suspended payment in the panic of 1837, in common with nearly all the banks in the country.

In the fall of 1836, Stevens was chosen a member of the convention which had been ordered by popular vote to consider amendments to the Constitution of the State. The convention assembled in May, 1837, and included among its members the ablest men of all parties. A majority of them, however, were Democratic in politics, and were evidently disposed to recast the Constitution upon partisan lines. This disposition was combated and very likely intensified by Stevens, who displayed all his natural radicalism in his treatment of the pro-

positions of which he disapproved. He doubtless could have exercised some influence in
moulding the new document, but, since it was
to be disfigured by any partisan blemishes, he
evidently preferred to retain the old Constitution with all its outgrown or inadequate provisions.

The stormy debates of this assembly fill thirteen large volumes, and appear to be more appropriate for a partisan legislature than a body
reforming the organic law of a great State.
Stevens did not regularly attend the sessions of
the convention, but when he was present he
contributed his full share of personalities to the
debates; he rarely lost an opportunity to take
a hand in a personal encounter, and his ready
and often bitter wit placed him easily at the
head in contests of that character. He generally opposed propositions to recognize class distinctions or to discriminate against any man on
account of his color. As finally adopted by the
convention, the Constitution limited the right of
suffrage to "white" citizens. Stevens refused
to affix his name to a document containing such
a race discrimination, and although delegates of
all parties finally signed it, his name is conspicuous by its absence.

At about this time Stevens also attended a
convention at Harrisburg, the members of which

styled themselves the "friends of the integrity
of the Union." The convention was called by
the supporters of slavery, who proposed to preserve the Union by repressing the agitation in
favor of freedom. In some way Stevens secured a seat in the body, but he was evidently
present for the purpose of making the movement ridiculous, and his efforts in that direction were crowned with complete success. It
would be difficult to find a better illustration of
his self-command in a deliberative body. He
held those views upon slavery which the convention was called to denounce, and yet he soon made
himself the central figure of the proceedings, and
by points of order, by objections to the form
of resolutions, by his eloquence and unsparing
sarcasm, the leaders of the movement were soon
thrown into dismay, and were glad to propose a
final adjournment. It was equally impossible
either to answer or to suppress him. The current newspaper report, which preserves a condensed statement of the proceedings, explains
in a parenthesis that "so electric was the effect
of Mr. Stevens's sallies here that no reporter
can touch their magic or picture their effect on
the hearers, who frequently renewed their applause a second time after the first burst had
subsided." The following will afford an example of these "sallies." In one of the discussions

Stevens so completely demonstrated the absurdity of a proposed resolution that one of the
members declared that, while he abhorred aboli-
tionism, he could never indorse such a doctrine.
This aroused a clergyman, who was apparently
the leading spirit in the movement, and he took
the floor to ask how a man with any sense of
honor, "knowing himself to hold the abominable
doctrines of the abolitionists, can come here in
sheep's clothing and sit among the friends of
the Union, while in his heart he is wishing to
throw his firebrands to consume it." Stevens
thereupon rebuked the clergyman for becoming
personal. "I meant no person in particular,"
was the reply. "Indeed," said Stevens, "I certainly understood the gentleman to more than
insinuate that my friend yonder," pointing to
his new recruit, whose hair was a bright red,
"looked very much like a firebrand."

Stevens served in the legislature of 1838, and
made a notable speech in favor of endowing the
colleges and higher institutions of learning in
the State. This speech lacks the fierce energy
of his free-school speech, but was more carefully
prepared.

In the same year he was appointed by Governor
Ritner a member of the Board of Canal Commissioners, which had charge of the expenditures
of large sums of money in internal improvements,

and during the heated political campaign of that
year he was charged with not being unmindful
of the interests of the Whig party in disbursing
the money. The campaign was a most exciting
one, and, as a result, Ritner, the Whig candidate for reëlection as governor, was defeated by
a slender majority. Stevens was again chosen a
member of the House. Both parties claimed
the legislature. There were two returns from
the city of Philadelphia, one made by the Democratic members of the returning board who
constituted a majority, and the other by the
Whig members. The former return declared
the Democrats to have been elected, and the
latter declared in favor of the Whigs. There
was a sufficient number of seats involved in the
controversy to determine which party should organize the legislature and elect a United States
senator.

The secretary of state recognized the return
made by the Whigs, and in doing so he did no
violence to his political convictions, as he was
the chairman of the Whig campaign committee.
He also indulged in a remarkable proclamation
announcing that the election of the Democratic
candidate for governor would be treated as a
nullity until an investigation could be held.
The legislature assembled in the most excited
frame of mind, and two hostile bodies of men,

sitting in the same hall, proceeded at the same time to elect a speaker. Stevens was the leader of the Whigs, and nominated his candidate, appointed tellers, and declared him triumphantly elected. In a somewhat similar fashion the Democrats elected their candidate.

The state-house was, of course, thronged with people who were partisans of one side or the other, and were not present entirely in the interests of peace. The struggle, as is not unusual in controversies of that nature, was attended with a great amount of noise, but no blood was spilled. The only one who appears to have been in any serious danger was Stevens himself, who was compelled to make his escape from the state-house through a window. The governor, doubtless with the approval of Stevens, if not at his instigation, issued a proclamation announcing that a "lawless, infuriated, armed mob" had assembled in the city for the purpose of overawing the legislature, and he called upon the civil authorities to restore order, and upon the military forces to hold themselves in readiness to render assistance.

Fearing that the militia might be called out, the Democrats made a demonstration, although an ineffective one, against the state arsenal. Some men, claiming to represent Stevens and the governor, agreed with the leaders of the mob that no arms should be taken from the arsenal for the use of the state forces. Stevens thereupon wrote a letter to a newspaper, declaring that he had held no communication with "the rebels," — which long remained with him a favorite epithet, — and that it would be "disgraceful to treat with the rebels on any subject."

It would scarcely be profitable to set forth here the details of the so-called "buckshot war," in which no one was killed, and not even a shot was fired, but which was made both noisy and ridiculous by proclamations, by calls upon the national government for assistance, and by acrimonious and insulting communications from the one party to the other. A contest, of which Stevens directed one side, could not be an indecisive one. Victory would certainly fall to one contestant or the other. There would be no compromise. In this case victory was with the Democrats. They retained possession of the representatives' chamber, inaugurated their governor, and the Whig representatives either surrendered by taking their seats in the Democratic House, or went home and abandoned the contest. Stevens refused to submit, and remained absent from the House during the whole session.

A special session of the legislature was called the following spring. There could be no

doubt that, as a legally elected member, it was
Stevens's right to be present. To make his
duty still more clear, and probably to relieve
him from the appearance of a surrender, his
constituents passed resolutions requesting him
to attend this session. Stevens replied that his
opinion of the legality of the "Hopkins House"
remained unshaken; that he believed it to be
"a usurping body forced upon the State by a
band of rebels," but that in obedience to the
wishes of his constituents he would attend the
House at the adjourned session in spite of his
repugnance. He accordingly was present when
the House again convened.

But his part had been too conspicuous in the
"buckshot war," in which the most deadly mis-
siles had been set in motion by his own tongue.
He was met by a resolution offered by Thomas
B. McElwee, the Democratic leader, calling
for the appointment of a committee to investigate whether he was elected, and if so, whether
he had forfeited his seat by "mal-conduct."
Stevens contemptuously refused to appear before
this committee, and replied to its summons by a
letter which conclusively established the illegality of the proceedings and his absolute right of
membership. The House then adopted a resolution by a party vote, declaring the seat vacant,
and ordering a new election. Stevens had de-

termined not to be a candidate again for the legislature, but this indefensible proceeding induced him to change his mind, and he at once issued an address to his constituents announcing that he would accept a reëlection to the seat which had been declared vacant.

It was evident, however, that he had not changed his opinion concerning the "Hopkins House." His address set forth that "a majority of that body, using the same unconstitutional and unlawful means which invested them with official authority, refused to allow me to occupy that seat to which I have been called by the free choice of my fellow citizens." He then denounced them as "tyrants," who had determined "to oppress and plunder the people." There was much more to the same effect. The people administered a fitting rebuke to the "tyrants" by again electing Stevens. This time he was permitted to take his seat, but as the legislature adjourned within a few days, there was very little opportunity for him to repay his persecutors. He had not long, however, to wait for his revenge. The legislature which met the following winter gave him expiation by expelling McElwee, the Democratic leader, who was responsible for the expulsion of Stevens.[1]

[1] Callendar, *Thaddeus Stevens, Commoner*, p. 49.

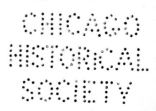

Once again, in 1841, Stevens was elected to the legislature, and rendered most useful service. The speech which he then made in favor of the right of petition produced an impression almost as profound as that in favor of free schools, and attracted the attention of the country. He also championed a resolution limiting the amount of the state debt, which passed the House by a large majority; also his speech against a bill hostile to the banks was most effective. With the session of 1842 his career as an occupant of state office came to an end. He retired from that service with the hatred and fear of the opposition party, and with the admiration, and possibly the fear, of his own. There can be no doubt that he had earned both these extremes of opinion. While an intense partisan, the influence of party could not restrain him when he differed with it, as he so often did. He had won an acknowledged position as the most formidable debater and perhaps the greatest orator at that time in public life in Pennsylvania. One of the leading organs of his own party, the "Harrisburg Telegraph," speaks of him at this time as a "giant among his pigmy opponents," and accords him "the most commanding abilities."

His fame had extended beyond the borders of his State. He took a conspicuous part in

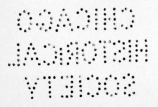

support of Harrison for the presidency in 1840, and it was believed in Pennsylvania that he was to have a seat in the cabinet.[1] The position he had attained in his party may be inferred from the fact that two years before his final retirement from the legislature, the friends of Harrison thought his support for the Whig presidential nomination of great value. Colonel McClure, who is high authority concerning Pennsylvania politics, makes the statement that Harrison sent to Stevens, through Mr. Purdy, "an autograph letter, voluntarily proposing that if Harrison should be nominated, and elected President, Stevens would be made a member of the cabinet." McClure adds that Stevens was one of the strongest of the leaders in the convention, and that "he finally controlled the nomination for Harrison."[2] Stevens appeared content to rest upon Harrison's promise, and was astonished, when the cabinet was announced, to find that it had been forgotten or repudiated, and that his name did not appear in the list.

The devotion of Stevens to politics had been

[1] "That Harrison had selected him for postmaster general is known with certainty, but through the open opposition of Clay and the wavering of Webster the appointment was given to Mr. Granger." Harris, *Biographical History of Lancaster County*, p. 582.

[2] McClure, *Lincoln and Men of War Times*, p. 261.

attended with the neglect of his private affairs.
Through the operations of a partner in the iron
business he found himself, at fifty years of age,
in debt to the amount of more than two hundred
thousand dollars. His temporary retirement
from politics had become imperatively necessary,
and to secure a wider field for his professional
practice he removed from Gettysburg to Lancaster. Alexander Hood, who was a law student in Stevens's office, and for many years
an intimate friend, is authority for the statement [1] that in 1843 his debts amounted to
$217,000. It is certain that when he estab-
lished himself at Lancaster, he was in deeper
poverty than when, a penniless young man, he
began his practice in Gettysburg a quarter of
a century before. But he had a reputation
as a lawyer and a public man, which preceded
him, and he had the necessary business talent
to straighten out the tangled affairs of his
iron business, and, to some extent, to retrieve
his disaster. In six years, according to Hood,
he succeeded in reducing his indebtedness to
$30,000.

He began practice at Lancaster in 1842.
The bar of that county numbered among its
members some of the ablest lawyers of Pennsylvania. Although already well known on account

[1] Harris, *Biographical History of Lancaster County.*

of his prominence in politics and his standing as a lawyer, he was again compelled to produce his passports, and to prove by actual contest his right to preëminence. The test came soon. He was retained in an important civil suit against Benjamin Champneys, the acknowledged leader of the bar. Stevens's mastery of his case and his method of presenting it so clearly established his superiority that he at once stepped into a position of acknowledged leadership, a position which he held unchallenged at the Lancaster bar until the day of his death. The rapid growth of his practice may be inferred from the fact that at the first session of the Supreme Court held in Harrisburg, after he settled in Lancaster, he was counsel in four of the six cases which came up from his county. In the next year he appeared in six of the eight cases, in addition to pleading cases from other counties. His practice brought him an income of from $12,000 to $15,000 a year, which may be esteemed an extraordinary amount when the time and the location are considered.[1]

His success was attested by the imitation with which he was flattered by his fellow members. When he came to the Lancaster bar its advocates were in the habit of making interminable addresses to the court and jury, but

[1] Harris, *Political Conflict in America*, p. 87.

Stevens soon cured them of this practice by the
force of his example. His speeches were condensed, brief, and terribly to the point, and
they were usually successful. He would unerr-
ingly detect the vital question, and he never
wasted his time upon side issues or trifles. His
example was soon followed by his professional
brethren. It was not his habit to take notes, but
no portion of the evidence escaped his marvelous
memory, and, disregarding the chaff, he fixed in
the minds of the jurymen that which was important to his side of the case, and demolished
with his ridicule the testimony which would
tell against him. While he had the choice of
causes at the bar, he did not confine himself
to those which paid large fees ; and especially
when proceedings were had for the return of
fugitive slaves, he was almost always found contributing his services to the defense of the negro.
His speeches in the fugitive slave cases were
the most eloquent and usually the most successful that he ever made in court. The evidence
against the black man for whom he spoke had
to be conclusive beyond all controversy whatever, or the white claimant had no chance to
prevail.

Stevens did not establish himself so quickly
in Lancaster County in politics as he did in
law. He was a Whig, but his devotion to the

lost cause of anti-Masonry had offended many influential members of his party who were Masons, while his radical views and methods of procedure led others to distrust his ability to become a safe leader. The "machine" of the Whig party in Lancaster offered him no encouragement, and he soon recognized the fact that he must fight his own way into the leadership or remain in the background. He at once decided to fight; but his political capital was not great. He attempted to revive the Masonic issue in the election of 1843, with the purpose apparently of diverting enough Whig votes to give the election to the Democrats of the county, and thus to prove that his support was necessary to the Whig party. This manœuvre ended in a disastrous failure. His faction polled fourteen hundred votes, but in spite of this division the Whig ticket was successful. This beginning was most unpromising; it still further separated him from the mass of the Whig party, and more closely identified him with an extreme and impotent faction. Not only was he not consulted, but his opposition soon became a passport to party favor. The nomination to Congress in 1844 was given to a man who was not only conspicuously hostile to the Stevens faction in the county, but who in the state legislature six years before, at the time of the "buckshot

war," had repudiated Stevens's leadership, and
voted to recognize the "Hopkins House."

Having failed to establish himself by fighting, Stevens concluded to try the effect of sulk-
ing, and the latter course proved the more effective. A situation soon arose in which his
services were needed. Henry Clay was nominated for the presidency in 1844, and it was
necessary for the Whigs to put forth every
effort to carry Pennsylvania. The Whig party
was so strong in the county that its leaders
could afford to indulge in the luxury of snub-
bing Stevens there, but in the State he was
easily the ablest man of his party, and his great
influence could not be disregarded. His opportunity had come. He could not only humiliate
the local leaders, but he could pay off an old
grudge which he had cherished toward Clay on
account of his failure to receive a cabinet appointment in 1841. He took to his tent. The
leaders were compelled to capitulate, and Clay
himself sent word to Stevens that in the event
of his election "atonement should be made for
past wrongs."

Thereupon Stevens took the stump and made
some powerful speeches for Clay. The most
notable occasion on which he appeared was in
Philadelphia, at a meeting which was made im-
mensely large by reason of the attraction of

Mr. Webster's name. The crowd was too great to be within hearing distance of the central platform, and another stand was erected in the outskirts, from which Stevens spoke. Mr. Webster spoke too often and was too great an orator to be uniformly eloquent. His great resources were, for the most part, called into play only on great occasions. It required the lashings of the tempest to stir up the depths of his nature. In a speech in an ordinary campaign, or one in which he was giving to a rival a not very cordial and almost perfunctory support, the godlike Daniel in his latter days could out-nod Homer, and could cause his hearers to nod also. On this occasion it soon became evident from the applause that those who were listening to Stevens were having a better time than those who were listening to Webster, and the platform from which the former was speaking soon became the principal one. This by no means indicated that Stevens was the greater orator, but that his wit, his power of keen argument, and his fund of good stories were more attractive to the crowd than was the profound and somnolent argument which Webster was very likely making on that day.

Clay was defeated after a very close contest, and the aspirations of Stevens for a seat in the cabinet remained then and ever afterward unsatisfied. He sought consolation again in his law practice, to which he gave his undivided attention. His qualities made him the idol of the young men, and a place as a student in his offices was greatly coveted. His prestige as a lawyer, as well as his good nature, may be inferred from the fact that he had as many as nine law students in his office at one time.[1] His contact with clients, witnesses, and jurymen rapidly widened his circle of acquaintances, and by attending strictly to his professional work he was fast acquiring popularity and a more solid basis of political strength than would ever have come from the political manœuvring in which he had sometimes indulged.

A half century ago, in a large and self-centred town, such as Lancaster was, a brilliant and successful lawyer like Stevens would almost certainly become the popular hero. The court-room was a common resort for all classes, and in the court-room in Lancaster County Stevens had reigned supreme ever since the day when he had shown his mettle against Benjamin Champneys. When the time came for the retirement of the member of Congress who then represented that district, Stevens became

[1] Harris is authority for the statement that a greater number of young men studied law with Stevens than with any other lawyer who had ever practiced at that bar.

the natural candidate. He still had the hostility of the men of his party who exercised the potent force which lay in the party machine. The leading party newspapers were against him. But the people had come under his spell, and in spite of the hostile party press and "machine," he was nominated as the Whig candidate for Congress by the narrowest of majorities. He showed his popularity with the voters by polling 9565 votes against 5464 votes for his Democratic antagonist.

CHAPTER V

The 31st Congress assembled in December, 1849, and Stevens for the first time took his seat as a member of the House of Representatives. He had almost reached the age of fifty-eight years, and therefore began his career in the House at a time of life when most men leave it, or have acquired from long service a position of leadership. It is undoubtedly true that an entrance into that body at an earlier age is more favorable to a successful career; but much depends upon previous occupation. Perhaps the most conspicuous figures in the history of the House of Representatives are John Quincy Adams and Thaddeus Stevens. Mr. Adams first took his seat there when more than sixty years of age. Both these men, however, had already had an experience which thoroughly equipped them for their work. Mr. Adams had served with distinction in the Senate, as secretary of state, as president, and in other important posts. Stevens had gained an

excellent parliamentary training in his long service in the Pennsylvania legislature, and his
practice at the bar had fitted him for the personal contests of the House of Representatives.
Both men were thoroughly equipped upon all
political questions, and they were also deeply
imbued with the spirit of our institutions. They
possessed those qualifications which a long service would naturally have created, and thus
their late appearance in the House really placed
them at no disadvantage.

The House at that time presented somewhat
greater opportunities to the new member than it
does to-day. Its membership was much less numerous, the country was not nearly so populous,
the amount of legislative business was greatly
less, and consequently the individual member, or
measure, stood a much better chance of recognition. The evolution of the rules had not
reached the point where, in order to secure the
rights of the House as a whole, it was necessary to suppress to so great an extent the privileges of the individual member.

But a career in the House at that time, as
now, was far from offering the fullest opportunity for statesmanship. The obvious difference
between the American government and other
free popular governments, of which the English
is the best model, is that in the American

government the essential powers are scattered among several departments, while in the English government those powers are practically concentrated in a single body and, essentially, in a single man; for so long as he can maintain himself in the Commons, the prime minister is the ruler of England. In the United States the President and his advisers can hold office to the end of the presidential term, however much they may differ with both houses of Congress, or even with the people as they may express themselves at the midway election between the beginning and the end of the term. The House of Representatives, the only direct popular branch of the government, has substantially the function of legislation, but jointly and equally with the Senate, and subject to the veto power of the President, which it requires a two-thirds vote of both legislative branches to overcome. The dramatic contests which mark parliamentary history elsewhere are of course not witnessed with us. An important measure may fail in the House, but no government falls in consequence; it may pass in the House and be defeated in the Senate, or it may pass both bodies to meet an executive veto; but none the less the steady routine of official existence will continue until the close of the term fixed by the Constitution. This condition of the Constitu-

tion doubtless conduces to conservatism in legislation, but it certainly does not conduce to the
development of the individual statesman. An
American statesman gets his power in install-
ments. In his early life he may try his hand
at legislation in the House; later he may appear
in the Senate, and in addition to legislative
work of practically the same character, he may
participate, in secret session, in the performance
of those executive functions, chiefly relating to
the filling of offices, which the Senate possesses;
and still later he may discharge the duties of
an executive officer as a member of the cabinet.
In the course of a long official career, therefore,
he will at different times very likely perform
substantially the same duties as a member of
the British government performs at one and the
same time.

The House in which Stevens took his seat
contained many men who were then well known,
or who afterwards became famous. In the dele-
gations from the New England States were Elbridge Gerry of Maine, Harry Hibbard of New
Hampshire, and Charles Allen, George Ashmun, Horace Mann, and Robert C. Winthrop,
of Massachusetts. Among the colleagues of
Stevens from Pennsylvania was David Wilmot,
the author of the famous proviso. Preston King
came from New York; Georgia sent Howell

Cobb, Alexander H. Stephens, and Robert Toombs. Ohio had among her members Joshua R.. Giddings and Robert C. Schenck; while among the Tennessee representatives were Isham G. Harris, who was then entering upon an official career destined to last for nearly half a century, and Andrew Johnson, to whose immortality Stevens contributed so greatly in the impeachment proceedings. The Whigs and Democrats were almost equal in number, and neither party was able to control the House. The Free-soilers and the radical Whigs held the balance of power.

While the devoted band of Free-soilers and the extreme Whig members, who soon ranged themselves behind Stevens as their natural leader, were too insignificant in number to elect the speaker, they were yet sufficiently strong to prevent either of the great parties from securing a majority. The Whig candidate was Robert C. Winthrop, who had been speaker of the preceding House, and was perhaps the most polished orator in that body. The Democratic candidate was Howell Cobb, an able man, but of a radically different political school. For three weeks the House fruitlessly balloted for the candidates. The contest was exciting and protracted beyond anything then known in the history of the House of Representatives. Although the

members had not been sworn in, and the only
business in order was to elect a speaker, or to
adjourn from day to day, the roll-call was re-
peatedly interrupted by threatening and inflam-
matory speeches.

Stevens soon appeared as a candidate, and
the vote for him included all the Free-soil members and an equal number of the Whigs. This
support was most respectable in character, and
it was no mean tribute to him that he should
receive it upon his first appearance in the House
of Representatives. It was impossible for any
candidate to obtain a majority. At length, by
general agreement, it was decided that a plu-
rality should elect, as the only solution of the
difficulty. The choice fell to Cobb, who was
only three votes ahead of Winthrop, but lacked
ten votes of a majority.

The Free-soil members agreed with Winthrop upon many political questions. They
disagreed with Cobb upon nearly all. It was
in their power to determine which should be
the speaker. But it illustrates the intensity of
the division, which then first appeared in the
Whig party, and finally led to its dissolution,
that its extreme members preferred an uncompromising enemy to a moderate friend. Their
object, however, lay farther in the future than
the election of the speaker of that House. They

aimed to force their party to take a more aggressive stand against slavery, or, failing in that, to disrupt it entirely, and organize a new party upon its ruins.

The slave question had reached a most acute stage, and overshadowed all other questions. Perhaps no Congress had met since the formation of the Constitution under such great excitement upon any domestic issue. The Mexican war had just been carried to a successful conclusion. Its principal result was the acquisition of a vast tract of territory, and, since the war had been emphatically a Southern war, the Southern leaders fondly hoped that the new domain would be carved into slave States, and thereby add to the strength of their peculiar "institution." Even if all this territory were not opened to slavery, the extension of the line of the Missouri Compromise to the Pacific Ocean would greatly augment the power of slavery.

Fortune, however, favored the cause of freedom. The new territory had scarcely been ceded to the Union when the discovery of gold in California set in motion a tide of immigration which, considering its volume, the energy of its motion, the distance it had to travel and the dangers it must overcome, may fairly be said to stand alone in the history of the transmigrations of the Anglo-Saxon race. Thousands of immigrants twice crossed the equator, and reached their destination over fifteen thousand miles of sea. Others took the shorter but scarcely less hazardous route by the Isthmus of Panama. Those who went overland dared the utmost dangers and privations, and were fortunate if they escaped slaughter at the hands of the savage.

In an incredibly short time California had a sufficient population to form a State, — a population that was liberty-loving, hardy, and brave. They were not the men to tolerate slavery. The territory itself, wonderful in its beauty, in its fertility, in its climate, and its wealth of resources, was fashioned to be the home of freedom. The people of California promptly adopted a free constitution and asked admission to the Union as a free State. The most that Congress could do was to refuse admission. The Democratic doctrine of popular sovereignty would not admit of an attempt to establish slavery there by national law, and, even if the attempt had been made, it would have been the most empty possible enactment, and one which never could have been put in force.

Nor was the question of slavery in the new territory the only irritating form which the slave problem assumed. The return of "persons held to service or labor," which was the

euphemistic term by which the framers of the
Constitution avoided the use of the word "slave"
in that instrument, had brought the wickedness
of the "institution" home to the people of the
free States.   They resented the apparent com-
plicity in the evil, which was involved in their
sending slaves back to bondage.   As a result
the laws upon the subject were very feebly enforced.   The people of the South believed that
the Constitution was being violated, and many
of their leaders threatened the dissolution of the
Union unless an effective law were enacted and
enforced for the return of runaway slaves.   The
slave problem, therefore, appeared in some form
or other in all the questions pressing for solution, and Stevens at the very threshold of his
national career was compelled to deal with the
question which had more intensely interested
him than any other.

The situation demanded the statesmanship of
Mr. Clay, who has had no superior in our history in ability to adjust, at least temporarily,
dangerous complications, and it was not an unfortunate circumstance that with this Congress
he again entered the Senate, from which he had
retired.   He was profoundly impressed with
the gravity of the crisis, and sincerely and patriotically desired to avert the perils with which
it was fraught.   He introduced a series of reso-

lutions covering the whole field, the important features of which were the admission of California as a free State, more effectual provisions for the return of fugitive slaves, territorial governments for New Mexico and Utah without any provision upon the question of slavery, payment of the debt of Texas, and the adjustment of her boundary, and the abolition of the slave trade in the District of Columbia.

Naturally enough this programme encountered hostility upon both sides. The provisions for the return of slaves and the establishment of the territorial governments without a prohibition of slavery were especially distasteful to the Whigs. The admission of California as a free State was equally distasteful to the Democrats. It is true that in all compromises between two parties something must be conceded upon both sides, but the extreme Whigs, of whom Stevens was the leader, were determined in this business not to yield anything.

He did not wait for the proposed compromise to reach the House, but on February 20, 1850, made a speech in which he violently attacked the proposition for the return of fugitive slaves, and broadly discussed the slavery question. This was his first set speech in Congress upon the subject, and he proposed to speak his mind frankly. "We can say anything," he said,

"within these walls or beyond them with impu-
nity unless it be to agitate in favor of human
liberty — that is aggression." While he announced his "unchangeable hostility" to slavery
"in every form and in every place," he declared
that he felt bound by the Constitutional provisions. Some of those compromises he greatly
disliked, and if they were still open he would
never consent to them, but he was precluded
from objecting. It was a matter of regret that
Congress had no power over slavery in the
States, and if it had, he would, regardless of
all threats, support "some just, safe, and certain means for its final extinction." He then
proceeded to discuss the wisdom of slavery in
a style which it is impossible to condense or
abridge without injuring the argument.

He first considered the question "in the low
light of political economy." That nation is the
most prosperous which has the most industrious and largest producing classes. "Those who
merely consume the fruits of the earth add nothing to the strength or the wealth of a nation."
Slave countries cannot have a large number of
industrious free men. "When the lash is the
only stimulant the spirit of man revolts from
labor." Never can such countries have a body
of small proprietors of the soil. The poor white
laborers are the scorn of the slave himself, and

are ranked with him. The soil occupied by slavery, he declared, is much less productive than a similar soil occupied by free men, because negligence and improvidence follow in its train. He illustrated his argument by a reference to Virginia.

"She has a delightful climate; a soil naturally fertile. She is intersected, as was well said by the gentleman from Virginia [Mr. Bayly], by the noblest rivers. Her hills and mountains are filled with rich minerals and covered with valuable timber. She has the finest water, I believe, in the nation, in the very heart of her State; and her harbors are among the best in the world. At the time of the adoption of the Constitution she was the most powerful State — her population was double that of New York. It was the boast of her statesmen that she was 'prima inter pares.' What is she now? The population of New York is more than double — I think the next census will show nearly treble hers. Her land, cultivated by unwilling hands, is unproductive. Travel through the adjoining States of Ohio and Pennsylvania, and you will see that the land produces more than double as much as the same kind of land in Virginia. In the free States new towns are everywhere springing up and thriving; the land is becoming more productive; smiling habitations are within hail

of each other; the whole country is dotted with
schoolhouses and churches almost within sight
of each other; and, except under peculiar circumstances, their manufactures and mechanic
arts are furnishing lucrative employment to all
their people; and their population is steadily
and rapidly increasing. Turn again to Virginia.
There is scarcely a new town, except at one or
two points, within her whole borders. Her
ancient villages wear the appearance of mourn-
ful decay. Her minerals and timber are un-
wrought. Her noble water-power is but partially
occupied. Her fine harbors are without ships,
except from other ports; and her seaport towns
are without commerce and falling to decay.
Ask yourself the cause, sir, and I will abide
the answer."

He thought it was vital to confine slavery to
the States in which it then existed, because that
course would bring the States themselves to its
gradual abolition. Permit the disease to spread,
and "it will render the whole body leprous and
loathsome." He again emphasized his cure for
slavery, which long dwelt in the memory of
Southern statesmen. "Surround it by a cordon
of freemen, so that it cannot spread, and in less
than twenty-five years every slave-holding State
in this Union will have on its statute books a law
for the gradual and final extinction of slavery."

This speech not only commanded the admiration of his friends and justified the votes they had given him for speaker, but it achieved the success of drawing upon him the fire of the opposition. It had strength and directness. It clearly expressed great ideas, which were not dressed up and concealed in any frippery of labored rhetoric. His trenchant power of argument, his courage, the force of his compact eloquence not merely established his position in the House, but they attracted the attention of the country. The proceedings of the House which most intensely interested Stevens were those relating to the slavery question. He was a member of the Judiciary Committee, and gave much of his time to the work of a technical and legal character which came before that committee; but his heart was with the slave, and his most elaborate speeches were made in his behalf.

When the California question came before the House, he seized the opportunity to state more fully his position with regard to slavery in the territories as well as to make more emphatic, if possible, his hostility to slavery everywhere. On June 10, 1850, he delivered another philippic, which was even more forcible and uncompromising than his February speech. He declared that in his opinion, so far as the constitutional power to admit new States was concerned, Congress only had power to admit such States as were formed out of territory previously belonging to the nation. He again expressed his unwillingness to violate any of the provisions of the Constitution, but displayed a good deal of legal ingenuity in the manner in which he construed some of those provisions. Aside from what he termed "the principle of eternal right," he would never give his consent to the admission of another slave State, unless bound to do so by some compact, "on account of the injustice of slave representation." He would not vote to give five slaves and their master the same voting power as four white men. From the eulogies which had been pronounced upon slavery, he would infer that the institution was a blessing politically and morally. Comparisons had been made between slaves and free working men much to the advantage of the slave. Instances had been cited "where the slave, after having tried his freedom, had voluntarily returned to resume his yoke." If this were true, he could not see any reason for being apprehensive as to the future of slavery. Slaveholders would never lack bondsmen. "Their slaves would remain, and many free men would seek admission into this happy condition." The North would not complain if they

would establish in the South "abolition societies
to abolish freedom."

He then referred to some of the glowing pic-
tures that had been painted of slavery. "If
these Southern gentlemen and their Northern
sycophants are sincere and correct, then I must
admit that they have just cause of complaint —
the only real aggression which the North ever
inflicted on them. For it cannot be denied
that for two centuries the North has mainly
contributed to secure to a particular race the
whole advantages of this blissful condition of
slavery; and, at the same time, has imposed
upon the white race the cares, the troubles, the
lean anxieties of freedom. This is a monopoly
inconsistent with republican principles, and
should be corrected. If it will save the Union,
let these gentlemen introduce a ' compromise '
by which these races may change conditions; by
which the oppressed master may slide into that
happy state where he can stretch his limbs on
the sunny ground without fear of deranging his
toilet; when he will have no care for to-mor-
row; another will be bound to find him meat
and drink, food and raiment, and provide for
the infirmities and helplessness of old age. Impose, if you please, upon the other race, as a
compensation for their former blessings, all
those cares, and duties, and anxieties. . . .

Homer informs us that the moment a man becomes a slave, he loses half the man; and a few short years of apprenticeship will expunge all the rest, except the faint glimmerings of an immortal soul. Take your stand, therefore, courageously in the swamp, spade and mattock in hand, and, uncovered and half naked, toil beneath the broiling sun. Go home to your hut at night, and sleep on the bare ground, and go forth in the morning unwashed to your daily labor, and a few short years, or a generation or two at the most, will give you a color that will pass muster in the most fastidious and pious slave market in Christendom." There were degrees in slavery, and having quoted Homer to illustrate its evils, he now cited a modern poet. "Dante, by actual observation, makes hell consist of nine circles, the punishments of each increasing in intensity over the preceding. Those doomed to the first circle are much less afflicted than those in the ninth, where are tortured Lucifer and Judas Iscariot — and, I trust, in the next edition will be added the Traitors to Liberty. But notwithstanding this difference in degree, all from the first circle to the ninth, inclusive, is hell — cruel, desolate, abhorred, horrible hell." He then recurred to the fugitive slave law. The owner of the slave had as effective remedies to recover his property as the

owner of a horse.   After citing the provisions
of the law, he said: "Is not this sufficient? It
is all the right which he would have if he claims
property in a horse, or other property, which he
might allege had strayed over the line.   Why
should he have any greater right when he claims
property in man?   Is a man of so much less
value than a horse, that he should be deprived of
the ordinary protection of the law?"   He then
drew a picture which was a most familiar one in
his experience.   "If an inhabitant of a free
State sees a wretched fugitive, who, he learns,
is fleeing from bondage, and gives him a meal
of victuals to keep him from starving, and
allows him to sleep in his outhouse, although his
master is not in pursuit of him, he is liable to
the penalty of five hundred dollars.   A judge in
Pennsylvania lately held that a worthy citizen
of Indiana County incurred such penalty by
giving a cup of water and a crust of bread to
a famishing man, whom he knew to be fleeing
from bondage.   A slave family escaped from
Maryland, went into Cumberland County, Pennsylvania, and obtained the reluctant consent of
a worthy farmer to sleep in his hayloft.   Their
owner did not pursue them for a week afterwards.   It was held by a state court that the
farmer was liable for the full value of the
slaves, besides the $500 penalty, and a jury

returned a verdict for $2000 and costs. Such
are some of the provisions of the law of 1793,
now in force, which these great expounders of
constitutional freedom hold to be too mild."

He commented with a good deal of asperity
upon the course of Webster and Clay. The
sons of the South were faithful, even though
its cause was that of human bondage. "But
the North, the poor, timid, mercenary, drivel-
ing North, has no such united defenders of
her cause, although it is the cause of human
liberty. Even her own great men have turned
her accusers." He declared his unyielding
opposition to the fugitive slave law. "The
distinguished senator from Kentucky [Clay]
wishes further to make it the duty of all by-
standers to aid in the capture of fugitives; to
join the chase and run down the prey. This is
asking more than my constituents will ever
grant. They will strictly abide by the Constitution. The slaveholder may pursue his slave
among them with his own foreign myrmidons,
unmolested, except by their frowning scorn. But
no law that tyranny can pass will ever induce
them to join the hue and cry after the trembling
wretch who has escaped from unjust bondage.
Their fair land, made by nature and their own
honest toil as fertile and as lovely as the Vale
of Tempe, shall never become the hunting-

ground on which the bloodhounds of slavery shall course their prey and command them to join the hunt."

The speeches of Stevens upon slavery in the thirty-first Congress were more rhetorical than those in his later style, and the faculty of wit which he could so successfully employ to provoke laughter and to promote a kindly feeling, displayed itself in these speeches in a biting, destructive sarcasm which grew out of his ineradicable hatred of slavery. They will, on the whole, bear comparison with any that were made during the entire history of the agitation.

It should be noted, also, that he did not speak one way and vote another. Clay's "omnibus bill," which contained the five features of the compromise, was defeated in the Senate, and having, in consequence, been resolved into its original elements, it came over to the House in the shape of five distinct bills. Stevens voted to the last against the fugitive slave law and the establishment of the territories without a prohibition against slavery. Enough of the Whigs, however, were willing to join with the Democrats to pass the Democratic features of the compromise, and enough Democrats united with the Whigs to pass the Whig features; thus ultimately the propositions of Clay all became embodied in law. The crisis was, perhaps, the most grave that had arisen under our government, and it was due in great measure to the statesmanship of Clay and the support he received from Webster that it was peacefully passed. The settlement, however, was only for the moment, and it was soon brushed aside by the impetuous slave leaders in their aggressive career, which finally culminated in war.

Stevens was reëlected to the thirty-second Congress. It assembled under much more peaceful conditions than had attended the meeting of its predecessor. The House organized without difficulty, and on the ballot for speaker Stevens received sixteen votes. Among his supporters were Charles Allen, Joshua R. Giddings, and Horace Mann. The compromise measures of Clay had temporarily effected a truce, and the great controversy in our politics was at that time dormant. Since the slavery agitation was suspended, Stevens had to be contented with the tariff, and his most elaborate speech in the thirty-second Congress was upon that subject. The speech was obviously intended for campaign purposes, and was made upon the Indian appropriation bill, under the rule or custom which makes all sorts of observations usual in a debate upon an appropriation bill except such as are pertinent to the bill.

He felt called upon at the outset to express sorrow at the "unhappy difficulties and dissensions which had destroyed the Democratic party," — a statement which was not strongly sustained by the election which soon followed, in which the Democratic candidate got nearly all the votes. His argument for the protective policy was an able one, but it dealt largely with the duties on iron, and was apparently directed to the voters of his own State.

One other extended speech he made in this Congress, and this time nominally upon the army appropriation bill. This also was a campaign speech, touching upon all the leading issues of the presidential election, containing ridicule of Mr. Pierce and praise of General Scott. He declared that Pierce could be relied upon to extend slavery and to aid in securing the admission of new slave States, notwithstanding that a speech which he was believed to have made had squinted in the opposite direction : — "If he ever did utter such sentiments — if he ever did fall into the path of rectitude, it was momentary and accidental, and for which he is not to be held responsible (renewed laughter) — for all his votes in Congress and all his public acts everywhere proclaim him the champion of slavery." [1] On the

[1] *Globe*, 32d Congress, 1st session, Appendix, p. 1029.

other hand, he alleged that Scott had nearly all
the virtues that could be desired in a presidential
candidate; that he was "deeply versed in municipal and international law;" that he was as
brave as Cæsar, "with no particle of his ambition;" that he believed it to be the moral duty
of slave States voluntarily to abolish slavery, —
and a good deal more in the same vein. In spite
of these ideal qualities as a candidate, Scott was
disastrously beaten. The people were getting
weary of the slavery agitation, and as the Democratic platform pledged the party to stand by
the compromise of 1850, the nation concluded
to take that party at its word. The signal Democratic triumph, however, was speedily followed by a repudiation of the compromise and
a radical reopening of the whole controversy.
But in the mean time Stevens had retired, as
he thought permanently, to private life, from
which he did not again emerge until his countrymen, aroused to fever heat, were about to
decide the question amid the clash of arms, and
he was to do the work which was destined to
make his name immortal.

CHAPTER VI

RESUMES LAW PRACTICE — AGAIN RETURNED TO CONGRESS — CAMPAIGN OF 1860

STEVENS retired from Congress in March, 1853, and it is probable that he did not expect to hold office again. In the very last hour of the session he arose to a personal explanation, for the purpose of disavowing any intention of disparaging a colleague in a speech he had made. "It is more than probable," he said, "that hereafter I shall never meet any member, here or elsewhere, officially, and I desire to part with no unfriendly feeling towards any of them." He returned to Lancaster, and resumed the practice of his profession with increased ardor, although he had not entirely relinquished it during his service in the House. During the latter part of 1851 he had appeared as counsel in the Hanway treason case, which was heard in the United States court in Philadelphia, and was probably the first important case, in Pennsylvania at least, arising under the fugitive slave law of 1850, which Stevens had so vigorously opposed in Congress.

Certain slaves of Edward Gorsuch, of Maryland, had escaped into Pennsylvania, and were
living in Lancaster County with other members
of their race. The owner proceeded under the
fugitive slave act, and, having obtained war-
rants for the fugitives, he went with the United
States marshal to point them out. The negroes
had secured arms, and energetically resisted the
officer in his attempt to serve the process. During the encounter Gorsuch was killed and two
other members of the marshal's party were
wounded. Two white men, of whom Castner
Hanway was one, and several others, were
arrested and tried on the charge of treason. It
is rare that any criminal proceeding has ever so
thoroughly aroused the country. The fugitive
slave act had only recently been passed amid
intense popular excitement. While an officer
of the law was proceeding according to its terms,
the Southern slave-owner had been shot down by
negroes. Not unnaturally the South was greatly
exasperated, and a numerous party in the North
supported the demand for the enforcement of the
law. On the other hand, there were not a few
who believed that a man, who was not accused
of crime, should have a right to fight for his
freedom, any statute or even the Constitution
itself to the contrary notwithstanding.

The trial closely held public attention during

the fifteen days that it lasted, and was memorable on account of the brilliant display of legal talent which it called forth. It appears to be conceded upon all sides that Stevens was the inspiration of the defense, and that its lines were laid down by him. But on account of his extreme anti-slavery views it was thought best to assign the part of leading counsel to a Democratic lawyer, and an extremely able one was found in John M. Read, who afterwards became chief justice of Pennsylvania. The trial ended in a verdict of acquittal, which was based upon the instruction of the court that the transaction did not rise to "the dignity of treason or the levying of war." [1]

The law practice of Stevens must have been very lucrative during the interval between the two periods of his congressional service. He had the choice of cases not merely in Lancaster, but also in the adjacent counties. He enjoyed a reputation second to that of no lawyer in Pennsylvania, and according to the best judges this reputation was thoroughly deserved. Colonel Alexander K. McClure, who was practicing law in a neighboring county during a portion of this period, knew Stevens intimately. After a long and honorable career in Pennsylvania,

---

[1] See McClure, *Lincoln and Men of War Times*, pp. 270, 271; Harris, *Political Conflict in America*, pp. 146-154.

in public life and as a journalist, which brought
him into close relations with the leading men
of his State, no man is more competent to place
an estimate upon the position of Stevens at the
bar, and I am fortunate in being able to present
his opinion, which I shall do in his own words.

"I had some experience with Mr. Stevens at
the bar from 1856 until ten years later, as he
attended all the Chambersburg courts and tried
one side of all the most important cases. I was
then a member of the Chambersburg bar, and
was Mr. Stevens's attorney in that county where
he had his large iron works. I have seen and
heard all the leading men of the Pennsylvania
bar who were contemporary with Mr. Stevens,
and I regarded him as the most accomplished
all round lawyer we had in the State. He was
thoroughly grounded in the fundamental principles of the law; was thoroughly familiar with
cases at home and abroad; was perfect in practice; elicited testimony from witnesses better
than any man I have ever heard in court, and
was one of the most skillful advocates that ever
addressed a jury. I was engaged with older
counsel against Mr. Stevens in the first important case I ever tried after my admission to the
bar, and felt much embarrassed in having so
accomplished an antagonist ; but he was one of
the most courteous men in the trial of a case,

whether engaged with or against him, and especially to the younger members of the bar, that
I have ever met. His invective, that was always
most wisely employed in the trial of cases, was
terrible, and the member of the bar who undertook to transcend the line of propriety was certain to pay dearly for his audacity; but he was
thoroughly manly and generous to all who mer-
ited such treatment. I have known many of
our great lawyers who were great advocates or
great in the skillful direction of cases, but he is
the only man I can recall who was eminent in
all the attributes of a great lawyer." [1]

For a short time after his retirement from
Congress, Stevens appears to have taken little
part in politics. He did not favor the compromising tendencies of the Whig party. His nature demanded something more radical, and he
probably regarded with a grim sort of satisfaction the disintegration of the political organization of which he had never been a very loyal
member, and which he had vainly endeavored
to make less conservative, first upon the question
of Masonry and afterwards upon slavery. In
1855 he attended a meeting in Lancaster, which
was held for the purpose of establishing the
Republican party in that county. The movement was not regarded with favor, and less than

[1] MS. letter, November 15, 1898.

twenty persons attended the meeting. The following year he was chosen a delegate to the Republican national convention, which nominated Frémont for the presidency. The formation of this new party, pledged to assume a more aggressive stand against the extension of slavery, rekindled his ambition to enter politics, and he reappeared in the national House as a representative from Lancaster at the December session of 1859.

Although he was then nearly sixty-eight years old, that which made his career memorable and most distinguished was still before him. He had doubtless shown conspicuous ability in every capacity in which he had thus far been called upon to act. He had never encountered his intellectual superior, either at the bar or in the Pennsylvania legislature, or in his four years' service in the national House. His work in establishing free schools in Pennsylvania was of transcendent importance, but it would probably not have extended his fame beyond the limits of his State. He had made one or two anti-slavery speeches in Congress, which deserve to take high rank in the literature of the crusade against slavery, and which are still gratefully remembered by the few survivors of the heroic band of those who stood with him in that great struggle. But there was probably never any

other political cause in which so much eloquence, good and bad, had been expended as
in the anti-slavery agitation, and his speeches,
standing alone, would not have caused him to
be longer remembered than some of the speeches
which he had made at the bar in behalf of fugitive slaves. Although he had shown himself
equal to every part he had been called upon to
play, yet his great opportunity had not come,
and if he had died at sixty-eight his name
would hardly have been mentioned in the history of his country.

It was evident that he himself had no premo-
nition of the work before him, and that he felt
conscious of the infirmities of age. Something
like an apology for his reappearance upon the
scene is found in a short eulogy which he delivered upon one of his colleagues, John Schwarz,
soon after his return to Congress. He said that
the loss of his colleague would perhaps have
been greater if he had been cut off in the prime
of manhood. "There are but few in this
House," he added, "who with me can appreciate the force of that suggestion. It were perhaps more graceful for those who are conscious
that age or infirmity has impaired their mental
and physical powers, who find by repeated trials
that they can no longer bend the bow of Ulysses,
to retire, and lay down the discus which they

have not the strength to hurl." How he might at an earlier age have done the work that was his to do can only be conjectured, but his supreme opportunity came to him in that far time when most men cease from their labors, and he then proved that he still retained enough of his youthful strength to take easily the lead in momentous events with which only a great man can deal, and for which a real leader is chosen, not because men consciously want him, but because the events seek him out by a process of natural selection.

By a curious coincidence the beginning of the second period of his congressional service was marked by a contest over the organization of the House not less exciting and even more protracted than that which had occurred when he first became a member of that body. As a result of its aggressive policy the new Republican party had elected a greater number of the members of the House than the Democrats had succeeded in electing. The Whig party had almost entirely disappeared, and its name was perpetuated in the House by only a single member. The Republicans, however, could not command the majority of all the members, which was necessary to a control, and the balance of power was held by the twenty-six members of the "American" party, so called, who were

somewhat less radical than the Republicans upon
the question of slavery, and were chosen, not
so much upon a platform for the restriction
of immigration, as from hostility to foreign-
born citizens.

At the outset the Republican strength was
divided on the vote for speaker between John
Sherman and Galusha A. Grow, the former of
whom has only recently retired from politics
after a highly useful and illustrious career, and
the latter is still serving in the House of Representatives with undiminished ability and with
all the enthusiasm and patriotic zeal which
characterized him as speaker during the presidency of Lincoln.   The Republican vote was
very soon consolidated upon Sherman; but although he received support from the "American" party he never quite secured the necessary
majority.

The proceedings were scarcely less turbulent
than when, in the thirty-first Congress, Mr.
Toombs had so easily outshone all competitors
in violence and intemperate threats.   The roll-
call was interrupted by long speeches, many of
them apparently made with the purpose of con-
suming time, and some doubtless to intimidate
Northern members with the well-worn threat of
dissolving the Union.   Stevens had been through
a similar contest, and he attempted to check

the flow of incendiary oratory by the point of
order, that the only business the House could
transact under the Constitution was to vote for
speaker or adjourn. Well founded as his point
of order certainly was, he was not conspicuously
fitted to fill the rôle of peacemaker, if indeed
he had taken the floor with so serious a purpose.
He grimly observed, amid Republican laughter,
that he did not blame Southern members "for
using this threat of rending God's creation from
the turret to the foundation." They had uttered
the menace a great many times, and a great
many times they had found "weak and timid
tremblers in the North who had been affected
by it." He then congratulated them upon their
ability to maintain grave countenances while
again attempting the same play.

This outpouring of vinegar instead of oil
produced its natural and probably its intended
result, and provoked interruptions and threats,
the angry sincerity of which could not be
doubted. "That is right," said Stevens, "that
is the way they frightened us before." This
irritating response added new fury to the storm,
and the members rushed together in the centre
of the hall amid the greatest excitement and
disorder. The clerk declared that he was powerless to enforce order. Stevens relieved the
strain and displayed his power over the members

by saying blandly: "This is a mere momentary breeze, sir, nothing else."

The contest continued for more than eight weeks. Stevens occasionally took a hand and rekindled the fury of his antagonists, when the proceedings lapsed into dullness; and sometimes, when the danger point was near, he averted the trouble by some happy remark which restored good humor. Mr. Anderson, a Democratic member from Missouri, proposed that all parties opposed to the Republican party should get together in a caucus and agree on an organization of the House, — a naïve suggestion which, if followed, would have given his party the control of the House. The gentleman, said Stevens, amid great laughter, had proposed "that happy family described in the 'Prairie' where the prairie wolf, the owl, and the rattlesnake live in one hole."

One day, late in the contest, Stevens arose with a very serious countenance, and said that a vote of his had been criticised in a newspaper, and he desired to make an explanation. He thereupon sent to the clerk's desk a paper, which he requested should be read. The clerk, after looking blankly at the paper, replied, amid the usual laughter that almost invariably attended the appearance of Stevens during that contest: "The paper is printed in German, and the clerk cannot read it." "Then," said Stevens, "I postpone my remarks until the clerk can read it."

There was certainly something in his ready and unfailing wit and in his manner that captured the House. The official record of the little speeches which he interjected into the proceedings are frequently punctured with the report of "laughter." The man himself and the circumstances of the moment formed a great part of what he said, and the effect cannot be reproduced by a repetition. There could hardly be a better tribute to his wit. It was never-failing, always sufficient, and it played like heat lightning over the proceedings of the House; yet sometimes it would show the force of the bolt that kills. "I never saw any one who was his match," said one who was a member of the House during the entire period of his second term of service, and who served with great distinction in both houses of Congress. "There was usually that quality in his wit which compelled you to join in the laugh he raised, even when it was at your own expense." [1]

It was, however, the exception for good humor to prevail during this long-drawn-out struggle for the speakership. The contest for that office was the occasion, but it was far from being the

[1] Hon. Henry L. Dawes.

cause, of those heated exhibitions of partisanship and violations of parliamentary decorum
which, during two months, signalized the proceedings of the House of Representatives. The
great contest over slavery had reached a climax.
The "irrepressible conflict" with freedom was
rapidly passing outside the domain of laws
and compromises and taking the inevitable form
of an appeal to arms. The crisis of 1850 had
been safely passed by a compromise which was
distasteful to both parties, as all real compromises are apt to be, but which a majority of the
people of the country were doubtless willing to
accept.

President Pierce, who had been elected by
an overwhelming vote, had declared in his first
annual message to Congress that the settlement
had resulted in giving "renewed vigor to our
institutions and restored a sense of peace and
security," and he promised that the repose which
had resulted from the compromise should not
be disturbed if he had the power to prevent it.
The convention which nominated him had given
a pledge against reopening the slavery question.
The leaders of the aggressive slavery party,
however, immediately proceeded to redeem this
pledge by the repeal of the "Missouri Compromise," which had been in force for a generation,
and which the people of the North regarded

only less reverently than the Constitution itself. This act of bad faith, followed as it was by the Dred Scott decision, the criminally conducted attempt to force the new State of Kansas to accept slavery, and the confident beginning of an agitation to wipe out the laws against the slave trade, aroused the spirit of the North and made a peaceful adjustment of the controversy well-nigh impossible. Of what use were compromises, when the most solemn ones were entered into only to be deliberately broken? The middle ground for conservatives to stand upon was each day growing narrower, and the people of the country were rapidly dividing into two parties, of which the advocates of slavery formed the one, and the friends of freedom the other.

It was in this condition of affairs that the thirty-sixth Congress assembled. It was hardly to be expected that all the niceties of parliamentary decorum should be observed when, after a long controversy, the passions of men had at last been kindled to the point of fighting. Stevens, who had nothing of compromise in his nature, found himself at last in accord with the prevailing popular temper, which demanded something radical instead of craving sedatives. He was enveloped by a very different atmosphere from that which pervaded the House when he was formerly a member, and one that was altogether more congenial; and although the interruption in his service had placed him to a certain extent in the position of a new member, yet he at once naturally assumed a more prominent place than he had ever held before.   The Democratic leaders had treasured up some of his declarations made against slavery during his former service, and their efforts to call him to account provoked responses which were received by his own side with unmistakable expressions of approval.   Mr. Clemens interrupted Stevens during one of his speeches in the speakership contest, and asked him whether he had not declared in a speech in Congress that the slave States should be surrounded by free States as by a cordon of fire until slavery like a scorpion should sting itself to death.   "If I did," replied Stevens, "it is in the books." Clemens pressed for a more direct answer, and Stevens then suggested that perhaps he was thinking of a remark of a friend of his from New York, who said he would surround the slave States "with an atmosphere of freedom, and that they should breathe it or die."   At the same time, Stevens declared that "republicanism is founded in the love of universal liberty and in hostility to slavery," and that if he had the power he would abolish human servitude everywhere.   But "the Constitution of the

United States," he added, "gives us no power
to interfere with the institutions of our sister
States."   While he denied that the Republican
party had any desire to disregard any of the
safeguards which the Constitution threw around
slavery, it would never favor any extension of
slavery upon this continent, and it would at an
opportune time abolish it in the District of Columbia, where Congress undoubtedly had jurisdiction.   The contest over the speakership at
last came to an end through the union of the
forces hostile to the Democratic party, and thus
a Republican speaker was elected.

The first important work to engage the attention of Stevens concerned the pressing needs of
the national treasury, which was in a most im-
pecunious condition.   The Committee on Ways
and Means, of which he was a member, reported
a bill for the payment of outstanding treasury
notes, to fund the debt, chiefly caused by the
deficiency in the revenues which had existed for
nearly three years, to repeal the tariff act of
1857, and to substitute a new measure for raising revenue, of which the important feature was
an increase of the duties upon imports.   The act
of 1857 had not shone brightly as a producer of
revenue.   During each year of its existence the
income had fallen far short of the expenditures,
and for the three years the deficit had amounted

in the aggregate to the sum of $50,000,000, which was an enormous amount upon a scale of national expenditures not one fifth so great as that of thirty-five years afterwards.

The revenue measure proposed by the committee to which Stevens belonged was exhaustively debated, and arguments which even at that time were far from novel, and certainly have not since been permitted to become unfamiliar, were offered in support respectively of protection and of free trade. Stevens made his contribution to the discussion in a speech, in which he made the somewhat paradoxical point that the repeal of the corn laws in Great Britain was essentially a protective enactment, because the only advantage possessed by American manufacturers over the British was in cheapness of food, and this was destroyed by the removal of the duty. He declared further that the British export duty on coal was also protective, because it compelled the manufacturers of France and other competing countries, poorly supplied with coal, to pay more for it, and to that extent gave the English manufacturer an advantage. This was ingenious, but hardly consistent with other arguments advanced on Stevens's side of the controversy, because both his propositions were based on the theory that laws which tended to give the manufacturers relatively cheaper raw material were in their nature protective. The bill passed the House by a large majority, and ultimately became a law in the closing days of the Congress, because of the withdrawal of the Southern senators, and because the President, in view of the approaching war, felt compelled to accept the increased revenue which the bill offered, although it was drawn upon principles antagonistic to his own.

Stevens also frequently took part in the debates on contested election cases, and it is worthy of notice that he condemned the system, under which the whole House assumed to act judicially upon the long and contradictory records usually found in those cases, and would then decide in almost every case, and with the best of intentions, upon partisan grounds. The obvious impossibility of securing the semblance of judicial fairness from a large body, composed of hundreds of members, of whom many were not lawyers, and of whom also not one in twenty would ordinarily have any knowledge of the evidence, strongly appealed to his common sense, partisan though he was, and impelled him to protest against a method which so often resulted in a mere travesty upon justice. He declared that it was a misfortune that we had not adopted the system prevailing in the British parliament, under which a committee was selected and sworn to try the case, and their report was accepted as final. Stevens, however, bravely survived this attack of non-partisanship, and at a later period in his career, after he had become hardened from a long practice at political surgery, he had advanced so far that upon one occasion he entered the House when a vote was being taken upon a contested election case, of the merits of which he was entirely ignorant, and in order that he might know how to cast his own vote he grimly asked of a colleague: "Which one is *our* d—d rascal?"

Since the system of which he complained had not been changed, he finally adapted himself to it. But it is significant that he condemned it and suggested a remedy, which since his day has been more than once proposed, for a system so certain of abuse, and which has cast reproach upon the House of Representatives.

He also kept a keen eye upon possible jobs aimed at the treasury. An instance is found in a project of an international character. The Senate had added amendments to the naval appropriation bill, appropriating $300,000 to enable the President to carry into effect a conditional contract between the secretary of the navy and the "Chiriqui Improvement Company," for securing coal and for harbor and other privileges in the Republic of Granada.

The project was supported by some very eloquent and patriotic speeches. It was said that it would result in placing a "commercial crown upon American brows;" that it would reëstablish our shipping industry and give us a large share of the East Indian trade, — and all for the small sum of $300,000, to be paid to the "Chiriqui Improvement Company."

Stevens unpatriotically moved to amend by striking out the proposition and appropriating a small sum to pay the expense of a commissioner to investigate the entire matter. He said that his information was to the effect that there was no coal and that there was no harbor. The statement that if we did not take it some other nation would, was made in the interest of speculators and to prevent an investigation. France and Great Britain had known about it for years, but the gentlemen controlling the scheme would not sell it to them, but would hold it for their own country, "because they are patriots of the first water." We should not be hurried into the appropriation. He then raised a laugh against the proposition by saying: "I think it time to put an end to this whole thing by an actual touch of the spear of Ithuriel and sending the angel out there."

One of the advocates of the measure replied that it was "not to be killed by the keen satire or the merciless ridicule of the gentleman from Pennsylvania;" but the House evidently thought differently, and adopted Stevens's amendment without a division.

The great Granada scheme, however, was not to be put down easily. An enterprise with so much money involved, and directed against the treasury, rarely is. During the following session, when the minds of members were engrossed with the effort to compromise with the seceding States, it stealthily put in an appearance in the House again. This time it fastened itself as an amendment upon the deficiency appropriation bill, which seems to have been then, what it has ever since remained, an attractive bill for jobs little suited to stand the ordeal of scrutiny and debate. But it did not escape the attention of Stevens, who assailed it in a half hour's speech, in which he refused to call anybody dishonest, but declared that the scheme was "as bold a thing as was ever gotten up by honest men." He caused the project to be laughed out of the House even more decisively than on the previous occasion.

The adjournment of the first session of the thirty-sixth Congress was followed by the most exciting presidential campaign in the history of the country. The great issue in the contest of 1860 necessarily grew out of the question,

whether slavery should be extended, or whether
it should be restrained within the limits in which
it was then confined. The slavery leaders had
only themselves to thank that at last their cherished institution was to furnish the substantial
ground of difference in a presidential election.
Had they rested content with the compromise
of ten years before, it is probable that it would
have stood for a generation. Undoubtedly there
would have been agitation, as the " institution," in the nature of things, could not endure
forever. But few men, if any, could have been
found at that time in public life willing to advocate the interference of Congress with slavery
in States where it had been established. Even
Stevens, with all his radicalism, was willing
that the provisions of the Constitution should
be enforced, although he would concede no
doubtful construction.

But scarcely had the compromise of 1850 become operative when the friends of slavery secured its repeal. By this action they succeeded
in alienating a large number of their supporters
whom they needed in the final contest. Douglas, who had yielded to the extent of aiding in
the repeal of the Missouri Compromise, had
more than redeemed his reputation by his courageous struggle against the attempt to force slavery upon Kansas. The bitter hostility of the

weak and obnoxious administration of Buchanan gave him a new title to popular favor, and while he was only less hateful to the ultra slave party than was Lincoln himself, he was idolized by the majority of his own party, and admired by many of the followers of Lincoln. In a personal campaign, which has since become somewhat fashionable among candidates for the presidency, but was then almost unknown, he displayed his remarkable capacity as a campaign speaker in widely separated portions of the country; and in the final disruption of his party, which was witnessed on election day, by far the greater number of its members were found following his standard.

The unfortunate leadership which had broken up the Democratic party was in striking contrast with the sagacious conduct of its antagonist. There was never a happier outcome from the uncertain chances of a political convention than the nomination of Lincoln. He was not less strong as a candidate because he could hardly have been classed among the leaders of his party. He had always been active in the politics of his own State, and was chiefly known to the country on account of the ability he had shown as a leader in Illinois and especially in the joint debates with Douglas. But his comparative obscurity gave him a great advantage over Seward, whose conspicuous national career had engendered antagonisms which showed themselves in the convention, and would have been sure to cause the loss of votes at the polls.

Stevens sat in the convention as a delegate from Pennsylvania. His delegation supported Simon Cameron, whose relations with him personally were not of the most cordial character, and who was brought forward on account of his prominence in the politics of his State. Stevens' real choice for the presidency was John McLean, who stood at the opposite extreme of the party from himself, and was probably the most conservative of all the candidates.[1] Cameron's strength, in common with that of the other candidates, was ultimately transferred to Lincoln, for whom Stevens voted upon the ballot which secured his nomination. With such a candidate supported by a young, expanding, and vigorous party, and with Douglas scarcely less hostile and more dangerous, because he endeavored to take a middle ground, the cause of slavery as an aggressive institution was doomed.

A good deal of importance has often been given to the fact that Lincoln was chosen president by a minority of the popular vote. It is true that the popular vote for the Lincoln

[1] McClure, *Lincoln and Men of War Times*, p. 259.

electors was much less than the combined vote
of the other candidates; but it is hardly significant, because it is also true that the supporters
of Douglas were nearer to the supporters of
Lincoln upon the question of the extension
of slavery than they were to the party of Breckenridge. Douglas had gone beyond the point
of political safety when he yielded upon the
Missouri Compromise. Later he had manfully
broken with his party and burned his bridges
behind him upon the Kansas question. The
forces, then, in favor of extending slavery are
measured by the vote for Breckenridge; the
forces against its practical extension are measured by the combined vote for Lincoln and
Douglas. No one appreciated this fact more
clearly than did the Southern leaders.

The meaning of the election appeared to be
that, in the territory at that time covered by our
flag, slavery should be confined to the States in
which it then existed, with the possibility of its
extension to the elevated and barren regions of
New Mexico. That was the probable meaning
of the popular verdict. But popular verdicts
are sometimes given away when put in the
keeping of intimidated representatives, as narrowly escaped illustration that very winter.
Such a limitation meant the loss of relative
political power to the South, and, with the

admission of new free States, with the rapid increase in population and wealth that was sure to come to the North, with the multiplication of free laborers armed with the ballot, who would not work in competition with slaves, and with a general advance in civilization, it also meant the ultimate abolition of slavery.

The Southern statesmen were able to read the handwriting upon the wall, and for the purpose of securing the safety of their cherished institution they determined upon the war which resulted in freedom. Peace very likely would ultimately have led to the same end, if, indeed, there could have been any real peace amid such antagonistic conditions; but the pathway that was chosen lay through the wilderness, and the goal was reached after the loss of more than six hundred thousand men, the destruction of enormous accumulations of wealth, and the creation of a condition of things in the revolting States which almost caused the extinction of civilization itself.

CHAPTER VII

THE thirty-sixth Congress came together again at the December session of 1860, under the shadow of impending war. The movement to disrupt the Union had been already well developed. The secession convention in South Carolina had been called, and her national senators had resigned their seats. A convention had been ordered in Georgia, and a large sum of money appropriated to arm the State. The legislature of every Southern State which had assembled had taken steps in support of the movement. There was no room to doubt that a grave crisis was upon the country, a crisis which demanded vigilance, energy, courage well-tempered with discretion, and, above all, patriotism on the part of the officers of the government.

Unfortunately, President Buchanan had few of the qualities so necessary to brave such a threatening storm. He was undoubtedly patriotic, and few men could write an abler state paper. But he was credulous, inefficient, completely under the domination of the Southern leaders, and so little alive to the real danger of the situation that he was apparently willing to use it for his own justification and to reprove the people of the North for electing Lincoln and casting so large a vote for Douglas. Throughout his administration he had been the blind instrument of those who were now seeking to overturn the government, and his conduct at the critical moment deserves to be regarded as the most conspicuously weak action of his whole career.

In his message to Congress, on the day on which that body assembled, he declared that "the long continued and intemperate interference of the Northern people with the question of slavery in the Southern States has at length produced its natural effects. I have long foreseen and often forewarned my countrymen of the now impending danger." The claim of Congress, or of the territorial legislatures, to exclude slavery from the territories, or the refusal of the States to enforce the fugitive slave law might, he said, have been endured by the South. The difficulty arose from the fact that this agitation has at length produced its "malign influence upon the slaves, and inspired them with vague notions of freedom." He then painted

in vivid colors the results of the apprehension
of a "servile insurrection," and added that "no
political union, however fraught with blessings
and benefits in all other respects, can long continue, if the necessary consequence be to render
the homes and the firesides of half the parties
to it habitually and hopelessly insecure. Sooner
or later the bonds of such a union must be severed."

Having delivered this powerful justification of
secession, he declared his conviction "that this
fatal period has not yet arrived." This declaration was doubtless sincere, but it proves that
the President did not comprehend the gravity
of the crisis. He then directed a strong argument to the South against breaking up the
Union, but made his argument ineffective by
subsequently reaching the conclusion that in
certain cases "the injured States, after having
used all peaceful and constitutional means to
obtain redress, would be justified in revolution-
ary resistance to the government of the Union,"
that the means of preserving the Union which
Congress possessed were only of a conciliatory
character, and that "the sword was not placed
in their hands to preserve it by force."

Jefferson Davis himself could not have written a message better suited to his purpose than
was here transmitted to Congress by the Presi-

dent of the United States. The grievance of
the South was admitted, its right to revolution-
ary resistance in this particular case was all
but admitted, and the power of preserving the
Union by force was denied. The harm done by
the message was beyond all calculation, not only
in the South, where it encouraged the belief
that there would be no resistance to secession,
but in the North also, where Mr. Buchanan's
personal influence was considerable and that of
his office was great.

The President was not long in seeing his fatal
mistake. The hostile comments of the Southern
press, the resignation of his venerable and patriotic secretary of state, Lewis Cass, and the
firm stand by the attorney-general, Jeremiah S.
Black, with reference to the reception of the
"ambassadors" from South Carolina, who came
to demand the surrender of the forts, brought
the President to his senses. Those members of
the cabinet who really represented secession,
and who had powerfully contributed by the use
of their positions to the cause of the disunion-
ists, now that their influence with the President
was gone, resigned, and proceeded to do openly
that which they had long been doing secretly.
His cabinet was speedily organized upon a
basis which put better influences in the ascendency. Jeremiah S. Black was made secretary

of state, and he brought his splendid ability to the task of extricating the President from the difficulty in which he had been placed by his argument against the power of Congress to maintain the Union by force, and in which Mr. Black himself had been responsible to a considerable extent for involving him. The result was the message of January 8, 1861, which displayed a radical change in tone from the message at the beginning of the session, and vindicated the right of the government "to use the military force defensively against those who resist the federal officers in the exercise of their legal functions, and against those who assail the property of the federal government."

It is significant that the keen eye of Stevens had already detected this loophole of escape for the President, and that his sense of leadership impelled him to take action. On the last day of December, nine days before the reception of the message, he presented a resolution to the House, calling upon the President to inform the House upon the condition of the forts, arsenals, and public property in the vicinity of the city of Charleston; "whether any means were taken to garrison them and put them in a defensible condition after it became evident that South Carolina intended to secede;" how many troops were there, and whether orders had been given for reinforcements. This resolution failed to receive the two-thirds vote which the rules of the House required for its passage, but it received a considerable majority, the vote being 91 to 62. This action conveyed an unmistakable intimation to the President that, in the opinion of a large majority of the House, it was the duty of the administration to provide for the defense of our forts and public property, and it must have infused into Mr. Buchanan a certain degree of that courage of which he so sadly stood in need.

But if the President had failed to comprehend the importance of the crisis, Congress proved itself fully alive to it. Indeed, it was so impressed with the magnitude of the danger, that it was willing, in order to avert it, to sacrifice freedom itself. Each House at once appointed a special committee to deal with the situation. The Senate committee was composed of thirteen members, which was equal in number to the States which formed the original Union. The House committee of thirty-three contained a member for each of the States then included in the Union.[1] The Senate committee soon reported a disagreement, and its work amounted to nothing.

The House committee was established by an

1 Blaine, *Twenty Years of Congress*, vol. i. p. 259.

amendment offered to a routine motion for the reference of the President's annual message. The amendment provided that so much of the message "as relates to the present perilous condition of the country be referred to a special committee of one from each State." The amendment was adopted by a vote of nearly five to one, but among the small minority were numbered Stevens and the more radical anti-slavery men, who had been educated by the experience of previous compromises to believe in their utter futility.

The sessions of the House committee were long and numerous, and its proceedings were interesting chiefly on account of the variety of remedies suggested and the extreme concessions which its members were willing to make for the preservation of the Union. It is only necessary to refer to a few of the more important propositions in order to appreciate the wide scope of the inquiry entered upon by the committee. Mr. Corwin, of Ohio, suggested a law declaring the inexpediency of abolishing slavery in the District of Columbia, "unless with the consent of the States of Maryland and Virginia." Mr. Houston proposed the restoration of the line of 36° 30', which was the line of the Missouri Compromise, and Mr. Taylor asked for a constitutional amendment providing that only persons of "the Caucasian race and of pure and unmixed blood" should be allowed to vote for any officer of the national government.

The proposition submitted by Mr. C. F. Adams was of far-reaching importance, and it would have effectually postponed to the millennium the peaceful abolition of slavery under law. He proposed to amend the Constitution so that no future amendment, proposing any interference with slavery, "shall originate with any State that does not recognize that relation within its own limits, or shall be valid without the assent of every one of the States composing the Union." The extreme character of this concession established Mr. Adams's high estimate of the value of the Union, and furnished material proof that he was indulging little in rhetoric, when, somewhat later, in a speech in the House in defense of the report of the committee, he said: "Rather than this [a division of the Union] let the heavens fall."

The remarkable thing in connection with this amendment was that it received nearly the unanimous support of the committee. There were few radical propositions made in favor of slavery which a majority of the committee were not disposed to favor. The leading recommendations of its report included Mr. Adams's amendment, the repeal of the so-called personal

liberty laws in the free States; the admission of
New Mexico with its slave laws; and the amendment of the fugitive slave law, so that a person
who was seized under the claim that he was a
slave should have his right to freedom tried by
jury, not in the State where he was seized, and
of which he might be a free white citizen, but
in the slave State from which he was accused of
having fled.[1]

This, then, was to be the result of the disruption of the Democratic party and the triumph
of the Republicans upon a platform hostile to
the growth of slavery! This was to be the
outcome of the first national verdict rendered
against that "institution"! The fugitive slave
law was to be armed with new terrors not only
against the slave, but also against free American
citizens living in a free State, and the Constitution was to be smeared all over with the muni-
ments of slavery. Stevens had voted with a
very small minority against the appointment of
the committee, and he remained its consistent
foe to the very end.

Not long after its appointment, and when
propositions of all sorts were being referred
to it, Stevens supplied a name for the committee which it had appeared to lack. The
"Committee on Incubation," he called it. His

[1] Blaine, *Twenty Years of Congress*, vol. i. pp. 260, 261.

attitude upon the proposed compromises it would not be difficult to conjecture. He not only opposed by his vote every feature of the report, but he made a speech of considerable length in the House, in which he showed little mercy to the committee. He said that, when States in open and declared rebellion seized upon public forts and arsenals, he had no hope that "concession, humiliation, and compromise can effect anything whatever." He alluded to the lack of a compromising spirit on the part of the Southern representatives, as shown by their vote the day before against the consideration of the bill to admit Kansas, "that source of all our woes." The time for compromises had gone by, and the virtue most needed in that perilous time was "courage, calm unwavering courage, which no danger can appall." If statesmen, "governed by such qualities, should be found at the head of this nation when danger comes, there can be no fear for the result. The Union will overcome all difficulties and last through unnumbered ages to bless millions of happy freemen."

He did not believe that the Southern States were to be "turned from their deliberate and stern purpose by soft words." He then turned his attention to Buchanan in a somewhat severer manner than he had been accustomed to employ

towards him.   He had usually alluded to him
as "my constituent," from the fact that the
President's home was in Lancaster, or in terms
of mock eulogy as "our intelligent and patriotic
President."   But the occasion was too solemn
for him to attempt to evoke the usual laugh.
He resented as an "atrocious calumny" the
President's charge, that the "long continued
and intemperate interference of the Northern
people with the question of slavery in the Southern States" was responsible for the crisis.   The
President well knew that the anti-slavery party
of the North never interfered with slavery in
the States.   Search the records of the legislatures and party conventions, and "you will find
them always disclaiming the right or intention
to touch slavery where it existed."   He dismissed the charge as a "calumny on the freemen of the North," made by one "who, during
his whole political life, had been the slave of
slavery."   He thought that the time had at last
arrived for determining whether secession was
a rightful act.   If it were, "then the Union is
not worth preserving for a single day;" for if
the emergency then existing should pass away,
"fancied wrongs would constantly arise" and
induce States to secede.   He then made a powerful argument against the right of secession,
and declared that the South had no just griev-

ance. "Rather than show repentance for the election of Mr. Lincoln, with all its consequences, I would see this government crumble into a thousand atoms. If I cannot be a freeman, let me cease to exist."

Returning to the committee of thirty-three, he said that it had shown its estimate of Southern grievances "by a most delicate piece of satire." As a remedy, and to lead back the rebellious States, the committee offered "to admit as a State about 250,000 square miles of volcanic desert, with less than a thousand white Anglo-Saxon inhabitants and some 40,000 or 50,000 Indians, Mustees and Mexicans, who do not ask admission, and who have shown their capacity for self-government by the infamous slave-code which they have passed, which establishes the most cruel kind of black and white slavery." He must admit, however, that Mr. Corwin, the chairman of the committee, seemed "to have become enamored of peonage. He looks upon it as a benevolent institution, which saves the poor man's cow to furnish milk for his children by selling the father instead of the cow." The slave States would be much better off in the Union than out of it. If secession became effective, there would be "one empire wholly slave-holding and one republic wholly free." While we should faithfully execute the present compact, "yet if it should be torn to pieces by rebels, our next United States will contain no foot of ground on which a slave can tread, no breath of air which a slave can breathe. Our neighboring slave empire must consider how it will affect their peculiar institution. They will be surrounded with freedom, with the whole civilized world scowling upon them."

Mr. Dawes, who was a member of Congress at the time, has preserved a striking picture of the effect of this speech. "No one," says Mr. Dawes, "could forget the scene in which it occurred, though all I can say of it and of him seems tame enough without the inspiration of the occasion and of his presence. This speech was delivered in that last session in Mr. Buchanan's administration, after the election of Mr. Lincoln, when the House was more like a powder magazine than a deliberative assembly. His denunciation of the plotters of treason to their face was terrible, and his exposé of the barbarism of the so-called civilization behind them was awful. . . . Nearly fifty Southern members rose to their feet, and rushed towards him with curses and threats of personal violence. As many of his friends gathered around him, and moving him in a sort of hollow square to the space in front of the speaker, opened before his assailants, and stood guard over him while he arraigned the slavocracy in an indictment for its crimes against humanity, surpassing in severity even the great arraignment by Mr. Sumner. He was then an old man approaching seventy, on whose frame and voice time had already made sad inroads, but still standing erect and firm as a man of thirty-five. Calm and self-possessed as a judge, he lashed them into a fury, and then bade them compose themselves at their leisure. The excitement aroused by his fiery denunciation and defiant scorn beggars all description, and can live only in the memory of those who witnessed it." [1]

Stevens was not a man to palter with a great crisis. His mind was eminently practical. He had little of the theorist or dreamer in his nature, and while the remedy which he might prescribe might not afford the wisest practical solution, he was unsurpassed in his keenness of vision and in his capacity to diagnose correctly a national condition. While he utterly repudiated the recommendations of the committee of thirty-three, as contrary to the principles by which he governed his political conduct, he saw that not only were they wrong in theory, but that they aggravated instead of removing the difficulty. His brave words did not avail to

[1] MS. Dartmouth College address: Thaddeus Stevens as a Leader in a Great Crisis.

defeat the compromise. The most important of the propositions of the committee were adopted. By more than the two-thirds vote required by the Constitution the House passed an amendment even more strongly guarding slavery than did that which had been put forward by Mr. Adams. The desired amendment of the fugitive slave law was also passed, but the bill for the admission of New Mexico failed.[1]

It is difficult at this distance to see what the authors of this astounding surrender to slavery hoped to gain by it. The radicalism of Stevens contained vastly the purer and also the more practical wisdom. The secession programme had been steadily carried out. State after State had adopted what was solemnly termed "the ordinance of secession." More than two weeks before the House voted upon the recommendations of the committee the Southern Congress had assembled, and its President, Howell Cobb, had declared that secession "is now a fixed and irrevocable fact, and the separation is perfect, complete, and perpetual." Before the vote was taken in the House, Jefferson Davis had been

---

[1] Mr. Blaine, usually so accurate, is in error in his statement that the bill to admit New Mexico passed the House. *Twenty Years of Congress*, vol. i. p. 267. It was laid upon the table, where it apparently always remained. *Congressional Globe*, 36th Congress, 2d session, p. 1327.

chosen President of the Southern Republic, his cabinet had been appointed, and, so far as governmental organization was concerned, the movement had been consummated. Nearly a month before that time Stevens had spoken his brave words, and had protested against the "cowardly counsels" that would operate to "unnerve the people." Instead of still further humiliating the spirit of the North by the passage of the Corwin compromise measures, it would seem too clear for doubt that the time had come for action of an opposite character. The proceedings of Congress at that grave crisis of our history were in keeping with the conduct of President Buchanan, and certainly cannot be regarded to-day with pride. Its members were unquestionably patriotic men; but they were overwhelmed by the magnitude of the peril, and they lacked a competent leader. Possibly the time had not yet arrived for aggressive leadership. And while the old remedy, which had been applied so often with only temporary success, was again prescribed, and wise men were endeavoring in vain to put off the "irrepressible conflict" by new concessions, the man for the crisis sat by, protesting and threatening, waiting for his time to come.

With the outbreak of the war the old forms

of the slavery question, which had for forty years engrossed the attention of the American people, were displaced and a new political chapter opened. It must not be forgotten that the people living in the South during the period of the controversy were not responsible for the existence of slavery. It had come down to them from a former generation. Most of the wicked profits of its establishment had gone to the owners of foreign ships, and some of them to people who lived in the North. The "institution" had existed in New England, and had vanished for the very good reason that it did not pay. It had at one time promised also to disappear from the South for the same reason. In most if not all of the slave States, during the years which immediately followed the adoption of the Constitution, slave property was not profitable, and in some of them it was believed to be an absolute burden. Some of the greatest of the earlier Southern statesmen, either during their lives or by will, gave freedom to their slaves. The very convention which framed the Constitution conferred upon Congress the power to abolish the slave trade after 1808, and without the supply of slaves which came from importation it was believed that the institution would languish and die. At the same time, Congress passed the great ordinance dedicating to free-

dom the vast territory given to the government
by the States, and chiefly by the slave State of
Virginia. But various causes, and chiefly the
increased production of cotton, had of late
years greatly augmented the value of slaves.
At the beginning of the war, the annual profits of slavery are conservatively estimated to
have been $300,000,000, which, according to
the rate then prevailing, represented the interest upon a capital of $5,000,000,000. If to
this enormous amount is added the value of
the plantations and other property, which was
believed to rest to a considerable extent upon
the perpetuation of slavery, a sum is produced
which represents by far the greater part of the
valuation of the property of the slave States.

The Southern people had been born and nur-
tured in the belief that slavery had a foundation
in the Scriptures. They had heard its benefi-
cence proclaimed from the pulpit, and had lis-
ened to sermons contrasting the deplorable condition of the negroes in Africa with the happy
lot of slaves upon the Southern plantations. So
long as slavery appeared to be simply a divine
institution it promised to disappear; but when
it began to pay, the enterprise of the statesmen
who represented it was at once exerted for its
extension and for laws that would make their
property more secure. Undoubtedly, too, the

agitation of the most extreme abolitionists produced an apprehension among the Southern
people which caused them to distrust the suffi-
ciency of constitutional safeguards alone for the
preservation of their institution. They felt impelled to extend the sway of slavery, not pri-
marily for the profits that it would produce in
the new territory which might be acquired, but
to maintain their political ascendency in the
country and to secure the safety which that
would bring.

It is impossible to question the high moral
quality or the wisdom of the abolition movement as a whole. It contributed indispensable
strength to the forces which finally gave to the
slave his freedom. But too much of the agitation was simply disruptive in its tendency, and
was marked by the affected superiority and the
narrow arrogance so often seen in those who
follow reform as they would follow a trade.
The abuse and vilification, which a few irrecon-
cilable spirits impartially bestowed upon the
South and upon every Northern statesman who
desired the ultimate end of freedom and labored
to discover some peaceful and effective means
for its accomplishment, tended less strongly to
freedom than to disunion and war. Violence
made few converts and many enemies, and doubtless to a considerable extent neutralized the

efforts of those who saw more efficacy in rational and temperate methods, such, for instance, as Lincoln employed, than in the calling of bad names. It is indeed remarkable that when the test came, in the secession winter of 1860–61, the abolition sentiment should have shown so little strength; that its representatives should have been denied a hearing in the most liberal cities of the North; that two thirds of the members of the House of Representatives should have voted for more odious compromises with slavery than had ever before been seriously proposed by its most extreme advocate, and that the Republicans of the Senate and House in creating territorial governments for the magnificent domains now included in Dakota, Colorado, and Nevada, unanimously recognized the very principle which Webster had enunciated in his famous Seventh of March speech with regard to New Mexico, and for which he had been so bitterly condemned.

The small class to which I have referred had indeed contributed in no small measure to the causes which produced secession and war, but they were powerless to keep the nation from being rent asunder, or to preserve the slave from the hopeless fate which would have been his under a republic dedicated to slavery. The force that rescued the slave and that saved the country was the sentiment of union; and the man who more than any other had created that sentiment was the great statesman whose last days were made bitter by the savage assaults of the abolitionists. It was the principles which Webster so powerfully proclaimed that raised and animated our armies; preserved the government, and made it possible for the slave to have his freedom; and from the attacks that were so unjustly made, history has not been slow in according him a magnificent vindication. If Washington created, Webster equally preserved, the Union.

CHAPTER VIII

LEADER OF THE HOUSE

President Lincoln was not long in displaying, after his inauguration, the moderate spirit which distinguished his administration. It was his great characteristic to refrain from any attempt to force public opinion, but rather to permit it to grow, and to take advantage of it at the opportune moment. He endeavored at the outset to unite his own party, and four of the seven members of his cabinet were taken from those candidates who, after himself, received the highest number of votes for the presidential nomination in the Chicago convention. Stevens had strong support for a cabinet place, and after Cameron's withdrawal as a candidate he had an excellent chance of success; but Cameron finally reëntered the contest, and his prominence as a presidential candidate secured him the position of secretary of war. Stevens did not relish being set aside for a man with whom he was not friendly, and appears to have got what consolation he could out of criticising the composition of the cabinet.[1]   The President, however, had made a safe choice.   He had secured advisers who were believed to hold moderate opinions, which was a great advantage when, in view of Northern sentiment, it was vital that the war should have no appearance of being one of aggression on the part of the national government.   They maintained also a high average of ability, and, with one or two exceptions, were well fitted for the work assigned them.

Lincoln took great care to avoid giving offense in his inaugural, and the caution which he displayed during his first month of office went far towards allaying the fears of Northern Democrats that his election was an act of hostility to the South.   The attack of the Confederate forces upon Fort Sumter brought the waiting policy to an end, and rallied the people of the North to a defense of the national authority, which had been violently assailed.   The sound of hostile guns dispelled the necessity for guarded action and made Lincoln's duty clear. He had the North behind him upon the issue of not permitting the Union to be dismembered and two independent and probably hostile gov-

[1] He said the cabinet was composed of an assortment of rivals whom the President appointed from courtesy, one stump speaker from Indiana and two representatives of the Blair family.   Blaine, *Twenty Years of Congress*, vol. i. p. 286.

ernments established upon its ruins. That was the principle for which he fought. He could wait until the sentiment of the North became equally strong for the abolition of slavery, either as a necessary measure for the preservation of the Union or from hatred of the institution itself, and in the mean time he could endure the abuse of those who desired a more radical course. He issued a call for Congress to meet on the Fourth of July, apparently intending to permit the issue to ripen, so that Congress should clearly perceive the necessity of preparing for war. He evidently did not desire the paralyzing effect of further attempts to compromise a hopeless situation.

In marked contrast with the protracted struggle in the preceding House an organization was at once effected. Mr. Grow was chosen speaker. The loss of the Democratic members from the seceding States left the Republicans with a large majority. Stevens was made chairman of the Committee on Ways and Means, which was the position of leadership. But he needed no formal christening as leader. He was, says Mr. Blaine, "the natural leader, who assumed his place by common consent." [1] Events had completely vindicated the position he had taken the preceding winter. The time for compromise had

---

[1] Blaine, *Twenty Years of Congress,* vol. i. p. 325.

gone by, and the occasion demanded a man of direct and positive force. At that time the Committee on Ways and Means had the jurisdiction now exercised by the same committee together with that of the Committee on Appropriations, which had not then been created. Thus he was at the head of the committee charged with the duty of devising means for raising the revenue to prosecute a great war, and also having charge of the appropriation bills which directed how the money should be spent. The burden was tremendous.

The message which the President sent to Congress presented the situation most judiciously as well as forcibly, and was, if possible, a more successful political document than even his inaugural address. He asked Congress to place at the disposal of the government 400,000 men and $400,000,000. "That number of men," he said, "is about one tenth of those of proper age within the regions where apparently all are willing to engage, and the sum is less than a twenty-third part of the money value owned by the men who seem ready to devote the whole." He thought that the time had arrived for giving an appropriate name to the movement against the government. The Southern people had been loyal to the Union, and their leaders had disguised from them the real character of the proceeding by employing a term which had to their ears a constitutional sound. The movement, rightly named, Lincoln said, was "rebellion" instead of "secession." This doctrine of "secession" had "drugged and insidiously debauched" the people of the South for thirty years. He expressed the deepest regret that he found the duty of employing the war power of the government forced upon him, but he said that he "must perform this duty or surrender the existence of the government." This message awoke an enthusiastic response in Congress. A large majority of both Houses were patriotic men who would go to any length in support of the policy of the President, and they at once set to work to meet the enormous demands that were made.

The position occupied by Stevens at the head of the great financial committee of that House of Congress which has the sole constitutional power to originate revenue bills most intimately associates him with all measures for raising or spending money to suppress the rebellion. The details of those measures would be irksome to the general reader, and are far too voluminous for insertion here. But a reference to the most important of them is absolutely necessary to a proper understanding of his work. The request of Lincoln for $400,000,000 was modified by the secretary of the treasury, who, in his detailed estimates, reduced the amount by nearly $82,000,000. But $318,000,000 was still a considerable sum of money to raise from two thirds of the country at war with the other third. It was five times the ordinary annual revenue which the government had before that time raised from the entire country, and seven times the actual annual revenue during the deficit-producing years of James Buchanan. The national credit, too, was at the lowest ebb, as a result, not perhaps so much of civil war, as of the incompetency which during four years had distinguished the management of the treasury. From 1857 to 1861 the average annual excess of the expenditures over the revenues had been about $20,000,000, which would correspond with a deficit of at least $120,000,000 on the financial scale on which the government was conducted in 1898, before the outbreak of the Spanish war. It is not to be wondered at that this enormous deficiency, so long continued, should have obliterated almost the last vestige of credit, and that when Lincoln was confronted with an empty and yawning treasury, he found the borrowing capacity of the government nearly exhausted.

During the preceding Congress a law had been passed, authorizing an issue of $10,000,000 in treasury notes to meet certain current obligations. The practical result of this issue proved that by January 1, 1861, the credit of the government had reached a twelve per cent basis. The new tariff act, which went into effect on April 1, greatly increased import duties, and, notwithstanding the decrease in importations anticipated on account of the war, it promised to augment the revenues. Secretary Chase, by great effort, and with the aid of the banks which patriotically coöperated with him to repair the government's credit, was able to raise at intervals a few millions of dollars; but on July 1 the cash in the treasury fell about $30,000,000 short of loans soon to mature and of unpaid appropriations for the previous fiscal year. In his estimate of expenditures of $318,000,000, which the secretary sent to Congress, he included the regular appropriations already made. The probable amount required to sustain military operations was put at $217,000,000, and the interest charge on the new debt, the deficiency for the preceding year, and the treasury notes about to mature or already due, would absorb more than $40,000,000 in addition. Congress was then asked to appropriate about $260,000,-000 of new money, and to provide new means for raising that amount, together with the deficiency between the appropriations already made, and the income already provided for the current year. It was asked to supplement existing and most inadequate sources of revenue so that in all $80,000,000 might be derived from taxation, and to authorize the raising of $240,000,000 by loans.

It was doubtless due in part to Mr. Chase's lack of experience in financial matters — a defect which the enormous burdens of his position speedily repaired — that he recommended raising so small a portion of the expenditures by current taxation, and that in time of war a wealthy people were asked to pay a smaller tax per head than they have at any subsequent time been called upon to contribute in time of peace.

Mr. Chase had been a prominent figure in the Senate, and had received a considerable vote for the presidential nomination in the Chicago convention of 1860. He was broad-minded, patriotic, and of absolute integrity. He was well fitted, as Horace Greeley said, to "command in the highest degree the public confidence." But he lacked the necessary experience and training to fit him for the difficult task to which he was called. The position was not attractive to him, and he at first declined it on the ground that he was not fitted for it "either by education or habits," and because the appropriate place for him was the Senate to which he had just been chosen again.[1] He finally consented to accept the office because, by refusing to comply with the request of the President, he might seem to "shrink from cares and labors for the common good which cannot be honorably shunned."[2] The sequel proved that he was endowed with many great qualities for the position, and that while it was expensive to the government to supply during the first years of the war his defects in special training, he is perhaps outranked only by Alexander Hamilton and John Sherman among our secretaries of the treasury.

Congress at once proceeded to the work of passing the necessary laws, and never was a response more promptly made. Within three days after he had been appointed chairman of the Committee on Ways and Means, Stevens reported a bill to the House, authorizing the secretary to borrow $250,000,000. On the next day he called up the bill under a suspension of the rules and with debate limited to one hour. This time was chiefly occupied by Mr. Vallandigham, of Ohio, who made a noisy and intemperate attack upon the President, which Stevens contemptuously permitted to go without reply,

---

[1] Bolles, *Financial History, 1861–1885*, p. 103.

[2] Letter of resignation to the governor of Ohio.

and the bill was then passed with only five dissenting votes.

Stevens immediately followed this bill with another appropriating $160,000,000 for the army. This measure encountered some opposition in debate, and the objection was made that the Military Committee had not yet recommended the increase of the army, for the maintenance of which the large appropriation was proposed. Stevens replied that he was only granting the demands of the administration. He proposed to make the appropriations so that Congress could adjourn at the earliest possible day. He assumed that the Military Committee would grant to the President what he asked; but he caustically intimated that if it should see fit to draw its bill upon different lines, the bill would be rejected. The House followed Stevens at once, and passed the bill, as it also did the naval bill, carrying $30,000,000 more, which Stevens called up on the same day. Within one week from the day on which Congress was called together, the House had voted substantially all the enormous sums of money asked for by the President to carry on the war, and had authorized a debt far greater than had rested upon the government at any time in its history.

The work of preparing the revenue bill was

much more difficult. Theories of taxation are
apt to be numerous and contradictory. But the
difficulty in formulating such a measure is not
so much with theories as with the practical application of them. The fish dealer, who wrote
to Sir Robert Peel that he believed in free trade
in everything except herring, illustrated the common tendency to modify theory so as to conform
with self-interest, and also the practical difficulties which representatives have to encounter
in framing revenue bills. A general tax, levied
equally upon all, is one which in a great emergency no one, unless a doctrinaire, would have
sufficient interest to oppose; but a tax levied
upon the banker or the farmer or the brewer
falls with special weight and inevitably provokes
protests from the affected classes even in time
of war, and according to their number and influence they are apt to be heard in Congress.

Stevens acted, however, with the expedition
suited to the emergency and forestalled a good
many of the ordinary political difficulties by
prompt action. With very little delay he brought
the revenue bills into the House. They increased the duty upon sugar and a great many
other articles, imposed very moderate duties
upon tea and coffee, levied a direct tax of
$30,000,000 upon real estate, which was appor-
tioned in the constitutional way among the States

according to population, and provided an income
tax upon all incomes of over eight hundred dollars derived from personal property, evidently
upon the theory that such a tax would not be
direct. It was estimated that these taxes would
produce about $50,000,000 a year, an estimate
which, it was afterwards discovered, did not
make sufficient allowance for the depressing influence of war upon business, and was therefore
much too great.

The direct tax upon real estate aroused the
opposition of members who represented agricul-
tural districts, and this feature was again and
again referred back to the committee. Colfax
and Conkling were especially hostile. The debate was most animated, and it was only after
consenting to reduce the tax by $10,000,000
and portraying with all his force the needs of
the country that Stevens was able to secure its
passage. He himself represented one of the
wealthiest farming districts in the country, composed of what he called "a close German population;" but he declared that he would vote for
the bill and submit himself "to their judgment,
their patriotism, their good sense," and if they
saw fit to reject him he would abide by the decision "without a murmur and without regret."
While no man could be more uncompromising
than Stevens when he had a large majority at

his back, he showed also by his management of
the direct tax that no one could be more conciliatory.

The "Crittenden resolution," so called from
its venerable author, aimed to set forth the objects of the war, and was perhaps the most important measure of this session, not of a financial or military character. It declared that
"the war is not waged in any spirit of oppres-
sion, or for any purpose of conquest or subjuga-
tion," or to interfere with "the rights or established institutions" of the Southern States, but
to maintain the Constitution and "preserve the
dignity, equality, and rights of the several States
unimpaired," and that after the attainment of
these objects "the war ought to cease." This
resolution passed the Senate and House with
practical unanimity so far as the Republicans
were concerned. But it did not have the support of Stevens, who stood almost alone in with-
holding his vote. He believed that the time
had gone by for preambles and explanations,
and that the nation should reserve to itself the
largest liberty in waging the war which had
been forced upon it. The contest had not proceeded far before the principles of the resolution were violated, and at the opening of the
very next session, when it was proposed to re-
affirm the resolution, Stevens moved to lay the

matter on the table, and the House sustained
his motion.

Stevens vigorously supported the "confiscation" bill which confiscated property "used for
insurrectionary purposes," and contained a special provision, in effect giving freedom to slaves
who were employed upon any fort or intrench-
ment or in any military or naval service against
the government. The bill was very much to
Stevens's liking. He had seen the fugitives
skurrying from the field of Bull Run, and he
was not disposed to talk much about the Constitution. He justified the measure, because,
under the laws of war, it would weaken the
enemy, and if it was justifiable to destroy an
enemy it certainly was permissible to weaken
him by taking away his means of aggression.
The time had come when the laws of war should
govern our conduct. He declared that, when
we had conquered a slave, we should never
shrink from saying "Go and be free." He
would not say that the war was made for that
purpose. "Ask them who made the war what
is its object." In the course of this speech he
declared that he did not like the Crittenden
resolution, because it looked like "an apology
from us in saying what were the objects of the
war." In his view the one object of the war
was "to subdue the rebels." He did not believe

the Northern people would long stand by and
see their sons and brothers slaughtered by
rebels, "and forbear to call upon their enemies
to be our friends and to help us in subduing
them." He predicted that, if the war continued,
the time would come when every slave "belonging to a rebel . . . will be called upon to aid
us in war against their masters and to restore
the Union." The House did not follow him at
that time, and rejected the bill; but at a later
time it verified his prediction by passing the bill,
and thus placing the nation upon his ground.

Congress adjourned upon August 6. In a
session of hardly a month it had transacted an
extraordinary amount of business. It had been
made to appreciate the gravity of the crisis by
an object lesson in war, for the battle of Bull
Run occurred during the session, and, as a result
of that bloody disaster, the capital itself was
for the moment believed to be in danger. It
devoted its attention almost exclusively to the
war, and generously supported the Administration. It provided for the increase of the army
to half a million of men. It greatly augmented
the navy. It provided a variety of new taxes,
estimated to add $50,000,000 each year to the
revenue. It authorized a loan, the magnitude
of which had never been approached in the history of the country, and it passed appropriation

bills carrying $265,000,000, — an amount equal to four times the annual peace appropriations of that time.   Upon nearly all these momentous questions it devolved upon Stevens to lead, and the results showed that he had not begun badly.

CHAPTER IX

THE LEGAL TENDER

THE war began in earnest during the special session of Congress, and it did not begin auspiciously for the Union. The disaster at Bull Run did not, however, shake the purpose of the North. It only proved that the contest was to be no dress parade affair, and thereby it inspired new efforts. The navy had been greatly strengthened. The offer of enlistments was far in excess of the number of troops called for, and before the end of 1861 more than 700,000 men had been mustered into the service.[1] But no decisive victory had yet come to the American arms, and the affair at Ball's Bluff was hardly less disheartening than had been the defeat at Bull Run.

The enormous preparation demanded, of course, enormous expenditures, even in excess of the great amounts appropriated at the special session. It will be necessary to consider the working of the measures with which Stevens

[1] Report of the Secretary of War, 37th Congress, 2d session.

was identified at the special session of Congress and the demands upon the treasury for which he was to be asked to provide at the first regular session.

Capital is proverbially as timid as men are brave, and the danger that inspires the one is very apt to put the other to flight. If in the preceding winter, in time of peace, the government had been able to borrow a few paltry millions only at an extortionate rate of interest, how could its friends now hope, since upon a broken credit there had been superadded the financial disturbance of a gigantic civil war, that it could obtain the hundreds of millions with which to contend for its existence?

Immediately after the adjournment of Congress the secretary set about borrowing money under the provisions of the loan bill. To this end he met the representatives of the banks of New York, Boston, and Philadelphia. The government's needs were imperative, and its credit poor. The secretary had nothing to offer which, under the circumstances, could tempt an investor. He was almost absolutely at the mercy of those with whom he was dealing. No hope could be entertained of getting money abroad, where the financial interests were hostile to the United States, and were hoping to profit by their dismemberment. There are few brighter pages in the history of the rebellion than that on which is written the conduct of the bankers at this crisis. Instead of attempting to take advantage of the government, instead of driving a sharp bargain, or even asking for compensation for the financial risk that could be fairly charged against the transaction, they arbitrarily raised the national credit to a far higher point than that at which it stood before the war.

The effect of the arrangement made by the secretary was that the banks received at par $100,000,000 of the so-called seven-thirty notes [1] of the government payable in three years, and $50,000,000 of its six per cent bonds "at the rate equivalent to par for the bonds bearing seven per cent interest;" [2] and they paid in coin for the whole subscription of $150,000,000. The entire capital of the banks associated together in the arrangement was only $120,000,000 — many millions less than the combined liabilities which they assumed toward a government whose very existence was seriously threatened by civil war. [3] It was one of the greatest and

[1] The transaction with regard to the seven-thirties practically amounted to a loan by the banks to the government, to be repaid out of the proceeds of the "popular loan;" or, if those proceeds should be inadequate, then when the seven-thirties should mature.

[2] Report of the Secretary of the Treasury, appendix, 37th Congress, 2d session.

[3] Bolles, *Financial History, 1861–1885*, p. 25.

most daring transactions that had ever been recorded in financial history, and it exhibited a form of patriotism which was as salutary as it was unusual.

This action of the banks enabled the secretary to meet pressing demands, and imparted an appearance of solidity to the treasury. But it was like throwing money into a maelstrom, and soon more was needed. Deeply involved as the banks already were, an effort was made again to secure their assistance, and that they were not able to help was largely due to the secretary himself. The banks had urged him to draw checks upon some single bank in each city, which bank should represent the syndicate, instead of requiring the entire subscriptions to be actually paid from the reserves of the banks in coin. These checks would to a large extent have performed the functions of money, and would therefore have increased the circulating medium, and they ordinarily would have been redeemed in the notes of the banks in the syndicate, which were all upon a specie-paying basis. The obvious advantage of this arrangement would have been to protect the coin reserves of the banks, and preserve the solidity so necessary not merely for themselves but for the future operations of the government.

But Mr. Chase was a " hard money " man in

so literal a sense that it ended in his becoming through necessity a "soft money" man.[1] He refused to grant the request of the banks, and received from them and paid out to the government's creditors the actual specie. The withdrawal of these large amounts of coin from the reserves of the banks and the scattering of the same over the country were, as the president of one of the principal banks well said, equivalent to pulling away "continually the foundations upon which the whole structure rested." Mr. Chase aggravated the evil results of his refusal by issuing from time to time demand notes upon the treasury, which must of necessity be redeemed in coin, if the credit of the government was to be maintained. These notes were very soon discredited, and while the banks were called upon to pay the government and their own customers in coin, they could not safely receive them as money from the people. Under these adverse conditions the coin reserves of the associated banks rapidly dwindled. The secretary refused to change his policy, and the banks, from having been in a remarkably strong condition so late as October, suspended specie payments on the twenty-eighth day of December.

[1] Sec. 6 of the Act of August 5, 1861, would appear effectually to authorize the suspension of the sub-treasury act, which Mr. Chase urged against the transaction.

The like suspension of the national treasury followed as a matter of course.

This event was of transcendent importance in the financial history of the civil war. Had the coin reserves of the banks not been bodily carried away by the government, when a payment in bank notes upon a specie basis would have been practically as good and more convenient; and had this mischief not been followed up by the unnecessary issue of demand notes by the treasury, it is practically certain that the banks could have maintained specie payments for a considerable time, and that they would have been most useful agents in getting government securities in the early days of the war, as they were near its close, into the hands of investors at par. It is indeed hardly probable, as some high authorities have declared, that the enormous expenses of the war could have been borne and the treasury not have succumbed to the strain; but, if the catastrophe could have been averted even for a year, the saving to the government would have been great in the higher price which it would have received for its securities in that interval, and in the difference between the price of supplies bought upon an inflated basis and the price at which they could have been bought upon a coin basis. It was unfortunate for the government that the departure from the specie basis was forced so early in the contest, when original and most valuable sources of financial aid were almost untouched and certainly far from being exhausted.

The secretary then had been at first successful in placing the loan authorized by Congress, although the temporary success had been followed by disaster. The first operations of the new revenue law had disappointed expectations. Mr. Chase was compelled to report in December that the revenues had greatly suffered from the conditions which were so adverse to foreign trade. The actual receipts for the year ending June 30, 1862, would probably fall twenty-five millions short of the estimates of the preceding summer. On the other hand, the expenditures had greatly increased, even far beyond the generous appropriations of the special session. The deficiency in appropriations would amount to nearly $150,000,000, which, added to the difference between the estimates of the revenue and the actual receipts, left an enormous sum of money to be raised in addition to the amounts provided for at the special session, in order to carry the country to June 30, 1862.

The secretary also gave the estimates for the fiscal year ending June 30, 1863, for which provision should be made at the session of Congress then about to open. These estimates showed

that the expenditures would amount to $475,-
000,000, and the receipts to $95,000,000, leav-
ing a deficiency of $380,000,000. From the
report of the secretary it thus appeared that the
December session of Congress would have to
provide about $600,000,000, either by loans or
additional taxes. If a comparison were made
on the basis of the wealth of the country, a
corresponding amount in 1899 would be fully
$3,000,000,000. This estimate, too, was made
while the country was upon a specie basis, and
it was certain to be largely exceeded. Surely
the financial outlook was appalling.

I have thus endeavored to describe the situation far enough to enable the exact character
and the magnitude of the work of Congress and
the special work of Stevens to be understood,
and to contribute to a better knowledge of the
legislation which followed and which made the
second session of this Congress the most important from a financial standpoint that was ever
held by any legislative body in the history of
the world.

The session opened on the first Monday in
December, 1861. The treasury and the banks
had not yet suspended specie payments, but that
event was sufficiently portended by the black
clouds which darkened the financial sky. Upon
the motion of Stevens those portions of the

President's message which related to the finances
and to the provision of additional revenue and
to the ways and means for "supporting and
meeting all public liabilities of the government"
were referred to the Committee on Ways and
Means.

The work of the session had hardly seriously
begun when the banks and the treasury suspended specie payments. This event was quickly
followed by the bill reported from Stevens's
committee for the issue of legal-tender notes.
A debate followed which was memorable for its
ability. The measure was violently opposed
by Mr. Conkling and Mr. Morrill, as well as
by the Democratic members. Stevens closed
the debate. His speech is an excellent spe-
cimen of his manner during the later period of
his service in the House. He rigidly discarded
ornament, aimed to express his ideas in the
most clear and direct fashion, and, speaking as
if he held rhetorical effort in contempt, he really
exhibited a high literary form. In force of
reasoning and in a lofty simplicity of style,
whether one agrees with its argument or not,
it is difficult to find its match among congressional speeches.

He called the bill a "measure of necessity,
not of choice." He would not willingly issue
a legal-tender paper currency, or "depart from

that circulating medium which, by the common
consent of civilized nations, forms the standard
of value." But such a measure, when rendered necessary by emergency, should not excite
alarm. Was the measure necessary? Buchanan
had left a debt of $100,000,000, and had also
bequeathed a formidable rebellion. This made
necessary the great loan authorized at the special
session. The efforts to carry their subscription
to this loan had broken the banks and compelled
them to suspend specie payments. Only the
day before they had managed to pay the last of
the loan, and now, with nearly $200,000,000 of
floating debt, the treasury was without money.
The expenses of the government were nearly
$2,000,000 each day. To carry the govern-
ment to the end of the next fiscal year about
$700,000,000 would have to be provided in ad-
dition to the $350,000,000 already appropriated.
How was this enormous sum to be raised? The
obvious method, he declared, was to sell bonds.
But the result of putting so large an amount upon
the market would be greatly to depreciate their
price; and even then they could not be sold for
coin, but payment would necessarily be made
in the depreciated notes of the suspended banks.
Taking the very lowest discount at which so
large an issue of bonds would sell, it would
require $1,500,000,000 of bonds to produce

sufficient currency to carry the government to
the end of the next fiscal year, a sum that was
"too frightful to be tolerated." Another course
had been suggested, and that was to borrow
money from the banks and pledge the bonds,
with a liberal margin, as collateral for the loan.
As it was not probable that the loan would be
paid when due, the bonds "would be thrown
into the market and sold for whatever the banks
might choose to pay for them. The folly of this
scheme needs no illustration."

To the proposition to strike out the legal-
tender clause and make the proposed notes re-
ceivable for public dues, he replied that this
would cause the notes to circulate at a ruinous
discount. No notes not redeemable on demand,
and not made a legal tender, "have ever been
kept at par. Even those who could use them
for taxes and duties would discredit them, that
they might get them low." If soldiers, contractors, and others were compelled to take them
from the government, they would have to "submit to a heavy shave before they could use
them." He did not believe the national banking project, suggested by the treasury, to be at
all adequate to the emergency; and although he
might favor it as a general system, he furnished
in a sentence an argument which ever since that
time has been the favorite argument against the

system. "To the banks I can see its advantage. They would have the whole benefit of the circulation without interest, and at the same time would draw interest on the government bonds."

Having, then, as he thought, "shown the impossibility of carrying on the government in any other way," he would consider the objections to the plan. He then argued most admirably, if not conclusively, that the legal tender would be constitutional. It was true, he said, that the power was nowhere expressly granted in the Constitution; but few of the acts which the government could perform were so specified. "It would require a volume larger than the pandects of Justinian or the code of Napoleon to make such enumeration." Every power necessary to carry out the granted powers was also granted. "If nothing could be done by Congress except what is enumerated in the Constitution, the government could not live a week." The express power to emit bills and the express prohibition against it were both considered in the convention which framed the Constitution. It was finally decided to omit both the express power and the prohibition, "leaving it to the exigencies of the times to determine its necessity." The right to emit bills had "for fifty years, by the common consent of the nation, been practiced," and the power to make them legal tender was consistent with it. "He who admits our power to emit bills of credit, nowhere expressly authorized by the Constitution, is a sharp and unreasonable doubter when he denies the power to make them legal tender." If Congress decided that the proposed law was necessary and convenient to "raise and support armies and navies, to borrow money, and to provide for the general welfare," it would be constitutional.

Having thus supported the constitutionality of the measure, he next sought to show that it was expedient. The necessity of the issue was admitted by all, but the objection was raised against making the notes money, that it would depreciate them. It was not easy to see "how notes issued without being made immediately payable in specie can be made any worse by making them legal tender." "Let him who is sharp enough to see it instruct me how notes that every man must take are worth less than the same notes that no man need take." As to the objection that the bill would impair the obligation of contracts, that prohibition did not exist against Congress, but against the States. This law, however, would impair no contract. "All contracts are made, not only with a view to present laws, but subject to the future legislation of the country." More than once the value of coin had been changed. Silver was at one time debased seven per cent, and made a legal tender.

But it was said that the bill would inflate the currency and raise prices. "How do gentlemen expect that using the same amount of notes without the legal tender will inflate it less? It will take the same amount of millions, with or without the legal tender, to carry on the war, except that the one would be below par and the other at par." The value of legal-tender notes depended on the amount issued, compared with the amount of business. The business of the country would require $150,000,000 more currency than it now had. The bank notes were depreciated, and coin had disappeared from circulation. The legal tender would furnish a needed currency with which to buy government bonds, and the government, again the possessor of the notes, could again use them, and again they could be employed in the purchase of bonds. He believed that the $150,000,000 authorized by the bill would be all that would be required.

He characterized the proposition of Mr. Roscoe Conkling to issue seven-per-cent bonds, to be sold or exchanged for the currency of the banks of New York, Boston, and Philadelphia,

as lacking "every element of wise legislation."
"Make a loan payable in irredeemable currency,
and pay that in its depreciated condition to our
contractors, soldiers, and creditors generally!
The banks would issue unlimited amounts of
what would become trash! Was there ever
such a temptation to swindle? If we are to
use suspended notes to pay our expenses, why
not use our own? Are they not as safe as bank
notes?"

He then proceeded to ridicule the proposition of the minority of the committee to issue
interest-bearing currency notes, and pictured
the shoemaker or laborer with his arithmetic,
calculating the interest on the note he had held
a week and wished to pay out. "This would
be rather inconvenient on a frosty day." He
recurred to the main argument, and said that
the notes of the Bank of England had greatly
depreciated during the Napoleonic wars, until
their fall was arrested by practically making
them a legal tender. He also cited the example
of Prussia in favor of a national paper currency. Yet the opponents of the bill had
"shown all the contortions, if not the inspira-
tions, of the sibyl, lest the government should
make these notes a uniform currency, rather
than leave them to be regulated by sharks and
brokers." He declared that he looked upon

"the immediate passage of this bill as essential
to the very existence of the government. Reject it, and the financial credit not only of the
government but of all the great interests of the
country will be prostrated." If the measure
were to be defeated he should be glad to resign
from the Committee on Ways and Means, and
leave it to the opposition to pursue some other
measure.

The bill passed the House by a vote of 93 to
59, and ultimately, with amendments presented
in the Senate, it became a law. Before it finally
passed, Stevens modified his statement that no
further issue would be necessary, and that the
notes would remain at par. He put the burden
for his change of opinion upon the Senate
amendments, which required the interest on the
bonds to be paid in coin, and which conferred
the legal-tender quality upon the notes already
issued. He declared that the notes would become depreciated, and that issue after issue
would be called for, "until our currency will
become frightfully inflated."

The legal-tender bill had no sooner become
a law than the abuse to which that system of
finance is liable began to show itself, and there
were propositions to issue more notes. The
leaders who were protesting in January, doubtless with entire sincerity, that the $150,000,000

provided by the bill would be sufficient, were in June of the same year asking for the passage of another measure authorizing another like amount. It is only just to Stevens to recall the modification of his opinion, which he based upon the Senate amendments. His statement of the effect of the amendment conferring the legal-tender quality upon notes already issued was not unreasonable. The amendment to which he most strongly objected was that which provided that the government should pay the interest on its notes and bonds in coin. By holding out a promise of coin payments, the requirement, it was urged, would have an opposite effect from that anticipated by Stevens and prevent a greater depreciation of the notes. He never ceased to recur to the objection to the end of his career. The promise of the ultimate payment of the principal of the bonds in coin would put them firmly upon that basis, but he argued with great force that, if coin had departed from circulation, and the government, or the importers upon whom it put the burden, were compelled to use legal-tender notes for the purchase of coin to pay the interest, the gold speculators would take advantage of the situation, "corner" gold, and push up its price. The notes would therefore depreciate. But the Senate amendments could not certainly be held responsible for the whole of the enormous increase of legal-tender notes. In one year from the time when the first step was taken, the legal-tender quality had been impressed upon more than $500,000,000 of paper.

Whether the resort to legal-tender issues could have been averted is a question which cannot be confidently answered, even with the wisdom which follows the event by a third of a century. Had the high taxation been resorted to at the outset, had even $150,000,000 been raised the first year instead of a beggarly $50,000,000, had the secretary of the treasury refrained from the policy which sapped the coin reserves of the banks and compelled the suspension of specie payments by them and by the treasury as a necessary result, it is certain that the issue of legal tender could have been much longer delayed, and it is even possible that it might have been avoided altogether. But when Congress was asked to authorize the first issue a great deal of the mischief had been done. The treasury and the banks had already suspended specie payments. We had been at war nearly a year and had raised very little by taxation. Many millions were due to the 700,000 soldiers and sailors who were fighting the battles of their country, and disaffection was beginning to appear among them; the last installment from

the sale of bonds to the banks had been dis-
bursed, and with an empty treasury the secretary was each month called upon to pay bills
almost equaling the total annual revenues of
two years before.   There were current demands
upon the government that were overdue, amounting to nearly $200,000,000, and it had the alter-
native of selling its bonds at a discount, not for
coin, but for the depreciated bills of suspended
banks.   The people, too, were without a safe
currency, and were exposed to the danger of a
wild and irresponsible inflation by the issues of
the non-specie-paying banks.   It is an easy
thing thirty-five years afterwards to say that
the government made a mistake; but a great
deal must be taken for granted, and it certainly
is not easy to point out the superiority of the
other plans, suggested for the difficulty, over
that which was actually adopted.

The men responsible for the measure were far
from being advocates of fiat money.   Indeed,
Mr. Chase had done infinite damage in hurry-
ing on the crisis by a too literal adherence to
views of an opposite character.   Before taking
the final plunge he hesitated long, with the apparent purpose of having a measure pass without responsibility upon him, which he believed
to be most necessary, but the principle of which
he profoundly disliked.   Stevens, Sumner, and

the other patriotic men who supported the bill,
were most reluctant to take the step. But they
were conscious that they were under the pressure
of an overwhelming necessity, and if one does
not conveniently forget some of the difficulties
which surrounded them, he will find it difficult
to impeach their wisdom. A bare statement of
the case is enough to put to confusion the text-
book statesmen who confidently condemn their
action. A great civil war inevitably has a disastrous effect upon national credit. Before the
rebellion the credit of the unbroken nation was
low; yet a fragment of the nation was compelled
in four years to raise nearly $4,000,000,000.
If, under these circumstances, we had not departed from a specie basis, we should have accomplished a feat for which history furnishes no
parallel. The aggregate amount raised by loans
and taxation by the French people during the
wars of the Consulate and Empire did not
greatly exceed $2,000,000,000. The people of
the North raised a billion more money in four
years than the united French nation had raised
in fourteen, some fifty or sixty years earlier.[1]
The issue of legal-tender paper followed the
suspension of coin payments as a logical consequence. With no coin in its vaults, what, it
was pertinently asked, could the government

[1] Blaine, *Twenty Years of Congress*, vol. i. p. 550.

pay to its creditors? How could it force upon them a currency which they in turn could not force their creditors to take?

The departure from a coin basis greatly increased the cost of the war, but the amount of this increase is usually exaggerated. The great item in the expense was the billion and a quarter that was paid to the soldiers and sailors; and this item, very unjustly no doubt, remained the same, when they were paid in a depreciated currency. The chief effect of inflation upon the cost would be seen in the prices of supplies. But these were mainly of domestic production, and prices of such articles did not rise with the fluctuations of gold to any such degree as did the prices of articles purchased abroad. Undoubtedly some hundreds of millions could have been saved, if the war could have been fought upon a gold basis; but it was out of the question to fight it on a gold basis at the time when Stevens advocated the first legal-tender bill.

The practical alternative to the greenback at that time was a bank currency, which probably would have been more expensive than the legal tender. Vastly the greater cost of the greenbacks has followed the war. They should have disappeared with the pressing necessity which called them into being. But it is not the fault of those who believed in them for a great emergency that they have been permitted to remain to cost the people, in one way or another, probably almost as great a sum as the entire money cost of suppressing the rebellion.

CHAPTER X

THE legal-tender notes directly extinguished several hundred millions of debt, but a much greater amount remained to be raised. This was done by the issue of bonds, and by current taxation. It would hardly be profitable to present in detail the different loan measures which were brought forward by the committee of which Stevens was chairman. It is sufficient to say that, including the loan of $250,000,000, authorized at the special session, loans of one form or another, not including the legal tender, were authorized and issued, during about four years, exceeding in amount $2,000,000,000. One important instrument in distributing so vast a burden of debt among the people was the national banking system, which Mr. Chase persistently urged, and which Congress finally adopted. The institutions thus created not only absorbed hundreds of millions of bonds to secure their note circulation, but in a single year more than three hundred and sixty millions were sold by them to their customers.[1] This indicates that, if Secretary Chase had protected the reserves of the banks, instead of destroying them, during the first year of the war, and if he had also urged an immediate resort to high taxation, the contest might have been fought to the end upon a specie basis.

The policy of raising large amounts of money by taxation should have been applied much earlier, but it was rigidly put in force during the last two years of the struggle, and greatly relieved the strain upon the borrowing capacity of the people. There existed at the outset a belief, which Secretary Chase appeared to share, that the war would be of short duration, and that the cost of suppressing the rebellion should not be borne by taxation upon a portion of the people, but that, after peace had been secured, taxation to meet the cost of the war should be imposed upon the guilty and the innocent alike. Mr. Chase, in his first report, recommended that provision should be made by taxation for paying only the ordinary expenditures and the interest and sinking fund upon the debt. Even this recommendation was not ungrudgingly carried out by Congress. Reference has already been made to the opposition which Stevens encountered in levying the direct tax of $20,000,000, and to

[1] Blaine, *Twenty Years of Congress*, vol. i. p. 482.

the concessions which he was compelled to
make in order to secure its passage. At the
same session also the small tax upon coffee was
violently opposed. No favor was shown to any
departure from the old method, or to even a
small tax which in ordinary times might promise
to be unpopular. Many members of Congress
were apparently not aroused to the fact that we
were really in war, and they conducted their
politics upon a peace basis. The taxation during the first year of the war produced barely
sufficient to meet the ordinary peace expenditures. The entire revenues during the year
ending June 30, 1862, including the produce of
the so-called war revenue measures, amounted
to about $2.50 for each one of the population,
which is barely half the annual rate of taxation
since the war.

At the opening of the December session of
1861 it had become apparent that we were involved in a war of tremendous magnitude ;
and it should have been apparent also that
the weakened credit of the government was
unequal to the task of borrowing the enormous
sums that were needed, and that a system of
high taxation should immediately be put in
force. But the secretary was slow in learning
the necessary lesson, and his mind was filled
with schemes for new loans. He still adhered

to the policy which he had announced in July: that provision should be made by taxation "for ordinary expenditures, for prompt payment of interest on the public debt existing and author- ized, and for the gradual extinction of the principal." This he declared to be "indispen- sable to a sound system of finance." It was unfortunate that he did not comprehend at that time that it was also indispensable to a sound system of finance that, when so many of the young men of the country were fighting at the front for only nominal pay, those at home should be called on to make the slight sacrifice which they were very willing to make, and pay sub- stantial taxes to carry on the war. By the issue of war bonds the interest charges of the govern- ment had been increased. To meet the expense which the secretary thought should be met from current revenues, he recommended that direct taxation be increased to $50,000,000, so that the entire annual revenue should be $90,000,000. In making this recommendation he declared that he was "aware that the sum is large," but he felt "that he must not shrink from a plain statement of the actual necessities of the situa- tion." Four years later, when the people were so much the more exhausted by war, they raised nearly $500,000,000 in a single year as against the paltry sum of $90,000,000, which the secretary was now recommending with apologies for its magnitude.

But the leaders in Congress were awake to the necessity of raising substantial amounts by taxation. Barely a month after Mr. Chase made his recommendation, Stevens and his associates upon the Committee on Ways and Means reported, and the House almost unanimously passed, a resolution declaring the purpose of Congress to provide an annual revenue of not less than $150,000,000. The House had not yet mastered the art of estimating the revenues to be produced by new taxes in time of war, and its first efforts at real war taxation were less productive than it intended. But the policy had been determined upon, and measure followed measure from Stevens's committee with a rapidity that proved their fixed intention of carrying it out. The same members who had opposed the taxes upon tea, coffee and sugar in July, were willing in December to pass almost without debate a further increase of several millions in these taxes. An internal revenue bill was passed which, with subsequent amendments, covered almost the entire field of industry and consumption.

These measures were interesting, not so much from any principle of taxation which they illustrated, as from the ingenuity of Stevens and his colleagues in discerning and exhausting almost every source of revenue. The great burden of the taxes fell upon malt and spirituous liquors. Stamps were required upon the most minute as well as the most important transactions of business. The butcher was required to pay a license fee, and in addition a certain sum for every beef or hog or sheep that he killed. The dealer who sold him the animals he slaughtered had also to pay a tax. A license was required for almost every imaginable calling and trade. Horse-dealers and peddlers, jugglers and lawyers, doctors and soapmakers, had each to contribute a fixed sum to the government. The dentist was required to pay ten dollars before he could pull a tooth, and the eating-house keeper a like sum before he could sell a meal. The manufacturer was compelled to pay a license fee and in addition a specific or an ad valorem tax upon the goods he made. A comprehensive idea of the great variety of pursuits and avocations which were followed in this country in 1862 can be gained by reading the internal revenue law. If, after paying the multitude of general and special taxes, one was fortunate enough to have more than $600 of annual income left, he was asked to pay three per cent to the government, and, if the surplus amounted to $10,000, ten per cent. At the end of the war the internal taxes were producing revenue at the rate of more than $300,000,000 a year. The tariff duties were revised and increased in number and amount until they annually brought to the treasury $180,000,000.

The practical instruments, then, for raising the fabulous amounts needed to prosecute the war were the high taxation measures, the enormous issues of loans, and the resort to legal-tender. Had the first of these expedients been more promptly adopted and a different policy pursued with regard to the banks in 1861, it might not have been necessary, as I have said, to resort to the third expedient. Yet what other men have ever done so well? With national credit almost destroyed, with property values greatly lessened, and with half the men of military age in the field in a civil war, 20,000,000 of people were called upon in four years to meet an expenditure of $3,500,000,000, and they showed themselves able to respond to the gigantic demand. The achievement not only stands without a parallel, but it stands unapproached. The credit was not chiefly due to leadership. What was demanded of the leaders was the ability to comprehend and the boldness to call into play the splendid capacity and the fervent patriotism of the people. But the one man who is as much entitled as any other, with the exception of the secretary of the treasury, to the glory of these financial achievements was the chairman of the Committee on Ways and Means and the leader of the House of Representatives.

CHAPTER XI

THE activity of Stevens was by no means confined to providing the means of carrying on the war and to supervising the appropriation bills. When any measure involving an important policy was before the House, he was pretty sure to be heard, and he himself presented a large number of important measures aside from those which were within the province of his committee. An important and ingenious measure was his bill to repeal the laws establishing Southern ports of entry. One of the great instrumentalities in bringing the war to an end was the destruction of the commerce between the Southern Confederacy and foreign nations.

The Administration, at the very threshold of the war, recognized the importance of preventing the South from sending abroad the vast quantities of cotton and other produce which could be raised by slaves without detracting from the fighting strength, and exchanging these for supplies and munitions of war. If the South could have had an uninterrupted commerce, she would have possessed a financial strength scarcely surpassed by that of the North. She had little manufacturing, and could make few of the articles which she might need to thoroughly equip her armies. But the labor of her slaves could be employed as well in war as in peace upon her plantations and cotton-fields, and if the produce of their toil could be exchanged for the products of the much more highly skilled labor of other nations, the slave would become a direct and important factor in winning the battle against his own freedom. The obvious thing for the North to do was to seal up the ports of the South. This could be accomplished by a blockade, but the disadvantage of that method was that its proclamation would involve a species of official recognition of the Confederacy, and it would also entail on us the obligation to make it effective. But if not by a blockade, how could the object be attained?

Stevens proposed to repeal the laws creating Southern ports of entry, and with remarkable foresight he reported a bill, before Lincoln was inaugurated, having that object in view. But he said in debate nearly a year afterwards that "there were too many peace conventions and border-state conferences, and too much amiable timidity in this House to allow it to pass — it might offend the rebels." [1]

He introduced it again in the following Congress, and supported it in a speech in which he declared that the government had suffered serious disadvantages because the bill had not been passed. We had been forced into a false position, he said, by closing our ports with a blockade, a proceeding which applied only to operations against a foreign nation, and involved an admission of the independent existence of the people blockaded. If a blockade were proclaimed, foreign powers had the right to question its efficiency. "Evading it, when imperfectly maintained, is legitimate trade." But a nation had a right to close its own ports, and that right other nations could not disregard. Harbors which were not ports of entry did not require a blockade to exclude commerce. "The law blockades them. Respect for that law is safer than fleets." The Confederate States might indeed create ports of entry, but foreign nations could not recognize these ports without recognizing also the independence of the Confederacy, and that would be an act of war.

He admitted that necessity for cotton was so vital to the industrial demands of England that she would do everything possible to keep open

[1] See *Congressional Globe*, December 30, 1861, p. 180.

the Southern ports. She had "made war upon the most innocent people of the world to compel them to take her opium," and had forced them at the mouth of the cannon to swallow $80,000,000 worth of the poison per annum. But if we should adopt a brave policy we should get the advantage of the anti-slavery feeling in England, which "among the masses is more intense than the greed for cotton." We ought to announce our purpose to abolish slavery, which "the whole civilized world now abhors." Our course had repelled sympathy, because the war had "virtually been made to rivet still stronger the chains of human bondage."

When Stevens delivered this speech it was too late to put his plan into effective execution, and he probably made it to justify his position. The President had, on the 19th of the preceding April, issued his proclamation declaring the blockade of Southern ports "in pursuance of the laws of the United States and the law of nations," and had declared that a competent force would be raised to prevent the entrance and departure of vessels. Whatever the disadvantages of a blockade, they had already been incurred even at the special session, when an important feature of the plan of Stevens was incorporated in one of the first bills to become a law.[1] But it is obvious that the method

[1] Acts of 37th Congress, chap. 3.

proposed by Stevens was not free from serious
objections. The friendship of foreign nations
would have been subjected to a severe test when
the legal difficulties which the plan imposed
could be evaded by the recognition of independence.   At any rate they would very likely have
refused to regard it after they recognized the
South as a belligerent power.

Stevens was ready to support the enormous
appropriations asked by the administration,
but he did not hesitate to criticise the lack of
energy and effectiveness shown during the first
year of the war, and he urged the strictest
economy in the expenditure of money. Very
likely his strictures were a little sharper on
account of his hostility to his fellow Pennsyl-
vanian, the secretary of war, and to the fact
that Lincoln moved too slowly for him in the
direction of emancipation.

In the discussion of a bill to raise a special
volunteer force for the protection of Kentucky
he uttered a warning note, and declared that
the continued increase of expense meant that
the "finances not only of the government, but
of the whole country must give way, and the
people will be involved in one general bank-
ruptcy and ruin." He said that the President's
message had given "a rose-colored view of the
condition of affairs in Kentucky." If, how-

ever, that State needed special protection, a
force should be sent from our existing armies.
"I understand there are 660,000 men under
arms somewhere," he said. "I do not know
where they are. I do not see their footsteps.
. . . I know they are lying about somewhere,
where they can very well be spared. They are
doing nothing. . . . But for Heaven's sake do
not let us go on piling mountains upon mountains of debt and taxation, until the nation
itself is finally destroyed in the operations of
this war."

The war had not proceeded far before it was
seen that the founders of the Constitution had
not contemplated a great civil war, and had not
made provision for it. The members were not
few in number who endeavored at each step to
justify their action under the Constitution by
a daring construction of that instrument, and
by drawing a meaning from its provisions of
which its framers never dreamed. Stevens,
however, did not permit himself to be disturbed
by any such scruples, or to make the Constitution ridiculous by forced and unnatural con-
structions. His mind clearly perceived the fact
that war existed. Whatever fictions might be
invented to prove that the seceding States were
in the Union, we were actually engaged in a
war for self-preservation, a civil war of greater

magnitude than had ever been witnessed. He regarded the Constitution as practically set aside in the seceding States, and wasted no ingenuity in trying to preserve the constitutional rights of those he was making every effort to destroy. Anything that would maintain the national authority, conquer its enemies, and, whenever it might be done, whether in the far or near future, restore the ultimate sway of the Constitution, was in his judgment the wisest policy to pursue.

A good illustration of his course upon constitutional questions arising within the area of the rebellion is found in his treatment of the bill for the admission of West Virginia as a State. The people of that portion of Virginia within the limits of the present State of West Virginia were opposed to secession. Like the inhabitants of the other mountainous regions of the South, they remained loyal to the Union. Their location by the side of the great free States of Pennsylvania and Ohio, their instinctive hostility to slavery, and the character of their industries, which demanded free rather than slave labor, naturally led them to sympathize with the Northern side of the controversy. When the parent State seceded they at once formed a state government, and chose state officers. They elected senators and representa-

tives to Congress, who were admitted to their
seats. But the patent absurdity of so small a
fraction of the people of Virginia claiming to
be the whole State was recognized from the outset, and it was determined to apply for admission to the Union as a separate State. The
Constitution prohibited the formation of a new
State within the jurisdiction of an existing
State without the consent of the legislature of
the State itself as well as of Congress. The
requisite consent therefore to the dismemberment of the State could not be obtained except
upon the extreme theory that the legislature
chosen by the people of West Virginia was the
legislature of Virginia. The war and the elastic
construction of the Constitution, which it produced, had not yet proceeded sufficiently far
for Congress to accept so extravagant a proposition, and the subject was postponed until the
December session of 1862. By that time distinguished representatives were prepared to
argue that the legislature chosen by the inhabitants of West Virginia was the legislature of
Virginia, and that it could constitutionally consent to the formation of the new State. Mr.
Dawes tersely stated the case when he said:
"Nobody has given his consent to the division
of the State of Virginia and the erection of a
new State who does not reside in the new State

itself." In other words, the people of the proposed new State gave the consent of the old State that it might be divided.

Stevens was willing to admit West Virignia, but his practical mind quickly rejected the fine-spun arguments to support the constitutionality of the proceeding. He began a speech upon the bill by declaring that he was not to be "understood as being deluded by the idea that we are admitting this State in pursuance of any provision of the Constitution." The constitutional argument was advanced by those who honestly held an erroneous opinion, or "who desire to justify by a forced construction an act which they have predetermined to do." In his judgment it was mockery to say that the legislature of Virginia had given its consent. Only 200,000 people out of a million and a quarter had chosen this legislature, while at the same time the State had a regularly organized government, which was the undeniable choice of the majority of its people and which had gone into rebellion. They were traitors undoubtedly, but they were still the State of Virginia. A very small number of respectable people in West Virginia had assembled, disapproved of the action of the State, and "with the utmost self-complacency called themselves Virginia." "Now is it not ridiculous . . . ? The State of Virginia has never therefore given its consent to this separation of the State. According to my principles operating at the present time, I can vote for its admission without any compunctions of conscience, but with some doubts about the policy of it."

He then announced his views concerning the legal status of the rebellious States, and these proved to be the principles upon which his policy of reconstruction was afterwards based, and which were accepted in substance by the nation. "This and other States have declared that they are no longer members of this Union — and have raised and organized an army and a power which the governments of Europe have recognized as a belligerent power." We ourselves, he declared, had unfortunately recognized them by declaring a blockade. We blockade an enemy's ports. We cannot blockade our own. We should have repealed the law creating these ports of entry. The Confederate States, therefore, were a power, and they became subject to all the laws of war. The Constitution had not the least effect upon them. It was idle to say that the obligations of an instrument were "binding upon one party while they are repudiated by the other. It is one of the principles of law universal . . . that obligations personal or national must, in order to be binding, be mutual and be equally

acknowledged and admitted by all parties. . . .
Hence I hold that none of the States now in
rebellion are entitled to the protection of the
Constitution." Where, he asked, did Lincoln
find any warrant in the Constitution for the appointment of military governors? "If he must
look there alone for authority, then all these
acts are flagrant usurpations." Stevens here
boldly and clearly announced the principle which
was hostile to the policy afterwards originated by
Lincoln and indorsed by Johnson, and which,
after a contest hardly less memorable than that
over slavery itself, and intimately connected
with it, was destined to prevail and to prescribe
the terms upon which the seceding States were
restored to the Union. Even in this speech he
foreshadowed his opposition to Lincoln's reconstruction policy, by declaring with a good deal
of asperity that, "while in a great majority of
instances in the rebel States he [the President]
has had but little regard to the Constitution, he
has upheld it in only one," referring to the
policy of confiscation.

While Stevens regarded the seceding States
as outside of the Constitution, he jealously upheld that instrument within the sphere of the
authority of the national government. Mr.
Roscoe Conkling presented a resolution, calling
upon the secretary of war for information as to

the responsibility for the disaster at Ball's Bluff, where, through a gross blunder, a detachment of our troops had been moved across the Potomac under most adverse conditions, and nearly a thousand of them had been lost. The secretary had replied that no inquiry to fix the responsibility had been held, because in the opinion of the general-in-chief it would be "injurious to the public service." Mr. Conkling introduced a second resolution, and supported it with a speech which excited a heated debate. The Constitution was, as usual, brought into the discussion. It was declared to be a violation of that instrument for the House to meddle with a military question of the character presented by the resolution. The President was made the commander-in-chief of the armies, and the question came within his jurisdiction, and was not an affair for the House. Stevens did not agree with this view of the case, and said that it had no foundation in the Constitution. The power to declare war, to raise armies, and to vote supplies was in Congress. "Has it come to that," he asked, "that this body is a mere automaton to register the decrees of another power? . . . It is the doctrine of despotism, better becoming that empire which they are attempting to establish in the South." The House passed the resolution, but the second reply of

the secretary contained no more information
upon the question of responsibility than the
first.

The bill presented to the House by Stevens,
to indemnify the President and others for the
suspension of the writ of habeas corpus, met
with determined opposition. The President
regarded it as a military necessity to suspend
the writ in the case of many persons who had
been arrested on the charge of aiding the rebellion. It was obviously impossible to conduct
the war in the courts or according to the rules
of law. If an officer of the army had caused
the arrest of a spy or of persons in a secret
conspiracy against the government, it would
not merely have been manifestly detrimental to
take him from his post of duty, but he could
not in many cases make without injury the dis-
closures which a judicial inquiry would involve.
The suspension of the writ in time of war was
clearly authorized by the Constitution. But
what power could suspend the writ? The President was advised by his cabinet that he could
do it. It was claimed, on the other hand, that
the suspension of a writ so vital to individual
liberty was not a mere executive act, but that,
if Congress were in session, its suspension must
first be sanctioned by that body. If the suspension had not been legal the executive officers

might be liable to heavy civil damages. It was also most important to the prosecution of the war that the writ should be suspended. Stevens proposed to settle all doubts by indemnifying the executive officers for arrests already made, and giving to the President authority to suspend the writ during the continuance of the rebellion. He had carefully studied the English precedents for the somewhat technical portion of the bill relating to the indemnity, and was able to answer all objections. He secured its passage in a summary fashion and with very little debate ; for when the opposition objected to assigning the discussion for some future day he abruptly demanded the previous question.

One of the acts of the thirty-seventh Congress which suffered a great deal of unpopularity was the act for "enrolling and calling out the national forces." In some portions of the North the number of those who were willing to volunteer had been exhausted. The conscription act at one step provided for drafting into the service, with a few exceptions, all the able-bodied men of military age in the country, or as many of them as the President should see fit to call out. The measure was the occasion for a prolonged and exciting debate, which, as party lines were closely drawn, took on the most partisan character. Some members objected to the drastic

features of the bill, which armed provost mar-
shals with the power to arrest for "treasonable practices." Of course, in the judgment of
others, it violated the Constitution. There was
a great deal of hot declamation to the effect that
the bill would completely destroy the liberty and
happiness of the people. Mr. Vallandigham
distinguished himself by the violence of his denunciation of the bill, and by a bitter attack
upon the President. Stevens was not at all dis-
inclined to take part in a partisan debate, and
the contribution which he made to the discussion affords a very good example of his style of
partisan speaking in the House. We should, he
said, have had sufficient volunteers had the Democrats not done all in their power to persuade
men not to enlist. They desired to keep Democrats at home in order that they might carry the
elections. Their policy had succeeded, he said,
in some districts, as the returns of the last election showed. He admitted that many loyal
Democrats had volunteered, but many also had
been dissuaded. To prove this statement, he said
that he would read from a speech of Mr. Vallandigham, in which the latter said: "The day
has gone by when a war for the restoration of
the Union can by any possibility be successful,"
and added that, if the war continued and no
relenting spirit was shown, the rebels ought to

be induced to invade the North. He had also asked in the same speech: "Will you send your sons again to the battlefield? Shall they be conscripted to carry on this war for two years more and for the negro?"

Vallandigham interrupted Stevens at this point to make a correction in the report of his speech. Stevens replied, "I will strike that out. The other is at least first cousin to it. The whole of it, if spoken anywhere else than under this government, would come very near to ' treasonable practices,' and therefore I intend to strike out that expression, for the partition between treason and treasonable practices, and between treasonable practices and the sentiments of that speech, is so very thin that any deputy provost marshal not skilled in these nice distinctions would be very likely to do great injustice by reporting the gentleman. (Laughter.)" [1] He then noticed the charge that we were not succeeding in the war because McClellan had been dismissed. He affected a reluctance to speak about McClellan, which, of course, he professed to do only under compulsion. Some idea of the character of his comments upon the less successful of McClellan's operations may be found from what he said about his important victory at Antietam. The President had ordered the

[1] *Congressional Globe*, February 24, 1863.

general to pursue the enemy. "He started after them with an army of 120,000 men before him, and marched that army at the rapid rate of six miles a day until they stopped and he came up with them. (Laughter.) He then fought the battle of Antietam. It was a quasi victory, but notwithstanding that, while the enemy were in sight of the river, and while he was within cannon-shot of the enemy, he suffered them all to cross the river, which was done by them deliberately and successfully to the last man and the last ambulance." The conscription bill finally passed by a vote of nearly three to one, and thus the first Congress which sat during the war voted "the last man," as it had already shown its willingness to appropriate "the last dollar."

One of the "war measures" adopted by Congress to suppress the rebellion was the confiscation of the property of the rebels. I have alluded to the act passed at the July session of 1861, which undertook to deal principally with the cases of slaves working upon forts and otherwise employed in the military service of the Confederacy. That was a mild enactment. As the war progressed, a great variety of bills, some of them of the most extreme character, were introduced. The action of the Confederate government in confiscating the property of "alien enemies," and the rigid manner in which it was enforced, were not without their effect upon Congress. This act was employed, not only against citizens of the North, but also against subjects of Great Britain and other neutral nations.[1]

Many harsh measures of reprisal were proposed in both Houses, and finally one of them, which seemed moderate only when compared with the others, was passed and received the reluctant approval of the President. Its chief features were the discretion which it gave to the court to impose the death sentence or a fine and imprisonment for the crime of treason; the power it conferred on the President to seize the estates of the military and the principal civil officers of the Confederacy; and the provision that all slaves of persons who should thereafter be engaged in rebellion, escaping or coming within the control of the forces of the United States, should be deemed captives and be "forever free."

The measure was, in fact, rendered somewhat ineffective by the passage of a resolution which Lincoln exacted as a condition to his signing it, and it does not appear to have been put into actual operation with any severity. This resolution did not give satisfaction to the advocates of confiscation, and an effort was subsequently

[1] Blaine, *Twenty Years of Congress*, p. 349.

made to amend it. It could safely be taken for granted that Stevens would support confiscation, especially of slave property, but he made use of the occasion chiefly for the purpose of again declaring his opinions upon the constitutional relations of the seceding States to the Union. This was a subject apparently always before his mind. In a speech which dealt very slightly with confiscation he ridiculed the claim that the rebel States were still in the Union, and that whenever our "wayward sisters choose to abandon their frivolities and present themselves at the door of the Union . . . we must receive them with open arms." If those States were in the Union he could see no reason why they should not elect the next President of the United States and senators and representatives to Congress. If that claim were correct, "then the rebel States, after having been conquered and reduced to utter helplessness through the expenditure of many billions of money and the shedding of oceans of loyal blood, may lay down their arms, which they can no longer wield, claim to be legitimate members of the Union, . . . retain all their lands and possessions, and leave the loyal States burdened with an immense debt, with no indemnity for their sufferings and damages and with no security for the future."

He then put the question whether the struggle was to be regarded as a "public war" under the rules of civilized warfare, or "only a domestic insurrection, to be suppressed by criminal prosecution before the courts of the country?" If it was an insurrection, then the insurgents had a right to "the protection of the Constitution and municipal laws." If it was a public war, "then they are subject to the laws of war alone." He then cited Vattel to show that, when a republic was broken into two armed factions, "this is called civil war;" that, although a sovereign might call all who resisted him rebels, yet if they had strength enough to oblige him to carry on war according to the established rules he must submit to the use of the term civil war, and that in such a case the combatants "stand in precisely the same predicament as two nations who engage in a contest." Could any one, he asked, deny to a contest of the magnitude of the rebellion the term "civil war"? The powers of Europe had recognized the Southern States as belligerents. What was even more conclusive, "with unfortunate haste we blockaded their ports," and thereby ourselves acknowledged their belligerency. We "had treated their captive soldiers as prisoners of war," exchanged prisoners, and sent flags of truce. "This is not the usage awarded to an

unorganized banditti." If public war existed,
he said, then it was clear that no compacts,
laws, and paper obligations could be relied upon
by the South against the North. This argument was in entire harmony with that which he
made soon after the war began and to which
he adhered to the end. He was unquestionably
a great lawyer. It is impossible to read his
speeches upon questions of a legal character
and not appreciate the grounds for the tribute,
said to have been paid him by another great
lawyer and a political foe, Judge Jeremiah S.
Black, that at the time of his death he had no
equal as a lawyer at the American bar.[1]

Being the thorough lawyer that he was, he
detected at the very outset the inevitable legal
question which would come with the ultimate
victory of the North. He investigated it,
weighed it most carefully, and when he had
once reached his conclusion he did not deviate
from it by a hair; it remained thereafter as
binding upon his mind as a decision of the
Supreme Court, and far more so than such a
decision which did not accord with his judgment. There was no partisanship about it, because his party had at the time no opinion upon
the question. Indeed that party had harbored
the loose generalization, which had become a

[1] *The Green Bag*, vol. iii. p. 260.

sort of cant, that the seceding States were in the Union, and it received his opinion at the outset with a species of horror. He was called radical and in advance of his party. Doubtless he was radical upon many propositions, but he was an apparent radical upon this question only because he studied and decided it first. It was not with him essentially a question of policy. It was almost purely a question of law. When other men came seriously to look into the problem most of them agreed with him, and ultimately the nation adopted his position.

The views of Stevens grew constantly more radical upon the question of confiscation, and he urged it both as a species of indemnity and as a punishment. He did not, however, believe in bloody penalties. While a member of the Pennsylvania legislature he had strongly opposed capital punishment, and he did not desire to apply it against the Confederates; but he would have been little constrained by considerations of mercy when it came to the infliction of pecuniary penalties.

Notwithstanding the great expense of the war Stevens appreciated the political and commercial advantage to the country of incurring new debts to provide for the construction of the Pacific railroads, and he took charge in the House of one at least of those great measures.

But he was discriminating in his support of public improvements and also of bills which disguised under a military title some formidable design upon the treasury. Among measures of the latter sort was one of which the patriotic title imported that it was designed to furnish a waterway "for the passage of armed and naval vessels from the Mississippi River to Lake Michigan." Stevens fought this measure successfully with the weapon of ridicule. He claimed that, as the Illinois River had very little depth of water, a connection between it and the lake would drain the latter and leave nothing but dry land. The war, which gentlemen favoring the bill were to have with Great Britain, "was to come off at the farthest in ninety days," and the canal through which our war vessels were to pass could not be finished in less than five years; and then, even if our gunboats could be brought to Chicago, a slight obstacle still remained to getting them into Lake Ontario, as it was necessary to run Niagara Falls, "which is said to be a little perilous in the spring of the year." No one could have been more relentlessly hostile to the schemes of those designing patriots, who always follow in the wake of war.

He was opposed to the policy of paying interest on the national debt in coin. He believed, during the war at least, that the principal of the bonds should be payable in coin, if the term for which they were to run should continue for a considerable time beyond the probable termination of the war, although at a later period he protested against paying in coin those bonds which according to their terms were payable in money; such a proceeding he termed "a swindle upon the taxpayers of the country." But his position during the war was that a general suspension of specie payments would cause gold to become an object of speculation, and that the government would have to submit to the exactions of the "gold room" in order to get the great quantity needed to meet its interest charge; and that, if it collected its customs duties in gold, the burden would only be shifted upon the importers, with the result in both cases of artificially putting up the price of gold as measured in greenbacks.

So late as the beginning of the last year of the war he again urged the adoption of his policy, making "one more effort," as he said, "probably the last I shall ever make upon this subject, for the purpose of arresting what I believe to be the rapid downward course to absolute ruin of our system of currency." [1] He was most tenacious of his belief upon this subject,

[1] *Cong. Globe*, June 23, 1864.

as indeed he was upon all others. He reiterated the view which he had expressed in the House soon after the suspension of specie payments. "I thought so from the first," he declared, "although it looks like tautology to repeat it every time when this question comes up." He pointed to the high price of gold, and consequently the high price of everything, as a vindication of his prophecy made more than two years before. "All our financial troubles," he said, "arise from the extraordinary demand for gold, when gold is not the currency of the country." When specie payments had been suspended he thought that the suspension should have been general and every industry and interest should have stood together, of course with the ultimate purpose to resume coin payments and with the hope of the "better and happier times when coin will be the currency of the country." If his plan was not adopted of making the principal of the bonds payable in coin and the interest in lawful money, he declared that gold was likely to go to 300 per cent. He hoped that he might prove a worse prophet than he had already been shown to be in regard to the same subject, but he had intended to paint the results in mild colors.

The House did not accept his policy, but whether the substantial fulfillment of his prediction vindicated his wisdom must remain a matter of conjecture. If we exclude the effect of speculation, there would appear to be no adequate reason, when the certainty of victory had become apparent, why the credit of the national government, as shown by the value of its currency in the purchase of gold, should have been barely a third as high as in the dark days of January, 1862. Its debt had indeed greatly increased; but, judged according to the standard of wealth and population, it still remained smaller than that of European nations which enjoyed a high credit.

Stevens was conservative in his financial views at the outbreak of the war, but he ceased to be orthodox before it closed. There is much in his later speeches to give comfort to the advocate of fiat money. The action of the legislative department was so often invoked to create money, and interfere with the natural laws of trade, that it was resorted to with constantly increasing frequency. He apparently came to have faith in the efficacy of legal nostrums, though his own experience should have taught him the danger of this course. Having aided in creating an enormous premium on gold by repeated issues of paper money, Congress chose to find the cause of that, for which it could fairly claim a large measure of responsibility, in the "gold room."

It accordingly applied a legislative remedy to the evil, and passed a rigid law restricting the transactions that could be made in gold. This extraordinary piece of legislation bore a striking resemblance in principle to some of the laws of the French Revolution. Although Stevens presented a gold bill to the House from his committee, he was probably no more responsible than many of the other members who supported the legislation. It had no more earnest advocate than Secretary Chase. The absurdity of the enactment was soon demonstrated by its own operations. It greatly aggravated the difficulty which it was intended to remove. In a short time the premium on gold bounded upwards thirty points, and fifteen days after the enactment of the law it was repealed by the very Congress which had passed it.

A review of the course of Stevens upon all the measures coming before the House would involve practically a history of legislation during the war. He was so unquestionably leader that no man was next to him, and his industry and energy responded so fully to the demands, that he was almost always upon his feet or in charge of measures before the House. When the enormous amount of committee work which he was called upon to perform is remembered, and especially the preparation of revenue and appropriation bills, which would alone be a sufficient tax upon the strength of an ordinary man, it is almost incredible that one at his advanced age should have been able to attend so constantly upon the sessions of the House and perform the part that he performed there. For the purpose of taking a glimpse of him as a working member in the ordinary routine of the House, I have instanced a few of the many matters with which he dealt, unimportant only when compared with the great financial measures to which I have referred in a previous chapter and to the measures of even greater consequence concerning emancipation and reconstruction of which I have still to treat.

CHAPTER XII

EMANCIPATION

PRIOR to 1861 the struggle over slavery was
principally involved in the effort to change the
line that separated slave from free territory;
and when the contest began to threaten the existence of the Union, the efforts of our statesmen
were directed towards adopting some expedient
which might temporarily restore the peace. As
usually happens, violence was an important
factor in determining the character of the compromise, and the most clamorous party either
got the best of the bargain, or, if it failed to
accomplish that, proceeded to set it aside with
little ceremony. Thus with alternations of
chills and fever the nation approached the
crisis. The only great party that had ever
assumed anything approaching an aggressive
attitude upon the anti-slavery side of the slavery question had triumphed, and elected a
President of the United States. Slavery had
been dealt a harder blow, so far as the ballot
could administer one, than it had ever received,

and it immediately became violent in proportion
to the force of the blow. Then the Southern
leaders began again to threaten rebellion and
secession. It is not strange that American
statesmen should have thought that they detected the favorite and well-known national
disease, and that they should have set about
prescribing the time-honored remedy of a compromise. The expiring effort of the old order
of statesmanship was seen in the offer of a
constitutional amendment, making it impossible
even to confer upon Congress the power to interfere with slavery in any State. This offer,
too, was made in the flush of the first great
anti-slavery triumph in the nation.

But the medicine had been tried too often,
and had finally lost all virtue. The violence,
which had so often demanded compromise, had
increased until it had at last reached the point
of causing war. Even after the appeal had
been taken to arms the old habits of thought
were still strong, and three months after Fort
Sumter had been fired upon, Congress almost
unanimously passed the Crittenden resolutions
which Stevens, without great exaggeration,
characterized as an apology for fighting, and
which, whether they were apologetic or not,
were cast in the old compromise mould.

But the education of the Northern people,

for which they were beginning to pay so roundly in blood and treasure, proceeded rapidly, and the same Crittenden resolutions, which passed almost unanimously in July, were, as we have already seen, upon the motion of Stevens, promptly laid upon the table when again offered in the following December. This action marked the beginning of the ascendency of the anti-slavery sentiment in Congress, and the absolute end of compromise upon the slavery question. Undoubtedly the North had taken up arms to uphold the Union, but the struggle had not proceeded far before two ideas became influential in the same direction, — the one, that emancipation was necessary as a war measure to destroy the rebellion; the other, that the Union, which had to be saved by such sacrifices, should be established upon a better and more permanent basis than the old Union, to which slavery had been a perpetual menace.

Any policy which led to emancipation Stevens was prepared from the outset to accept. In supporting the mild confiscation bill at the July session of 1861, he did not hesitate to declare his opinion that the slaves should be armed if the war continued.[1] On the day of the opening of the very next session he introduced a resolution, declaring that slavery caused the rebel-

[1] *Cong. Globe*, August 2, 1861.

lion; that there could be "no solid and permanent peace and union" in the republic so long
as slavery existed within it; that slaves were
"used by the rebels as essential means of supporting and protracting the war," and that by
the law of nations it was "right to liberate the
slaves of an enemy to weaken his power." His
resolution also provided "that the President be
requested to declare free, and to direct all our
generals and officers in command to order freedom to, all slaves who shall leave their masters
or who shall aid in quelling this rebellion."
It also contained a clause for the compensation
of loyal citizens for losses under the resolution.[1]
He supported his resolution in an extended
speech on January 22, 1862. He declared that
the rebellion was inevitable, and that "now is
the appropriate time to solve the greatest problem ever submitted to civilized man." He did
not believe that the North could conquer until
it had adopted a new method of warfare. The
Southern soldiers were as brave, their generals
were as intelligent as those of the North, and
they had valuable allies in their swamps, their
inaccessible mountains, their climate which
would prove fatal to the Union armies, and
most of all in their slaves. A vast number of
Northern men of military age would be compelled

[1] *Cong. Globe*, December 3, 1861.

to stay at home to till the soil and keep in motion the mechanical and manufacturing industries, but every Southern white man fit for war could be spared for the army without taking a single hand from the industrial pursuits.

"The protecting summer," which would destroy our armies, "would enable them to cultivate their fields . . . to furnish them the sinews of war." While the black man did not carry a gun, he was in reality " the mainstay of the war." He declared that he would take the slaves from the fields, and set them to "fighting for their liberty." He thought it a "puerile inconsistency" that the North should be willing to kill the rebels in order to prevail, and yet would not use the freedom of the slave as an instrumentality to the same end. He believed that manumission was merciful, but would admit for the sake of argument that it was "the most terrible weapon in our armory." That was no argument against its use. "Instruments of war are not selected on account of their harmlessness. You choose the cannon that has the longest range. You throw the shell that will kill the most men by its explosion. You grind to its sharpest edge the sabre bayonet. But you object to emancipation because it liberates the slaves of traitors!" He proposed his resolutions, not only as a war measure, but as a per-

manent peace measure. "The principles of our
republic are wholly incompatible with slavery.
They cannot live together. While you are
quelling this insurrection at such fearful cost,
remove the cause, that future generations may
live at peace."

He spoke with still less reserve in a speech
later in the same session upon the course of
General Hunter in arming a regiment of black
men.[1] He warmly approved the action of
Hunter, and accused the administration of being under the influence of "Kentucky council-
ors," so far as the employment of slaves in the
war was concerned. He did not believe in
keeping the runaway slaves employed in some
menial work until the war was over, in order
then to send them back to their masters "un-
hurt, under the fugitive slave law." He declared that he was in favor of sending the army
through the slave populations of the South and
asking them "to come from their masters, to
take the weapons which we furnish, and to join
us in this war of freedom." He denounced the
charge that "the blameless sons of Ethiopia"
were inhuman soldiers. In the uprising in San
Domingo the blacks had done all they could
to save their masters, against whom they were
fighting.

[1] *Cong. Globe*, July 5, 1862.

Stevens was then ahead of public opinion in his ideas of emancipation, although that opinion was moving rapidly, and he was not far in advance of it in point of time. On December 11, 1861, he made a pungent speech on a resolution requesting the President to direct General Halleck to withdraw an order he had made, prohibiting negroes from coming within the lines of our armies, and sending back those already there.[1] On March 6, following, the President sent a message to Congress, asking for the passage of a joint resolution declaring that the United States ought to coöperate with any State which may adopt gradual abolishment of slavery, giving to such State pecuniary aid, to be used by it in its discretion to compensate for the damage, public and private, produced by such change of system. On March 10, Mr. Roscoe Conkling introduced a resolution in the precise terms of that recommended by the President, and it was passed by a vote of 89 to 31. Stevens voted for it, but he regarded it as of very little importance. On a motion to postpone, he said he could not see why one side was "so anxious to pass it, or the other side so anxious to defeat it. I think it is about the most diluted milk-and-water gruel proposition that was ever given to the American nation.

[1] *Cong. Globe*, December 11, 1861.

(Laughter.) The only reason I can discover why any gentleman should wish to postpone this measure is for the purpose of having a chemical analysis to see whether there is any poison in it. (Laughter)." [1]

On April 10th, on motion of Stevens, the House proceeded to consider the bill to abolish slavery in the District of Columbia, and on the next day the bill passed by a party vote and soon became a law. On May 9 he warmly supported Mr. Lovejoy's bill prohibiting slavery in all territories then existing, or to be thereafter acquired, and also in forts and other public places and in ships on the high seas. This bill also passed. Thus the tendency towards emancipation appeared general and inevitable, and nine months from the day on which Stevens made his speech in support of his resolutions for freedom, Lincoln issued his proclamation of conditional emancipation. Undoubtedly Lincoln's action was also a little ahead of public opinion. After a winter and summer spent in futile attempts to secure compensated emancipation in the border states, and after the abolition of slavery in the District of Columbia, and the passage of confiscation acts, he had the wisdom to see that enough had been done to alienate those who were opposed to interference with sla-

[1] *Cong. Globe*, March 11, 1862.

very, but not enough to attract the radical and progressive element who believed that freedom would be a potent war measure, or who saw little to be desired in a Union which retained the ancient source of contention. Without a doubt Lincoln earnestly desired ultimate freedom, but he wanted the time to be ripe for it, and he was really conservative. If he could have had his way he would almost certainly have preferred a gradual process both for emancipation and the suffrage. But his hand was in a sense forced. Vallandigham and orators of his stripe were not lacking in material which they could use in their harangues to shock the Union Democrats with the idea that they were fighting an "abolition war." On the other hand, the severest critics of the administration were found among the abolitionists themselves.

Lincoln determined that the bravest course was the safest course, and he put emancipation as a war measure squarely before the people only a few weeks before the Congressional elections of 1862. He declared that all slaves in those rebel States which should not have submitted before January 1, 1863, "shall be then, thenceforward, and forever free." It was in the power of the Confederates to avoid the proclamation by laying down their arms. They were not compelled to continue the war. On the other hand, if they were to keep on fighting indefinitely they could not expect the North to cherish their institution any longer.

It was well that Lincoln displayed all his consummate skill as a politician in framing the issue as he did frame it, for the election was of transcendent importance. A hostile Congress meant, not merely delay and probably destruction to the emancipation policy, but it meant also reduced appropriations for the war and great encouragement to the Confederates. The Democrats accepted the issue; indeed they were anxious to raise it. In the Pennsylvania convention, which had met nearly three months before the emancipation proclamation was issued, they resolved that "this is a government of white men, and was established exclusively for the white race," and that the policy which would "turn loose the slaves of the Southern States to overrun the North, and to enter into competition with the white laboring masses, thus degrading their manhood by placing them on an equality with negroes, is insulting to our race, and meets our most emphatic and unqualified condemnation." This declaration was temperate and conservative in comparison with the platforms of the same party in other States. They could not with any show of success make the issue against fighting for the restoration of the Union. Upon that ground there was room for only one party. But if they could make it appear that the war was prosecuted to interfere with the "institutions of the States," or to establish political equality between the black man and the white, they would stand some prospect of success. The sentiment to which they appealed was then waning; but one year earlier it would have swept the country. The stake was tremendous, and the result was looked forward to with great anxiety.

The early elections were disastrous. In Ohio the Democrats carried fourteen districts out of nineteen; in Indiana eight out of eleven, and in Pennsylvania after a desperate struggle they divided the delegation equally with the Republicans, and enjoyed the satisfaction of polling a formidable vote against Stevens, who at the preceding election had been practically unopposed.[1] New York was carried by the Democrats, as was also the President's own State of Illinois, where the Republicans secured only three members out of fourteen. In the great cordon of free States, beginning with New York and New Jersey on the Atlantic, and extending to the Mississippi, the Democrats received a majority of twenty-three members.

[1] In 1860 Stevens received 12,964 votes against 470 for all others; in 1862, 11,174 against 6,650 for Steinson, Democrat.

But the cause of freedom was upheld by the extreme East and the extreme West, and, strangely enough, by those slave States which remained in the Union. Massachusetts sent a solid Republican delegation, as also did Iowa and California, and the new States of Kansas and Minnesota. Out of twenty-six members, the slave States returned twenty-one Republicans, which proved to be almost the exact number of the Republican majority in the House. The administration losses had been serious when compared with the two-thirds membership which it had held in the House during the thirty-seventh Congress. The heavy burdens of nearly two years of indecisive war could undoubtedly be charged with some of this loss, and if some of it also was to be attributed to emancipation, at least it was a great gain that the final plunge had been taken and that a majority had sanctioned freedom.

When the last session of the thirty-seventh Congress opened in December, the policy of emancipation had been settled upon, and it only remained to devise a method for making the decree effectual. Slavery had been withdrawn as a subject of controversy except as between the two great political parties, and the questions that grew out of it no longer remained to divide seriously the party that was responsible by the vote of the people for the government of the country. But there still existed a wide diversity of opinion as to the method of getting rid of it. The President believed in the wisdom of gradual emancipation, and in his annual message to Congress in December, 1862, he somewhat checked the hopes of the extreme abolitionists by recommending a plan providing compensation for any State abolishing slavery at any time before the year 1900. A bill was introduced for the emancipation of slaves in Missouri on the lines of the message, but it was defeated by filibustering, and similar bills with reference to other States were thereupon abandoned. On January 1, Lincoln, true to the promise of his proclamation of the preceding September, issued a proclamation, declaring that, as "a fit and necessary war measure," all persons held as slaves within a designated area of rebellion became on that day free men.

Stevens still kept up his fight for the enlistment of negro soldiers. After waiting in vain for action by the military committee, he boldly presented his bill to the House, and secured an assignment for its consideration without awaiting the report of any committee. This unusual course excited violent opposition, and an attempt was made to prevent a vote upon the measure by repeated roll-calls upon motions to adjourn and other dilatory propositions. After an all night session, the House adjourned without action, but the struggle was resumed at its next meeting and continued for a week. Stevens concluded the debate by a speech which did not lack bitterness, and which also did not lack eloquence. He had spoken so many times for the cause that he could not refrain from making one more effort to secure to the black man the right of fighting to be free. He did not expect to see the day when in a "Christian land merit shall counterbalance the crime of color;" but he proposed "to give them an equal chance to meet death upon the battlefield. . . . The only place where they can find equality is in the grave. There all God's children are equal." His efforts were at last crowned with success; the bill passed by 83 to 54, and the hundreds of thousands of black soldiers who enlisted before the end of the war refuted by their conduct the predictions that they would be guilty of inhumanity.

The election of 1862 had made emancipation a party question. The Republicans were committed to it. The Democrats, on the other hand, were encouraged, by their enormous gains in the great free States, to believe that they had at last found a winning issue. The ill-fortune which pursued our arms produced disaffection in the North, and the draft was contributing to make the war unpopular among those who would be patriotic, provided that they might be permitted to stay at home. The equal interest which the soldier had in the country, for which he was willing to fight, was recognized in a few of the States, and laws were passed giving him the ballot; but many times more than enough to turn the tide in a reasonably close election were practically disfranchised, and the expression of the public opinion of the country was in effect restricted to those who pursued the arts of peace. Under all these favoring circumstances the opponents of Lincoln cherished no ill-founded anticipation, when they believed that they would be able to carry the country at the next general election.

But while the great mass of the soldiers were deprived of the right of suffrage, they proved that they could settle by their valor the issues which they were forbidden to decide by their votes. Early in July, 1863, the decisive battle of Gettysburg marked the high-water point of the rebellion, and from the moment when the great Confederate commander led from the field what remained of his magnificent army, the cause for which he fought steadily declined. The decisive blow struck by Grant at Vicksburg followed Gettysburg by only a day, and the result of these two great victories put an end to Democratic hopes.

At this time the freedom of the slaves had been proclaimed only for the rebel States, and not in those slave States which remained loyal, and it rested only upon an executive order. It was now determined to set the matter forever at rest, and to write the decree of freedom in the Constitution. Soon after the assembling of the thirty-eighth Congress Mr. Ashley, of Ohio, proposed an amendment to the Constitution, abolishing slavery, and later on the same day Mr. Wilson, of Iowa, introduced a similar resolution. On March 28, 1864, Stevens proposed an amendment very similar in phraseology to the one which was finally adopted. It required a two-thirds vote of both Houses to submit the amendment for adoption to the States. The Senate was strongly Republican, and the requisite majority there was secured with little difficulty. In the House, however, the Republicans had a bare majority of 20 in a membership of 162, and upon the first vote taken in June, 1864, it failed to receive the necessary two-thirds vote. A motion was made to reconsider, and the subject was postponed until the next session.

In the mean time the Union arms were everywhere successful, and the rebellion was reduced to the point of collapse. Lincoln was elected over McClellan by more than ten to one of the electoral vote. The Democrats were disastrously beaten in the Congressional elections, and the Republicans secured many more than the necessary two thirds of the House. Under these circumstances, the amendment was again called up, and when the vote was taken, it was found that enough of the Democratic members had patriotically bowed to the inevitable to secure its passage by more than the necessary two-thirds vote. The ratification of the amendment followed in due time, and this muniment of freedom, forever prohibiting slavery in the United States, became established in the Constitution.

Emancipation was, above even union itself, the great contribution which the war made to the progress of mankind; but it was only the wisest statesmanship that so shaped and directed the varying issues of the war that freedom was secured and the Union saved. In a great institution like slavery, as it existed, firmly intrenched by law over a great portion of the country, there is so much that quickly becomes vested, so much, too, that is sure to be interwoven into the fabric of society, that nothing short of a great national convulsion can remove it. It was not difficult for those who were not financially interested in it, and who looked upon it from a safe distance, to become impressed with a sense of its wickedness. But how to do away with it was a problem for the profoundest statesmanship. The most casual survey of the course of slavery to its extinction will convince one both of the danger of agitation and of the danger of compromise, when each of them is taken alone, but of the potency of each in finally setting in motion the resultant force which brought forth freedom. Very many patriotic people were found who were willing to make the best of the evil in order to be at peace, or who would at the most employ palliatives and trust to time to do the work of regeneration. Others desired to resort to methods which were excessively heroic, and would have killed the patient in order to destroy the disease. The progress and very existence of society lay in the fact that neither of these extreme views could have its way, but that, as a result of antagonistic, or certainly not concurrent, forces a middle and safer pathway was pursued. Whether slavery could, within any reasonable period, have been blotted out, except through war, is a question which is even now debated; but there can be little doubt that, after war had been entered upon, the rational and conservative course was taken, and instead of sacrificing the Union by a premature attempt at freedom, or delaying freedom until the Union was lost, the time and the methods were chosen which made freedom more certain, and made it also an instrumentality for preserving the Union. It was fortunate that men like Stevens foresaw the ultimate result and prepared the minds of men to receive it. It was fortunate that Lincoln apparently drifted with public opinion and waited until the moment was ripe. The immortal event was finally consummated, not by one side or extreme of humanity, but as a result of the combined wisdom of all.

CHAPTER XIII

THE BEGINNING OF RECONSTRUCTION

THE manner in which the Union might practically be restored, and the national government again set in operation in the Southern States, after peace returned, was anxiously considered long before the war ended. Stevens, indeed, had the subject in view at the very beginning of the war, and had a theory to meet the case. I have already referred to the fact that at the session of Congress beginning in December, 1861, he had declared that the States in rebellion had forfeited all their constitutional rights, and that a condition of public and recognized war existed between them and the national government. The view which the Republican party was willing to accept at the beginning of the war was set forth in the Crittenden resolutions. The purpose of the war was declared to be to "maintain" the Constitution and to "preserve" the Union and "all the dignity and equality and rights of the several States." Stevens, however, dissented radically from that

doctrine at the outset. The rights of the seceding States under the Constitution were already
destroyed, according to his theory, by their
own action; when they should be conquered, it
would then be for the conqueror to determine
what terms it would be expedient and just to
impose. The members who had voted for the
Crittenden resolutions in July may not have
changed their minds by December, but they
did not care to vote for them a second time,
and when they were again presented many of
those members supported Stevens's motion to
lay them upon the table, where they and the
doctrine of the equal and unimpaired rights of
loyal and rebellious States remained forever
afterwards.

In December, 1862, Mr. Vallandigham, of
Ohio, presented some resolutions reaffirming the
Crittenden theory, with the obvious purpose of
censuring the President for the departure from
that theory involved in his first proclamation
of emancipation. The resolutions were defeated
by a party vote. The Democratic position on
this vote was that maintained by both parties
at the beginning of the war, and it was consist-
ently maintained by the Democracy to the end.[1]
The course of the President and the House was

[1] Chadsey on the struggle between President Johnson and
Congress.

thus showing a gradual approach to the position of Stevens, that the Southern States could not claim the benefits of that Constitution and those laws which they were fighting to overthrow.

In the spring of 1862 the national forces captured New Orleans and obtained a firm foothold in Louisiana. A government was soon organized, and two members of Congress were chosen who were ultimately admitted to seats, although upon what theory it is difficult to comprehend, unless as an exercise of the war power which was sufficiently elastic to be made to include anything. Upon the proposition to admit them Stevens voted in the negative.

No step of much significance, however, was taken until the meeting of Congress, in December, 1863, when the President declared in his message that "the Constitutional obligation of the United States to guarantee to every State in the Union a republican form of government, and to protect the State in such cases, is full and explicit. . . . An attempt to guarantee and protect a revived state government constructed in whole or in preponderating part from the very element against whose hostility and violence it is to be protected is simply absurd. There must be a test by which to separate the opposing elements so as to build only from the sound, and that test is a sufficiently liberal one which accepts as sound whoever will make a sworn recantation of his former unsoundness." This was somewhat metaphysical, but the meaning was clear. With reference to Louisiana the President held that the obligations of the government to guarantee a republican form of government extended to the States in rebellion. Clearly, then, they were not altogether outside of the Constitution.

The President at the same time issued a proclamation in which he set forth a comprehensive plan of reconstruction. He granted to all persons who had participated in the rebellion, with a few exceptions, a full pardon "with restoration of all rights of property except as to slaves," upon condition that they should first take an oath to faithfully support and defend the Constitution and the Union, and to support and abide by the laws and proclamations relating to slavery, "so long and so far as not modified or declared void by decision of the Supreme Court."[1] He required that enough must take the oath in any State to cast one tenth as many votes as were cast in that State for President in 1860. On that condition a government established in any State which had seceded should "be recognized as the true government of the State, and the State shall receive thereunder the

[1] Blaine, *Twenty Years of Congress*, p. 38.

benefits of the Constitutional provision which declares that the United States shall guarantee to every State in this Union a republican form of government." The question of the admission of senators and representatives would be decided by the respective Houses of Congress.

State governments were established in Louisiana and one or two other States, in pursuance of the President's proclamation, and constitutions were adopted which contained provisions abolishing slavery.

The plan proposed by the President was not favorably received by the leaders of his party in Congress. They thought that so important a matter should have been determined by legislation, and not by a mere executive proclamation, and the requirements were believed to be loose and easily evaded. Stevens was the last man to be satisfied with such a settlement of the question as the President proposed. At the opening of the December session of 1863, he had curtly moved to strike the names of the three Louisiana members from the roll where the clerk had placed them. He supported the proposition to create a special committee to consider the President's plan of reconstruction, and he opposed the admission of members of Congress elected under that plan in the States which had adopted it.

A sharp issue was soon drawn between the President and Congress. The senators and representatives chosen by the reorganized state governments, which he had declared he would recognize, were refused admission to seats. This conflict made the situation doubly confused. So long as Louisiana clearly had the status of a rebel State, it was either in or out of the Union according as one adopted the Republican or the Democratic theory. But under the President's plan it was partly in and partly out, and in a position of great uncertainty. So far as executive recognition had validity, it was in; but so far as the most important function of representation in Congress was concerned, it was out.

The leaders in the two Houses were not content with merely refusing to recognize the States which the President had reconstructed, but they proceeded to form a plan of their own, and to send it to the President embodied in a bill, which, if he should sign it, would settle all controversy. The congressional plan, with which the name of Mr. Henry Winter Davis is particularly associated, provided that the President should appoint a provisional governor in each of the States in rebellion, and that so soon as resistance to the national authority had ceased in any State, the governor should enroll the white male citizens; and if a majority of them should take an oath to support the Constitution of the United States, then the election of delegates to a constitutional convention should be ordered. The state constitution should contain provisions imposing disabilities upon certain civil and military officers of the Confederacy, prohibiting the payment of all debts incurred in aid of the rebellion, and abolishing slavery. When all requirements had been complied with to the satisfaction of Congress, the President should recognize the state government, and the State should thereupon become entitled to representation in Congress. The measure did not contain a provision for negro suffrage.[1]

Although the bill contained more stringent provisions than the President had imposed, Stevens would not accept it. He said that it "partially acknowledges the rebel States to have rights under the Constitution, which I deny, as war has abrogated them all." He objected to it further, because it adopted "in some measure the idea that less than a majority may regulate . . . the affairs of a republic," and because it took away the right of confiscation.

In the speech which he made upon this bill he stated again his position that those who sup-

[1] Chadsey, *Reconstruction*, p. 21.

ported the Confederacy were belligerents, that the right of confiscation existed, and he desired such an important right to be preserved; not that he would enforce it against non-combatants and those who were forced into the war, but he would hold it against the most guilty. "To escape the consequences of my argument he [Mr. Blair, of Missouri] denies that the Confederate States have been acknowledged as a belligerent or have established and maintained independent governments *de facto*. Such assurance would deny that there is a sun in the heavens. They have a Congress, in which eleven States are represented; they have at least 300,-000 soldiers in the field; their pickets are almost within sight of Washington; they have ships of war on the ocean destroying hundreds of our ships, and our government and the governments of Europe acknowledge and treat them as privateers, not as pirates. From whom do privateers get their commissions except from a power independent either *de jure* or *de facto*? There is no reasoning against such impudent denials." He congratulated himself that the House had already accepted the proposition for which he had contended. "I have lived to see the triumph of principles which, although I had full faith in their ultimate success, I did not expect to witness. If Providence should spare

me a little longer, until this government shall
be so reconstructed that the foot of a slave can
never again tread upon the soil of the republic,
I shall be content to accept any lot which may
await me." The bill passed the House by a
few less than the usual party majority, Stevens
saying, amid laughter, "I refuse to vote under
protest."

It did not reach the President until within
ten days of the day of adjournment of Congress,
and by his abstention from signing it, it failed
to become a law. The President justified this
"pocket veto" by a proclamation, issued soon
after the adjournment, in which he said that
he did not wish by signing the bill "to be in-
flexibly committed to any single plan of restoration," or to declare that the state governments
already established should be "set aside and
held for naught, thereby repelling and discouraging the loyal citizens who have set up the
same."

The plan which the President had proclaimed
was not carefully framed, and it was at best
incomplete. It provided for a recognition by
the executive department alone. If Congress
should fail to extend recognition to a reëstablished state government, it would remain practically a military government with no clearly
defined status. It was manifestly the part of

wisdom, before beginning upon the work of reconstruction, for Congress and the President to agree upon some plan which, when put into effect, would complete the work of restoration. There was little practical wisdom in a course which might lead to contradictory action upon the part of the great departments of the government, when the task was grave enough to demand every resource which could be brought to bear through harmony and coöperation.

The plan proposed by Congress was prepared with much greater care. The work of reconstruction under it would doubtless have been more slow, but it would have been more certain to be lasting. It was more exacting than the President's plan, but mild in the extreme when compared with that which was ultimately adopted. Had Lincoln given it his approval, the long conflict with President Johnson and his impeachment would probably have been averted, and the anarchy into which some of the Southern States were plunged, and many of the other unfortunate consequences which ensued, would very likely have been avoided also.

The disagreement between the President and Congress stopped the work of reconstruction for the time, but it was only postponed. With the end of the war it was sure to press for a final solution. The controversy was dropped so far as the President was concerned, but Congress at its next session returned to the subject by passing a resolution, "declaring certain States not entitled to representation in the electoral college," which was clearly aimed at Lincoln's "ten per cent States," as they were called by his opponents who desired to be facetious.[1] The President avoided a renewal of the controversy by signing the resolution, and he sent a message to Congress, announcing that he did so "in deference to the view of Congress implied in its passage." He added, however, that the President had nothing to do with the counting of the electoral vote, and he disclaimed "that by signing said resolution he had expressed any opinion" on its subject matter or on the recitals of the preamble.

It is not very profitable to conjecture what the course of reconstruction would have been had Lincoln lived, but it is certain that he clung to his views with much pertinacity, and in a carefully prepared speech, which he read only three days before his death, he warmly defended the "Louisiana plan." He declared, with reference to the men responsible for the newly organized state government of Louisiana, that, "if we now reject and spurn them, we do our utmost to disorganize and disperse them.

[1] Blaine, *Twenty Years of Congress*, pp. 2–45.

We say to the white man, you are worthless or worse. . . . To the black man we say, this cup of liberty which these, your old masters, hold to your lips we will dash from you. . . . If this course, discouraging and paralyzing to both white and black, has any tendency to bring Louisiana into proper practical relations with the Union, I have so far been unable to perceive it. If, on the contrary, they recognize and sustain the new government of Louisiana the converse of all this is made true." All this could only mean that he believed in the wisdom of the plan he had proposed, and if that is conceded, there can be little doubt that he would have adhered to it in its substantial parts. Indeed it is hard to resist the conclusion, after reading his elaborate speech, that he made it with the purpose of preparing the public mind for the action which the destruction of the rebellion would thrust upon him. "It may be my duty," he said, "to make some new announcement to the people of the South. I am considering, and shall not fail to act when satisfied that action will be proper."[1] In the Hampton Roads conference, February 3, 1865, he promptly declared, when questioned on the subject, that it was his opinion that the Confederate States ought to be admitted to representation

[1] *Life of Lincoln*, by Nicolay and Hay, vol. ix. pp. 461–463.

in Congress, when the war was ended; and that it was also his opinion that, "when the resistance ceased and the national authority was recognized, the States would be immediately restored to their practical relations to the Union."

In addition to Lincoln's expressions of opinion on this question, near the time of his assassination, and his own intimation that he was about to make "some new announcement," not to Congress, but "to the people of the South," there is strong direct testimony as to the character of this announcement. Mr. McCulloch, who was appointed secretary of the treasury almost immediately after his second inaugural, and continued in that position under President Johnson, declared that the work of reconstruction under Johnson "was taken up just where Mr. Lincoln had left it. The very same instrument for restoring the national authority over North Carolina, and placing her where she stood before her attempted secession, which had been approved by Mr. Lincoln, was presented by Mr. Stanton at the first cabinet meeting which was held at the Executive Mansion after Mr. Lincoln's death, and, having been carefully considered at two or three meetings, was adopted as the reconstruction policy of the administration." [1] Not improbably the "two or three meet-

[1] McCulloch, *Men and Measures of Half a Century*, p. 378.

ings " were necessary to convert Mr. Andrew
Johnson, who had protested to Lincoln against
the leniency of the terms of the surrender at
Appomattox, and who, by his early presidential
speeches upon the blackness of the crime of
treason and the necessity for punishing it, confirmed the general belief that he regarded his
predecessor's policy towards the rebels as too
mild.[1]   Mr. McCulloch's statement is confirmed
by General Grant,[2] and is powerfully corrobo-
rated by the fact that the identical cabinet
which served under Lincoln remained in office
under Johnson, and at so early a time after the
accession of the latter concurred unanimously
in the plan of reconstruction.   The plan itself
contained more stringent provisions than were
embodied in Lincoln's proclamation put forth
less than a year and a half earlier.   There
is little room for doubt that Mr. Lincoln had
practically decided upon the plan of reconstruction which, six weeks after his death, was promulgated by Andrew Johnson, which gave rise
to the long and bitter conflict between Congress
and the President, and led to a condition of
things similar to that in England during the
Revolution when Parliament was supreme.   If

[1] Blaine, *Twenty Years of Congress*, vol. ii. pp. 8, 14, 65.
[2] Testimony, July 18, 1867, before Impeachment Committee.

that great man had lived, his fine political sagacity and his popularity with the people might
not have been strong enough to carry through
his plan of reconstruction, but we can at least
feel sure that his moderation would have averted
any serious rupture; that he would not have
been dragged to the bar of the Senate in impeachment proceedings, and that Congress, under the lead of Stevens, would not have wielded
the supreme power.

CHAPTER XIV

THE JOHNSON PLAN

ANDREW JOHNSON took the oath of office as President, April 15, 1865. Although coming from a State which had joined the rebellion he had shown the most unflinching loyalty. His devoted service to the Union had won him the nomination for the vice-presidency. Stevens, who was a delegate to the convention of 1864, voted for him, although with the greatest reluctance.[1] He was a man of rugged honesty and of no little egotism as well, and was a good deal given to declaiming about the Constitution and his own virtues, after the fashion of a school of statesmen somewhat numerous then and by no means extinct now.

But his selection as a possible President was due to any consideration except that of fit-

[1] Stevens said to Colonel A. K. McClure, who was also a delegate, after the latter had voted for the nomination of Johnson: "Can't you find a candidate for Vice-President in the United States, without going down to one of those damned rebel provinces to pick one up?" *Lincoln and Men of War Times*, p. 260.

ness for the position. He did not possess the special training and natural aptitude necessary for the administration of the office even in quiet times; and in the patience, discernment, political tact and constructive capacity, so requisite for leadership in the task of reëstablishing civil government in so many States upon a permanent basis, he was conspicuously lacking. He was not long in demonstrating that his selection had been a mistake. In the speech which he made upon taking the oath as President, immediately after the death of Lincoln, he said nothing about the latter, little about the country, and much about himself. "Toil and an honest advocacy of the great principles of free government," he observed, "have been my lot." Then, with characteristic modesty, he added· "The duties have been mine, the consequences God's." His reticence about all things except himself did not produce a good impression, and the fear that it portended a severe policy towards the South was soon strengthened by his violent denunciation of traitors, who, he declared, must be punished and impoverished. "If you take the life of one individual for the murder of another, . . . what should be done with one who is trying to assassinate this nation . . . ? The time has arrived, my countrymen, when the American people should be educated and taught what is crime, and that treason . . . is the highest crime that can be committed, and those engaged in it should suffer all its penalties. I know it is very easy to get up sympathy and sentiment where human blood is about to be shed, easy to acquire a reputation for leniency and kindness, but sometimes its effects and practical operations produce misery and woe to the mass of mankind." [1] These sentiments, uttered not merely in one speech, but reiterated again and again, produced general uneasiness, and extorted even from that stern old radical, Benjamin F. Wade, an entreaty that he would limit the number to be hung to a good round dozen and no more. [2]

Under the instruction of Seward and the other statesmen who composed Lincoln's cabinet and whom he still retained, the President made rapid progress. In six weeks after his inauguration he promulgated his plan of reconstruction. The plan was contained in two papers — one a proclamation of amnesty applicable to all the rebellious States, and the other an executive order having reference only to North Carolina, but soon after applied by successive orders to all the rebellious States not

[1] Johnson's speech to citizens of Indiana, April 21, McPherson's *Reconstruction*, p. 45.

[2] Blaine's *Twenty Years of Congress*, ii. p. 14.

included in proclamations issued by Lincoln.
The amnesty proclamation was almost identical
with Lincoln's proclamation, issued in December, 1863, except that its terms were not so
liberal. It granted a pardon for treason to all
who should take an oath to support the Constitution and the Union, and to obey all laws and
proclamations which had been made with reference to the emancipation of slaves. Thirteen
classes were exempted from the privileges of
the proclamations as against only seven classes
in the proclamation of Lincoln, and the terms
of exclusion were much more sweeping and
severe. With regard to these classes it was
provided that special application for pardon
should be made in each case.

The North Carolina order was exactly one in
theory with Lincoln's "Louisiana plan," and
was based upon the clause of the Constitution
which provided that the United States should
guarantee to each State a republican form of
government. It declared that the forces of the
rebellion, now almost overcome, had destroyed
civil government in North Carolina, and that it
had become necessary to carry out the obligations of the United States to the people of that
State and secure to them a republican form of
government. It appointed a provisional governor of North Carolina, and ordered him at the

earliest practicable time to prescribe rules for "convening a convention," composed of delegates chosen by the loyal people of the State, for the purpose of amending the state constitution, and for adopting such a republican form of government "as will entitle the State to the guarantee of the United States therefor." The "loyal people" were to include only those who should take the oath and receive the pardon provided for in the amnesty proclamation, and they were required to be qualified voters according to the laws in force at the time of secession. The military commander in the State was ordered to assist the governor; the postmaster-general was instructed to establish post offices and post routes, and the heads of the other departments were directed to enforce throughout the State the national laws under their respective jurisdictions. Thus the work of reconstruction was imposed upon the white race, and in effect was put in the control of those who had participated in the rebellion. Since the latter were greatly in the majority, the formation of the new Constitution which was to establish the conditions of the suffrage and of other fundamental rights, was to be committed to their hands.

The conventions called for by the successive proclamations were quickly held, the old state constitutions were repaired, and in a wonderfully short time the legislatures were in session passing laws, and senators and representatives for the national Congress were chosen. The first acts of the provisional governments were regarded by the people of the North with the most intense and friendly interest. The passions of the war had not wholly subsided; but there was heartfelt rejoicing that the bloody contest was over, and a general desire to witness the reëstablishment of state governments at the South and the complete restoration of the Union. Andrew Johnson, too, had won golden opinions by his patriotic course as the "war governor" of Tennessee, and enjoyed a high degree of popularity in the North. The one point which excited the most interest was the treatment that was to be accorded to the negro by the new governments.

There was a wide difference of opinion even among Republicans as to the wisdom of conferring the ballot upon the newly liberated slave, but there was no difference of opinion, among all loyal men of whatever party, as to the necessity of maintaining inviolable the freedom which had been won for him at such great cost. It was unfortunate, although it was not unnatural, that the new legislatures should not have appreciated the great importance of leaving the negro alone, if they could not treat him without discrimination. But most of them speedily proceeded to enact laws expressly aimed at the freedmen. A sufficient reference to these laws to illustrate their general character is necessary, because they had a vital effect in determining future legislation upon reconstruction, and especially in producing the antagonism between Congress and the President, of whose policy they were the first fruits.

The legislature of Mississippi passed laws requiring certain officers to report to the probate courts all free negroes under the age of eighteen, whose parents were without the means to support them or refused to do so, and that the court should thereupon order them to be apprenticed until they became of age. In choosing the master for the new apprentice the former owner was to have a preference. Severe penalties were enacted in case the "apprentice" ran away, or if any person furnished him with food and clothing. When poverty was so universal among both blacks and whites very few colored people could judicially prove that they had the means of supporting their children. The same legislature enacted that all free negroes over eighteen years of age, found with no lawful employment or business, should be deemed vagrants, and be subject to a heavy fine. If unable to pay the fine the freedman was to be "hired out," preferably to his old master, for a term sufficient to produce the amount of the fine.[1]

Another act was passed relating to the "employment" of freedmen, with provisions of forfeiture of rights for violation of the contract, which left the payment of wages practically optional with the employer. Any negro who should quit the service of his "employer" before the expiration of his contract became practically an outlaw, and any one giving him food or clothing became liable to an action for damages by the "employer," to a heavy fine, and to possible imprisonment.

The laws of South Carolina were drafted upon the same lines as those of Mississippi. "All persons of color" making contracts of labor were to be known as servants, and their employers as masters. In order to follow any pursuit, except one of the most menial character, a colored man was required to pay a license fee, which was practically prohibitory, and which was not required of a white man.

Special crimes were created and special penalties imposed upon the black race. The unequal character of these laws led to the intervention of General Sickles, the military commander of that department, who issued an order which

[1] Act of November 24, 1865.

caused the military law to shine for once in comparison with civil justice. It practically set the code aside and declared that "all laws shall be applicable alike to all the inhabitants," and that a freedman should not be obliged "to pay any tax or any fee for a license, nor be amenable to any municipal or parish ordinance, not imposed upon all other persons." [1]

The Johnson legislature in Alabama passed bills relating to contracts for labor, which went far towards doing away with the emancipation proclamation. They devised an easy way back to slavery for men and women, and one that was even more effective for children. Perhaps the most vicious of these statutes was the new charter of Mobile, which attached to the crime of poverty, universal and inevitable among the black race at that time, a penalty of six months' labor for the benefit of the city, and made it possible to rebuild its neglected streets, wharves, and other public works out of the un- compensated labor of the freedmen. Some of the worst of the bills failed to become laws through a courageous use of the veto power by Governor Patton. [2]

The laws of Florida created a criminal court, with jurisdiction to try for vagrancy and other

[1] Order of January 17, 1866.
[2] McPherson's *Reconstruction*, p. 21.

crimes for which capital punishment was not provided. In the proceedings of this court no indictment or written pleadings were required. If any fine should not be paid, the "vagrant" might be put to such labor as the county commissioner should direct, or might be "hired out" by that official to any person who would take him for the shortest time and pay the fine and costs.[1] Special criminal statutes were passed, aimed at the negro, and providing for contracts for labor with "persons of color."

These "contracts" were given a peculiar sanctity so far as the obligations of the black man were concerned. A violation on the part of the employer would subject him to a mere civil liability, in the shape of a proceeding for damages, for breach of contract; but a violation on the part of the black man constituted a heinous crime, for which he was liable to be pilloried, or whipped with thirty-nine lashes, or "hired out for one year."

But it is monotonous iteration to review the early legislation of the reconstructed governments established under the proclamation of the President. In most of the States the laws established a condition but little better than that of slavery, and in one important respect far worse; for in place of the property interest,

[1] Act of January 11, 1866.

which would induce the owner to preserve and
care for his slave, there was substituted the
guardianship of penal statutes; and the ignorant
black man, innocent of any intention to commit
a wrong, could be bandied about from one
temporary owner to another who would have no
other interest than to wring out of him, without regard to his ultimate condition, all that
was possible during the limited term of his
thraldom.

An attempt has been made to excuse these
laws by the assertion that similar statutes
existed in Northern States.[1] This amounts to
a very slender justification. In the first place
the Northern statutes, which are called similar,
applied impartially to all races. Most of the
statutes which I have referred to were leveled
at the negro alone and discriminated against
him. Doubtless a great many unwise laws, the
accumulation of a century, could be found on the
statute books of the older States, which had escaped the attention of the people and legislators
alike, and had become obsolete. But it would
surely have been a scanty display of political
wisdom for the newly established state governments of the South to extract these vicious
principles and embody them in laws against the
black race, in their very earliest exercise of

[1] *Why the Solid South?* H. A. Herbert, pp. 32–36.

legislative power, and when the eyes of the
nation were upon them to see whether the freedom which resulted from a great war could be
safely intrusted to their hands. It was most
unfortunate, in view of the formative condition
of opinion among the Northern people, that
those particular statutes should have been enacted at that particular time. A most unfavor-
able impression was produced at the North.
The people there felt that emancipation was
liable to be nullified to a considerable extent by
state laws, if the making of the laws was exclusively intrusted to the former master. Then,
for the first time, the opinion became widespread
that the newly acquired freedom must be armed
with the ballot. The first results of Johnson's
reconstruction policy thus established its unpopularity at the North and paved the way for
a radical reaction.

CHAPTER XV

WHILE the new legislatures of the Southern States were about the work of passing their vagrant and labor laws, the thirty-ninth Congress assembled for the first time. The overwhelming Republican victory in 1864 had secured to that party a great majority in both Houses. For a second time the policy of a Republican President upon the reconstruction of the rebellious States was to come before Congress. It came now with even greater sanction, because Johnson's policy had been Lincoln's, and because, too, the war was now ended. The issue was a momentous one. Would Congress break with the President and refuse to recognize his state governments?

The clerk of the preceding House of Representatives, whose duty it was to make up the list of members-elect, had excluded from the roll the names of those who presented credentials of election from the reconstructed Southern States. The issue was raised at the outset, and the strongest possible case was first presented by the Democrats. Before the speaker was elected, Mr. Brooks demanded to have it decided whether Mr. Maynard, a prominent Republican from Tennessee, was entitled to his seat. If Tennessee is not in the Union, Mr. Brooks argued, the President of the United States, who comes from that State, must be a foreigner and a usurper. The Congress immediately preceding that one had permitted the members from Louisiana to take their seats and vote for speaker. Why should the members of the same State be excluded now? The clerk, Mr. Brooks declared, had excluded the Southern members from the roll because of a resolution passed at a caucus of Republican members. He intimated to Stevens that he should be glad to know "at what period he intends to press this resolution, of which he is to be the organ."

Stevens sat with the resolution in his pocket which was to work the commencement of that memorable conflict between the President and Congress, which transcends in importance any other political struggle in our history. He had a large majority at his back, and was about to see the beginning of the triumph of the ideas which he had long advocated, and for which he had been denounced as a radical. If he was impressed with the gravity of the crisis he cer-

tainly did not show it. He could not even refrain from making Brooks the victim of a general laugh. "I have no objection to answer
the gentleman," he said in a tone of mock seriousness. "I propose to press it at the proper
time."

The House proceeded at once to elect its
officers, and after that had been done, and before the reception of the annual message of the
President, Stevens offered his resolution, which
provided for a joint committee on reconstruction, to be composed of nine representatives
and six senators, who should inquire into the
condition of the Southern States and "report
whether they or any of them are entitled to be
represented in either House of Congress; . . .
and until such report shall have been made
and finally acted upon by Congress, no member
shall be received into either House from any of
the said so-called Confederate States." He
moved to suspend the rules and also for the
previous question, which cut off all debate, and
his resolution passed by 133 to 36.

As a mere piece of political strategy this
move was admirable. In all probability the
House would not at that time have voted to
condemn the policy of the President. It was
regarded as the policy, not only of Johnson,
but also of Lincoln, and the influence of Lin-

coln had never been so potent as during the
year which followed his assassination. Moreover, the Southern legislatures had not yet proceeded far in their work of passing discriminating laws, and the tendency of the new system was
not generally seen. Stevens, however, already
discerned the unpopularity to which the policy
of the President was predestined, and he desired
to give time for the storm to gather. What
could be more fitting than to have the whole
matter carefully considered by a committee of
Congress before it should be decided? And so,
without even learning the plea which the President's message contained, he shrewdly procured
an adjournment of the question while a committee should investigate, and the presidential
policies, working out their own destruction,
should at last give way to the ideas for which
he himself had contended. Before that day
Stevens had been the leader of the House of
Representatives. Henceforth he was to be its
dictator and the leader of his party throughout
the country.

Stevens was made the House chairman of the
Committee on Reconstruction, and among his as-
sociates were such prominent men as Bingham,
Washburne, Boutwell, Conkling and Morrill.
The appropriation bills were taken from the
Committee on Ways and Means, from which

Stevens retired, and given to a new committee. Stevens was appointed chairman of the first Committee on Appropriations. Important as was the work of the latter committee it was largely of a routine character, and his attention was absorbed by the great problem of reconstruction and kindred subjects. On the second day of the session he proposed a series of amendments to the Constitution, prohibiting the payment of the Confederate debt by any State or by the United States; apportioning representatives among the States according to the number of their respective legal voters, and declaring that all national and state laws should be equally applicable to every citizen without discrimination on account of race.

Nearly all these propositions were afterwards incorporated in substance in the fourteenth amendment to the Constitution, which Stevens reported from the Committee on Reconstruction during the same session, but in a form which in one important particular was far less effective. His proposition to base representation upon the number of legal voters, to be ascertained by the national census, was self-operating, and would have been far more effective than the mere generalization which took its place in the Constitution, and which, though often violated, has never once been enforced.

He lost no opportunity to impress upon Congress his views upon the constitutional status of the Confederate States. He opened the debate on reconstruction, in a somewhat lengthy speech, for him, on December 18, 1865. He attacked the position of Lincoln and Johnson, which assumed that reconstruction was within the province of the Executive. "There is," he said, "fortunately, no difficulty in solving the question. There are two provisions in the Constitution, under one of which the case must fall. The fourth article says that ' new States may be admitted by the Congress into this Union.' In my judgment this is the controlling provision in this case. Unless the law of nations is a dead letter, the late war between two acknowledged belligerents severed their original compacts, and broke all the ties that bound them together. The future condition of the conquered power depends on the will of the conqueror. They must come in as new States or remain as conquered provinces. Congress — the Senate and House of Representatives, with the concurrence of the President — is the only power that can act in the matter. But suppose, as some dreaming theorists imagine, that these States have never been out of the Union, but have only destroyed their state governments so as to be incapable of political action, then the fourth section of the fourth article applies, which says: ' The United States shall guarantee to every State in this Union a republican form of government.' Who is the United States? Not the Judiciary; not the President; but the sovereign power of the people, exercised through their representatives in Congress with the concurrence of the Executive. It means the political government, the concurrent action of both branches of Congress and the Executive. The separate action of each amounts to nothing, either in admitting new States or guaranteeing republican governments to lapsed or outlawed States."

After expounding his well known arguments upon this proposition, he said that those States should not be admitted to the Union until the principles embodied in his proposed amendments to the Constitution should be established in that instrument, and especially the amendment basing representation upon the number of legal voters. If they were admitted with the basis unchanged, they would, with the aid of Northern Democrats, " at the very first election take possession of the White House and the halls of Congress." They might then assume the Confederate debt, repudiate the Union debt, and reëstablish slavery. He proposed to take no such chances while the North was the conqueror. He boldly proposed negro suffrage, and declared that, if the blacks were given the right to vote, "there would always be Union white men enough in the South, aided by the blacks, to divide the representation, and thus continue the Republican ascendency." If they were not given the right of suffrage in the late slave States, the representation of those States would, under his amendment, be so reduced as to "render them powerless for evil."

He referred to the legislatures of the President's reconstructed States as "the aggregation of whitewashed rebels, who, without any legal authority, have assembled in the capitols of the late rebel States and simulated legislative bodies." The doctrine that this was a "white man's government" he declared to be "as atrocious as the infamous sentiment that damned the late chief justice to everlasting fame, and I fear to everlasting fire."

When Stevens delivered this speech he had evidently not advanced to the position of requiring the concession of negro suffrage as a condition of the readmission of the Southern States; but he proposed, by basing representation upon the number of legal voters, to make it to their political interest to grant the franchise, and to leave the question in that form to the decision of each State. He did not believe that the negro should count in the representation, if he were not permitted to vote. He estimated that those States would have eighty-three representatives, if the blacks were counted, and forty-six if they were excluded, and that the opportunity to multiply their representation almost by two would induce them to confer the suffrage upon the negro.

This speech mortally offended the administration, and it was determined that a reply should be made at once, in order to check its influence upon the country. The friends of the President's policy were few in number among the Republicans of the House; but one was found, Mr. Henry J. Raymond, who was ready to defend it, and who did so with very great ability.

Mr. Raymond was not a lawyer, and he failed utterly to turn the coldly logical position which Stevens had so long held, that a condition of public war had existed, and that the Southern States could not be heard to set up any constitutional or other rights against the conqueror, except such as were granted by the laws of war. But as an argument in favor of the adoption of a liberal policy towards the South, regardless of what her strict legal rights were, the speech was admirable. Mr. Shellabarger, of Ohio, replied to the legal propositions of Mr. Raymond in a speech of great eloquence, and the debate thus inaugurated was spun out indefinitely and with constantly increasing acrimony.

Neither was it confined to the House of Representatives, for the President himself was not long in taking part in it. The appointment of the Committee on Reconstruction and the speech of Stevens wounded him deeply, and, as reticence could not be numbered among his virtues, he took an early opportunity to free his mind. In the course of a speech, very formidable in length, made on February 22, 1866, he desisted from self-eulogy long enough to denounce the Committee on Reconstruction as "an irresponsible central directory, 'which had usurped' nearly all the powers of Congress." "Suppose," he added, with that charming disregard of the proprieties of his position so characteristic of him, "I should name to you those whom I look upon as being opposed to the fundamental principles of this government, and as now laboring to destroy them. I say Thaddeus Stevens, of Pennsylvania; I say Charles Sumner, of Massachusetts; I say Wendell Phillips, of Massachusetts. . . . An honest conviction is my sustenance, the Constitution my guide." Then he returned to his favorite themes, — Andrew Johnson and the Constitution.[1]

[1] McPherson, *Reconstruction*, pp. 60, 61.

The President's speech gained no favor for his cause among his enemies, and the egotism and undignified character of the performance disgusted many of his friends. Stevens made his second important contribution to the discussion on March 10, 1866. He taunted Mr. Raymond with failing to support himself with a single authority against the contention that the rebellious States possessed any rights under the Constitution. "The gentleman," he said, "denies the correctness of Vattel's doctrine, . . . but he gives us no authority but his own. I admit the gravity of the gentleman's opinion, and with the slightest corroborating authority should yield the case. But without some such aid I am not willing that the sages of the law whom I have been accustomed to revere, — Grotius, Rutherford, Vattel, and a long line of compeers, — sustained by the verdict of the civilized world, should be overthrown and demolished by the single arm of the gentleman from New York. . . . I pray the gentleman to quote authority; not to put too heavy a load upon his own judgment; he might sink under the weight. Give us your author."

Stevens denied that his doctrine involved the efficacy of the secession ordinances, "which amounted to nothing either in law or in fact. It was the formation of a regular, hostile government, and the raising and supporting of large

armies, and for a long time maintaining their
declaration of independence, that made them a
belligerent and the contest, war." He disputed,
with only apparent inconsistency, the theory that
loyal citizens alone made a State. A State was
made up of all legal citizens, good or bad, within
its jurisdiction, and the " control of republics
depends on the number, not the quality, of the
voters. This is not a government of saints.
It has a large sprinkling of sinners." He then
proceeded to a serious eulogy of the President,
who, he said, had " stood too firmly for the
Union in the midst of dangers and sacrifices to
allow me to doubt the purity of his wishes."
But he must denounce his opinions when they
were wrong. " I should have forgotten the oblo-
quy which I have calmly borne for thirty years
in the war for liberty, if I should turn craven
now." He was evidently prepared to overlook
the gross and unbecoming personal attack which
the President had made upon him ; but one of
the Democratic members interrupted him, to ask
if the Thaddeus Stevens whom the President denounced in a speech was the same person who
was now eulogizing him. This produced the
effect upon Stevens that was evidently intended.
Did the gentleman suppose, Stevens replied,
that the President ever made that speech ? He
then convulsed the House with a mock defense

of the President, and insisted that he could not possibly have made the speech attributed to him. He was glad of an opportunity to exonerate the President. The story was a Democratic slander. Of course the charge was not serious. " My friend before me, if he were trying in court a case *de lunatico inquirendo*, and if the outside evidence were doubtful, leaving it questionable whether the jury would adopt the view that insanity existed, would cautiously lead the alleged lunatic to speak upon the subject of the hallucination, and, if he could be induced to gabble nonsense, the intrinsic evidence of the case would make out the allegation of insanity. So, Mr. Speaker, if these slanderers can make the people believe that the President ever uttered that speech, then they have made out their case. [Laughter.] But we all know he never did utter it. [Laughter.] " Then, he said, the Democrats had also cunningly invented circumstances to give the story an air of truth. They said that while the President was speaking he was supported by a late "rebel mayor of this city, who was gratuitously furnished lodgings in one of our penal forts for some time. [Great laughter.] The people may have been deceived, but we who knew the President knew it was a lie from the start. [Renewed laughter.] Now, sir, having shown my friends that all it is built upon is fallacious, I hope they will permit me to occupy the same friendly position with the President I did before. [Laughter.] " [1]

After this diversion Stevens proceeded with his argument. The President had in fact adopted the " conquered province " theory. He had appointed military governors, had fixed the qualifications of voters, and prescribed the kind of constitutions the States should adopt. What part of the Constitution gave him such powers over a State in the Union? He then called ridicule into his service, of which no countryman of his has ever been a more adept master, in describing the proceedings in the different Southern States under the President's proclamations. What could be better, for instance, than his reference to the case of Virginia, which " had assembled the free representatives of fragments of about eleven townships, out of one hundred and forty-two counties; elected in spots between the contending armies, on disputed ground, . . . twelve men, . . . who met within the Federal lines, called itself a convention, formed a constitution, ordered elections for the whole State, and Governor Pierpont received about 3300 votes for governor, . . . and was proclaimed in the market-house of Alexandria governor of imperial Virginia, the mother of statesmen. In ' reconstruc-

[1] *Congressional Globe*, March 10, 1866.

tion' the President acknowledged him as the
governor, and those twelve as the representatives of a million and a quarter of people, and
counts this Virginia as one of the twenty-seven
States that adopted the constitutional amendment. I am fond of genteel comedy, but this
low farce is too vulgar to be acted on the stage
of nations. Are these free republics, such as
the United States are bound to guarantee to all
the States in the Union? Should these swindles,
these impostures, bred in the midst of martial
law, without authority from Congress, be acknowledged here?" He then exposed the inconsistencies in which the President was involved by
his theories, and urged again the adoption of the
principles of his proposed constitutional amendments as a part of any plan of reconstruction.

The relations between the President and his
party in the two Houses of Congress had by this
time drifted into hopeless antagonism. The first
open rupture came on the veto of the Freedmen's Bureau bill. This veto, which was sent
to Congress on February 19, 1866, had narrowly escaped the two-thirds vote. A few very
conservative Republican senators were not prepared to break finally with the President, and
voted to sustain him. A second bill of the same
general character, but free from some of the objections urged against the first bill, was promptly

passed. This bill was also vetoed. The House at once passed it over the veto by a vote of more than three to one, and the Senate, very likely influenced by the decisive action of the House, recorded more than the necessary two-thirds vote against the veto.

About the same time the civil rights bill was passed by the two Houses, and received the Executive veto, which was promptly overridden by more than the required vote in both Houses, and amidst unmistakable expressions of public approval. From that time forth a veto of the President was little more than an idle formality, to be promptly brushed aside by the great Republican vote of the two Houses, and the will of Congress became absolute.

On April 30, 1866, Stevens reported to the House the important fourteenth amendment for submission to the States, and with a few changes in form it ultimately became a part of the national Constitution. The amendment broadly declared that "all persons born or naturalized in the United States and subject to the jurisdiction thereof are citizens of the United States and of the State wherein they reside," and prohibited any State from abridging the privileges of citizens or denying to any person "the equal protection of the laws." Representatives were apportioned according to population; but if in any State the right to vote were denied to any male citizens twenty-one years of age, except for crime, the representation should be proportionately reduced. It imposed a disability, which, however, might be removed by a two-thirds vote of Congress, upon those who, having before the war held office and taken an official oath to support the Constitution, had afterwards taken part in the rebellion. The validity of the national debt was established, and the payment of claims for the emancipation of slaves and of all debts incurred in the prosecution of the rebellion was prohibited.

A bill was reported by Stevens, at the same time, declaring that when the fourteenth amendment should have become a part of the Constitution, and "any State lately in insurrection should have ratified it" and adopted a constitution and laws in conformity with its terms, such State should be admitted to representation in Congress. The measure was not acted upon and went over to the next session. It was then abandoned for more stringent measures, chiefly because the provisional governments of the Southern States contemptuously refused to accept the fourteenth amendment, which of course put an end to the comparatively mild condition set forth in the plan to base reconstruction upon the acceptance of that amendment. They them-

selves were far from being free from responsibility for the harsher system that was finally
imposed.

The Committee on Reconstruction dealt with
the situation in an extended report, which was
presented to the Senate by Fessenden and to
the House by Stevens, and in almost every line
of which the influence of the ideas of the latter
can be traced. The report declared that the
action of the insurrectionary States had destroyed their constitutions " in respect to the
vital principle which connected their respective
States with the Union and secured their federal
relations." It conceded that the President in
his military capacity might " permit the people
to form local governments," but declared that
Congress alone possessed the power to establish
the conditions under which the States might
receive again their rights as States. Their people had fought until they were " reduced to the
condition of enemies conquered in war, entitled
only by public law to such rights, privileges,
and conditions as might be vouchsafed by the
conqueror." Under these circumstances they
could not " complain of temporary exclusion from
Congress." The argument in favor of the " conquered province " theory was then stated with
extraordinary force.

" It is moreover contended, and with apparent

gravity, that, from the peculiar nature and character of our government, no such right on the part of the conqueror can exist; that from the moment when rebellion lays down its arms and actual hostilities cease, all political rights of rebellious communities are at once restored; that, because the people of a State of the Union were once an organized community within the Union, they necessarily so remain, and their right to be represented in Congress at any and all times, and to participate in the government of the country under all circumstances, admits of neither question nor dispute. If this is indeed true, then is the government of the United States powerless for its own protection, and flagrant rebellion, carried to the extreme of civil war, is a pastime which any State may play at, not only certain that it can lose nothing in any event, but may even be the gainer by defeat. If rebellion succeeds, it accomplishes its purpose and destroys the government. If it fails, the war has been barren of results, and the battle may be still fought out in the legislative halls of the country. Treason, defeated in the field, has only to take possession of Congress and the cabinet. . . . The question before Congress is, then, whether conquered enemies have the right, and shall be permitted, at their own pleasure and on their own terms, to participate

in making laws for their conquerors; whether
conquered rebels may change their theatre of
operations from the battlefield, where they were
defeated and overthrown, to the halls of Congress, and, through their representatives, seize
upon the government which they fought to destroy; whether the national treasury, the army
of the nation, its navy, its forts and arsenals,
its whole civil administration, its credit, its
pensioners, the widows and orphans of those
who perished in the war, the public honor, peace
and safety, shall all be turned over to the keeping of its recent enemies without delay, and
without imposing such conditions as, in the
opinion of Congress, the security of the country
and its institutions may demand."

The report insisted upon the imposition of the
conditions prescribed in the bill, to which I have
just referred, the passage of which the committee recommended. The bill, however, did not go
so far as Stevens desired. On the last day of the
session he offered amendments to it, giving the
blacks an equal right of suffrage with the white
race, and supported these amendments in a speech
of great seriousness. He was at the time worn
out with the work of the session, his health was
slender, he bore the burden of more than the
allotted number of years, and very probably the

[1] Report of June 18, 1866.

fear that he might not be permitted to return
to his seat in the House imparted an unusual
solemnity to his manner and inspired him "to
make one more — perhaps an expiring — effort
to do something which shall be useful to my
fellow men; something to elevate and enlighten
the poor, the oppressed, and the ignorant in this
great crisis of human affairs." The black man,
he declared, must have the ballot or he would
continue to be a slave. There was some allevi-
ation to the lot of a bondman, but "a freeman
deprived of every human right is the most de-
graded of human beings." Without the protection of the ballot-box the freedmen were "the
mere serfs," and would become "the victims, of
their former masters." He declared that what
he had done he had done for humanity. "I
know it is easy," he said, "to protect the interests of the rich and powerful; but it is a great
labor to guard the rights of the poor and down-
trodden, — it is the eternal labor of Sisyphus
forever to be renewed. . . . In this, perhaps my
final action on this great question, I can see
nothing in my political course, especially in regard to human freedom, which I could wish to
have expunged or changed. I believe that we
must all account hereafter for deeds done in
the body, and that political deeds will be among
those accounts. I desire to take to the bar of

that final settlement the record which I shall this day make on the great question of human rights. While I am sure it will not make atonement for half my errors, I hope it will be some palliation. Are there any who will venture to take the list with their negative seal upon it, and will dare to unroll it before that stern Judge who is the Father of the immortal beings whom they have been trampling under foot, and whose souls they have been crushing out?"

His speech made a profound impression. It had the tone of a farewell message; but his time was not yet to come until he should see his own sympathy and his inextinguishable love of liberty engraven still more deeply upon the statute books of his country.

The session ended before the Congressional plan of reconstruction had been fully developed, but its general lines were clearly indicated and the difference with Johnson had passed beyond the point of compromise. The hostility of the President to the fourteenth amendment produced a cabinet crisis, and three members resigned; but Mr. Stanton, still to all appearances loyal, retained his position, wherein he was soon to become a thorn in the side of the President and ultimately the occasion of his impeachment.

The issue between the President and Congress was clearly defined, and was ripe for presenta-

tion to the people in the Congressional elections
which followed the adjournment of the first session of the Thirty-ninth Congress. A campaign of great excitement followed. The course
was taken, somewhat unusual in elections when
the presidency is not at stake, of holding national conventions.

Ill luck attended the Johnson demonstrations.
The elements which supported him were so antagonistic that they either neutralized each other
and produced a result which was a nullity, or
afforded ready material for effective popular
ridicule. On the other hand, the Republican
conventions were imposing affairs. Mr. Speed,
who had retired from the office of attorney-
general because of his disagreement with the
President, presided over one of them with dramatic effect. But the great meeting of citizen
soldiers and sailors who came together to denounce the President's policy, composed as it
was of the most conspicuous volunteers in the
war for the Union, set the popular current irresistibly in favor of the radical policy of Congress.

As the campaign progressed the agitation in
favor of granting suffrage to the negro as a
necessary muniment of his freedom became
more marked. The bold and extreme ideas,
which Stevens had advocated, were far more

likely to prevail in times of popular passion and
when the patriotism of the people was stirred to
the depths, than was any policy which bore upon
itself the appearance of a surrender. The people had faith in the efficacy of laws for any
condition, and it was not enough that the em-
bers of rebellion should be permitted slowly to
die and a new system gradually take shape and
grow out of the chaos which covered the South;
rather some great enactment was demanded
which should be in keeping with the greatness of
the war. It was a ripe time for decorating the
Constitution with magnificent reforms. That
they would prove effective was taken for granted
from the fact that they were to have a place
in so imposing an instrument. That they could
even prove injurious, if they were in advance of
the times or in any respect at variance with the
laws of nature, was not thought of. The edict
of so mighty a people could, in the popular
mind, accomplish anything; could even at one
fiat raise up four millions of the African race
from the depths of slavery to the dignity of
equal membership in a self-governing and highly
civilized nation.

There appeared to be no middle course which
was practically attainable. Lincoln was not
living, to urge his conservative plan of gradual
enfranchisement, beginning with those who were

most intelligent or had served in the Union
armies, and cautiously extending the right to
all who were, or should become, fitted to discharge the duties of citizenship. Moreover, the
President's plan had worked abominably with
the hostile negro laws which were so promptly
enacted under it and the bloody riots in which
many freedmen were killed.

Stevens, more than any other man, supplied
his party with an issue, but his personal part
in the conduct of the campaign was small.   His
health at the adjournment of Congress in July
was very slender, and his physician had enjoined
upon him an abstinence from work. He was
certain of reëlection, and he employed himself
in recuperating from the exhausting labors of
the previous session and preparing himself to
endure the heavy burdens that he was still to
carry.   But the grotesque performances of the
President in his pilgrimage to the tomb of
Douglas, which he converted into the most vulgar sort of a campaign tour, tempted Stevens
to depart from the strict rule which he had
prescribed for himself. This expedition of
Johnson's, which suggested the name that is
likely always to adhere to it, — " swinging round
the circle," — remains and is probably destined
to remain without a parallel in our history. He
had with him a distinguished retinue composed

of members of his cabinet, including Mr. Seward, General Grant and Admiral Farragut. The presence of these distinguished men would ordinarily have secured him large audiences and a respectful hearing. But he was not long in dispensing with this advantage together with the dignity of his office.

He violently attacked Congress, and chose to assume that the only obstacles which stood between himself and a dictatorship lay in his own self-control and his attachment to the Constitution. There was no necessity for his declaring, as he did in his speech at Cleveland, " I care not for dignity "; for in the same speech he said that, " though the powers of hell and Thad Stevens and his gang were by, they could not turn me from my purpose." In the same speech also he asked : " Why not hang Thad Stevens and Wendell Phillips ? I tell you, my countrymen, I have been fighting the South, and they have been whipped and crushed, and they acknowledge their defeat, and accept the terms of the Constitution ; and now, as I go around this circle, having fought traitors at the South, I am prepared to fight traitors at the North." [1] The inquiry why Stevens should not hang was evidently a favorite one with the President, and he again propounded it at St. Louis.

[1] McPherson, *Reconstruction*, p. 137.

Stevens apparently did not permit his serenity to be disturbed, and did not stand in great fear of being executed, if one may judge from a little off-hand speech which he made to his constituents a short time before the election. " I come not to make a speech," he said, " but for the want of one. When I left Washington I was somewhat worn by labors and disease, and I was directed by my physician neither to think, to speak, nor to read until the next session of Congress, or I should not regain my strength. I have followed the first injunction most religiously, for I believe I have not let an idea pass through my mind to trouble me since Congress adjourned. The second one — not to speak — I was seduced from keeping ; and I made a speech at Bedford, — the only one I have made. The one — not to read — I have followed almost literally. It is true, I have amused myself with a little light, frivolous reading. For instance, there was a serial account from day to day of a very remarkable circus that traveled through the country, from Washington to Chicago and St. Louis, and from Louisville back to Washington. I read that with some interest, expecting to see in so celebrated an establishment, — one which from its heralding was to beat Dan Rice and all the old circuses that ever went forth, — I expected great wit from the

celebrated character of its clowns.   [Laughter.]
They were well provided with clowns ; instead
of one, there were two.   One of these clowns
was high in office and somewhat advanced in
years ; the other was a little less advanced in
office, but older in years.   They started out with
a very respectable stock company.   In order to
attract attention they took with them, for instance, a celebrated general; they took with them
an eminent naval officer, and they chained him
to the rigging so that he could not get away,
though he tried to do so once or twice.   But
the circus went on all the time, — sometimes one
clown performing and sometimes the other.   For
instance, the younger clown told them, in the
language of the ancient heroes, who trod the
stage, that he had it in his power, if 'he chose,
to be a dictator.'   The elder clown pointed to
the other one, and said to the people, 'Will
you take him for President or will you take him
for King?'   [Laughter.]   He left you but one
alternative.   You are obliged to take him for
one or the other, either for President or King,
if 'My policy' prevails.

"I am not following them all round.   I shall
not describe to you how sometimes they cut outside the circle, and entered into street broils
with common blackguards ; how they fought at
Cleveland and Indianapolis.   But, coming round,

they told you, or one of them did, that he had been everything but one. He had been a tailor, — I think he did not say drunken tailor, — no, he had been a tailor. [Laughter.] He had been a constable. [Laughter.] He had been city alderman. [Laughter.] He had been in the legislature. God help that legislature! [Great merriment.] He had been in Congress; and now he was President. He had been everything but one, — he had never been a hangman, and he asked leave to hang Thad Stevens. [Laughter.] " [1]

The elections had not proceeded far before it became evident that the cause of the President was lost. The Republican majority in some of the States was unprecedented, and the result was a sweeping victory, the Republicans electing 143 members against 49 Democrats. With more than two thirds of the membership of both Houses, the congressional leaders had nothing to fear from the presidential veto, which they could override at pleasure. What the President had been from the beginning of his term he was destined to continue until its close, — a mere nullity as a factor in partisan legislation. Reconstruction was now sure to come, and upon more radical lines than had ever been proposed. The triumph of the theory of Stevens was complete.

[1] *Thaddeus Stevens, Commoner*, by E. B. Callender, pp. 158–161.

CHAPTER XVI

RECONSTRUCTION LEGISLATION AND ITS RESULTS

THE message which the President sent to Congress at the December session of 1866 was a strong and dignified paper, but it afforded no evidence of the truth of that statement which he had so often made about himself, that he bowed to the will of the people. It contained a powerful vindication of his own course, and urged upon Congress the wisdom of admitting the senators and representatives from the rebellious States. The two Houses at once proceeded to exhibit equal devotion to their own policy. On the second day of the session Stevens offered a resolution for the establishment of the Committee on Reconstruction, which, being a joint committee, had expired with the previous session. Both bodies concurred in the resolution, and the committee set itself to work to develop a bill which Stevens finally reported to the House, February 6, 1867. At that time every one of the legislatures of the insurrectionary States had voted upon the fourteenth amendment; and with the exception of Tennessee, which had promptly accepted it and been admitted to representation in Congress, they all had rejected the amendment, and, in some instances, by a unanimous vote. It was useless, therefore, to entertain the plan proposed by the committee during the preceding session, and events irresistibly pressed Congress more closely to the radicalism of Stevens. He was so constituted that it was impossible for him to change his opinions upon the question. They were firmly imbedded in his sense of justice, and, what had scarcely less force with a great lawyer, he believed them firmly imbedded in the law. He adhered to his position upon reconstruction as persistently as Johnson adhered to his. He would not have yielded had he been in a minority; he certainly could not be expected to yield after the emphatic expression of the people of the loyal States at the November election.

He pressed on the work in his committee, where he was providing for provisional military governments for the South; and he also seized every opportunity to impress upon the House the wisdom of requiring that the constitution of the Southern States should establish negro suffrage as a condition of readmission. He presented again, in a new form, the arguments which he had so frequently employed, and he called upon Congress to show at last that it had the boldness to act. " In the acquisition of true fame," he said, " courage is just as necessary in the civilian as in the military hero. We may not aspire to fame, but great results fix the eye of history on small objects and magnify their meanness. Let us at least escape that condition."

That he would not deviate from what he believed to be sound legal principles even in the hour of victory was shown by his opposition, at the opening of the December session, to a bill, reported by the law committee of the House, repealing an ancient statute of limitations, and providing that all persons guilty of treason might be tried at any time for the crime. He declared that the bill appeared like an attempt to permit judicial murder; and while he was convinced that "none of these traitors" could ever be convicted of treason under the laws then existing, he " would rather let every man of them run unpunished forever than to make a law now by which they could be punished." He was willing enough to punish traitors, but he thought that by the proposed measure " our government would be endangered in its future existence, in its sense of justice, in its character before the world." He believed, too, in a statute

of limitations for treason, for, although it was a
high crime, there were " generally so many engaged in the crime of treason and rebellion that
there must be some quieting law." He desired
that bloodshed should cease with the war, but
he was strenuous in urging the confiscation of
property as a punishment for the leaders of the
rebellion.

The reconstruction bill, which his committee
finally brought into the House, recited that
" the pretended state governments of the late
so-called Confederate States afford no adequate
protection for life or property, but countenance
and encourage lawlessness and crime ; " and
that it was necessary to enforce order until loyal
state governments could be established. To
that end it provided that the " so-called States "
should be divided into five military districts.
The President was ignored, but the general of
the army was to assign to the command of each
district an officer of the regular army not below
the rank of brigadier-general, who was armed
with full authority to protect life and property,
suppress insurrection and preserve order, and
might permit the civil tribunals to try offenders ;
or he could in his discretion employ military
commissioners ; but the sentence of a military
tribunal affecting life or liberty should not be
executed until approved by the officer in com-

mand of the district.   The bill was a brief and drastic measure of military government.   As Garfield aptly said, in a speech in support of the measure, "it was written with a steel pen made out of a bayonet."

There was, undoubtedly, at the time almost a paralysis of civil government at the South. The organizations established under the President's plan were denied recognition by Congress, had been discredited by the elections, and had no practical efficiency as governments.   Some vigorous sort of authority was demanded to secure the ends of government over that area which had been the seat of war, and was then the theatre of a social revolution so profound as that involved in the emancipation of slaves. Political assassinations were not infrequent ; and riots and insurrections made the reign of disorder in some sections almost supreme.

I have already referred to the bill, reported at the preceding session by Stevens, for the permanent reorganization of the state governments, which had not been finally acted upon by the House, although he had urged action.   As the thirty-ninth Congress was about to come to an end he desired that the bill establishing military governments should become a law on account of temporary necessity.   Something, he thought, should be done to preserve order while Con-

gress was settling upon a scheme of final restoration. The measure gave rise to a long and
exciting debate. Some of the Republicans,
prominent among whom were Mr. Bingham and
Mr. Blaine, insisted that the two measures
should go hand in hand, and that Congress
should not set up military governments in the
Southern States, without at the same time prescribing the terms by which these States could
be freed from them, and to which their permanent civil governments should conform. Mr.
Blaine offered an amendment substantially prescribing the most important conditions for readmission, which had been already set forth in the
bill reported by Stevens at the preceding session and in certain extreme amendments which
he had proposed. But Stevens for some reason
did not wish to see the two measures combined,
although they were both substantially his own.
He strenuously resisted the adoption of Mr.
Blaine's amendment, which he stigmatized as a
" step towards universal amnesty and universal
Andy-Johnsonism." He asked the House to
adopt the military government bill in the form
in which he had presented it. He declared that
it was not intended as a reconstruction measure,
but " simply as a police bill to protect the loyal
men from anarchy and murder, until this Congress, taking a little more time, can suit gentle-

men in a bill for the admission of all those rebel States upon the basis of civil government." Curiously enough his resistance was made effective only by the aid of Democratic votes, and after an acrimonious discussion, to which he contributed some characteristic ridicule, he secured the passage of the bill in the precise form in which he desired it to pass.

The contest was renewed in the Senate by the advocates of the Blaine amendment, and that body incorporated its essential features in the measure. The House, however, refused to yield except upon the insertion of conditions which, after a conference, the Senate agreed to accept; and the bill then went to the President. It was now the 20th of February, 1867. As the Congress expired on the 4th of March, and the President was given ten days in which to consider the bill, its fate was even yet in doubt. If he should take the full time allotted him by the Constitution before sending in his inevitable veto, only two days would remain in which to pass it again through both Houses; and this time might be consumed by dilatory tactics, and thus the bill might fail through lack of final action before the termination of Congress.

Johnson comprehended the situation, and held back his veto until the last moment, transmitting it to the House on the afternoon of

March 2, which was Saturday. The Congress expired on the following Monday at noon. Stevens saw that no time was to be lost, and at once demanded consideration, but yielded for brief statements from Democratic members, who protested that the bill meant the dissolution of the Union and "the death knell of republican liberty." One of them declared that the bill should not pass unless he was "overpowered from physical exhaustion, or restrained by the rules of the House." Stevens, in closing the debate, said that he had listened to the gentlemen, because he appreciated "the melancholy feelings with which they are approaching this funeral of the nation," but as he desired the passage of the bill he asked Mr. Blaine to move a suspension of the rules. Mr. Blaine accordingly made the motion, and after an ineffectual attempt at filibustering, the bill was at once passed by a vote of 135 yeas to 48 nays. The Senate speedily took similar action, and thus the reconstruction bill became a law.

The measure was shortly after amended in technical details. It was also changed from time to time to meet the difficulties growing out of the unfriendly attitude of the President, who had charge of its execution; but it embodied the essential principles upon which civil government at the South was reëstablished, and the rebellious States restored to the Union. As it finally passed it contained the provisions of the original bill for the military governments, except that the commanders of the different departments were to be appointed by the President instead of by the general of the army, and that no sentence of death should be executed without the approval of the President. It also enacted that when the people of any of the insurrectionary States should have adopted a constitution conforming in every respect with the national Constitution; and passed by a convention of delegates chosen by male citizens, not disqualified by crime, twenty-one years old and upwards, " of whatever race, color, or previous condition," who had been residents of the State one year; " and when such constitution shall provide that the elective franchise shall be enjoyed by all such persons as have the qualifications herein stated for electors of delegates ; and when such constitution shall be ratified by a majority of the persons voting on the question of ratification who are qualified as electors for delegates ; " and when the constitution should have been approved by Congress; and the fourteenth amendment adopted by the State, and have become a part of the national Constitution, " said State shall be declared entitled to representation in Congress."

It will thus be seen that the plan of reconstruction which was finally put in operation conformed in a singular manner, in its essential principles, with the ideas that Stevens had long advocated. It was promulgated by Congress, and not by the Executive, as he had never ceased to contend should be the case since Lincoln had put forth his "Louisiana plan." It applied a radical dogma, which he had long proclaimed with the voice of one crying in the wilderness, and practically treated the Southern States as conquered provinces and as entitled to no rights under the Constitution. It prescribed universal suffrage for the black as well as for the white man, not merely in the formation of the new state constitutions but as an enduring part of those instruments.

The permanent efficiency of Stevens's plan was much impaired by a departure from the form which he advocated in that clause of the fourteenth amendment fixing the basis of representation in Congress. By one of the so-called compromises in the Constitution, one kind of property was exalted above all other kinds, and representation in Congress was based upon slaves equal to three fifths of their number. Stevens always contended that this was wrong; but it was in the Constitution, and he showed that sort of willingness to abide by it which springs out of compulsion. But after emancipation had raised the negro above the dignity of property, and had transformed him from a chattel into a man, Stevens very justly contended that this dumb representation should end; and he did not propose, by apportioning representatives directly according to population, to give to the war the effect of augmenting the political power of the conquered, as would be the case if the white man alone were to exercise the suffrage, and all, instead of three fifths, of the negroes were to be counted in establishing the basis of representation.

He therefore proposed, as I have stated, during the early period of the controversy with Johnson, to divide the representatives among the States according to the number of legal voters, to be ascertained by the national census. Under this provision, which was to have universal application throughout the Union, any State which saw fit to exclude black men or any other men from the suffrage would do so at the expense of its representation in the national House. If the excluded classes could not have representatives of their own choosing, they were to have none chosen by somebody else. His proposition, in the form in which he made it, was not adopted, but was set aside in order to adopt in its place the language now standing in the Constitution, and which, while it was doubtless intended to have the same effect so far as the black man was concerned, still awaits that positive legislative action necessary to give it vitality.

I have thus endeavored to outline the principal steps in the adoption of the plan of reconstruction, avoiding, as far as possible, the technical history of various propositions and amendments, of slight value except to the special student, which would demand a long narration and be of no corresponding advantage in securing a general understanding of the final result. The legislation itself is of transcendent importance; and it constitutes the great contribution which Stevens made to the history of his country, although for some of the details he is not to be held responsible.

Whether the conditions that were imposed upon the Southern States were wisely imposed or not, there can be little doubt that Stevens was right in discarding the pedantic and technical phases of the question and treating reconstruction as a practical problem. It was purely a question of what was best for the future, and not of constitutional rights of the seceded States. At this distance of time it seems inconceivable that men should have seriously advanced the proposition, as a basis for practical action, that the States were never out of the Union, and that when peace returned they were of right entitled to representation in Congress. The laws had been violently set aside, and the sword appealed to, in what proved to be the greatest civil war in all history. The work of conquering the people of the rebellious States, defended as they were by climate, by vast areas of territory, and by their own splendid valor, presented to the North one of the most difficult tasks that ever confronted a nation. They continued to struggle to the very end, and only laid down their arms because they could fight no longer. After the victory had been won through the destruction of seven hundred thousand men and seven billions of dollars' worth of property, it was seriously proposed that no safeguards should be exacted for the future, if the framers of the Constitution three-fourths of a century before had not provided for such a contingency.

Stevens clearly saw that it would be criminal folly to throw away any advantage of so costly a war in order to preserve a constitutional fiction, and that those who were charged with the responsibilities of the victory would be false alike to the victor and to the vanquished, if, on account of any scruples about the Constitution, they should neglect a single precaution against the recurrence of strife, or should fail to provide the most careful safeguards for the future safety of all. Within the theatre of the war the Constitution had been set aside, and there had been a cessation of all the processes of the law. Stevens believed in the Constitution, but he did not believe in parchment worship or that the earth should be held in bondage to a dead generation. A new crisis had been reached in our affairs, and the supreme considerations in dealing with it were those of common sense and expediency.

But while the point of view from which he regarded the problem was the correct one, the question of the wisdom of the remedy which was prescribed is a very distinct question. That must be determined to some extent, at least, by its actual operation and effect. In the course of time, necessary state governments were established upon the basis of the congressional act, the substantial conditions governing readmission were complied with, and the senators and representatives of the Southern States were admitted to both Houses of Congress. During the formative period of the new state governments and under the era of military rule a fair degree of order was maintained. That kind of government was obviously not destined to be popular among a people accustomed to free institutions, but it was probably as effective and as little harsh as any military government could have been in the face of the difficulties with which it contended, and it was better than anarchy.

The important point is the effect of the negro suffrage so suddenly and so universally imposed. The presence of federal soldiers was favorable to the working of this experiment, since they protected the black man and made his right to vote a practical as well as a theoretical right. What happened was precisely what might have been expected to happen when the roots of society were upturned, and when its lowest strata were at once forcibly imposed upon the top. What followed lacked even the one element of justice, which it would have possessed if the poor colored man had shared in the spoliation which resulted, and had gained some portion of the fruits of his extorted and uncompensated labor. But instead of being a beneficiary he was made the innocent instrument of plunder by as unprincipled a set of political scoundrels and public robbers as ever looted a defenseless treasury. Undoubtedly there were some honest and patriotic men who removed to the South immediately after the war and participated in politics, but they were in a minority, unable materially to restrain and powerless to control.

The administration of most of the Southern state governments had long been characterized by economy and frugality even in the time of

their prosperity. Public officers performed
their duties for small salaries, in public buildings of primitive construction, and amid surroundings where any elements of luxury would
be sought for in vain. But the simplicity and
economy, which had been so long practiced from
inclination, were imperatively demanded in the
conditions following the war, when poverty was
well-nigh universal, and the once wealthy possessor of hundreds of slaves had become as poor
as the meanest black man he had once owned.

The barest survey of the facts will suffice to
show the first effect of the new order. In the
State of Florida in 1860 the combined salaries
of the principal executive officers were $26,200
upon a taxable valuation amounting to about
$67,000,000. In 1869 some of these officers had
been given the sounding title of "cabinet officers," and they were paid in a way to maintain
"the dignity of the office." The tax valuation
of the State had decreased more than one half,
but the salaries were nearly trebled. The legislative expenses in 1860 were $17,592; in 1869,
$67,620. The total annual state expenditures
in the same period bounded from $118,000 to
$375,000. In the four years from 1868 to 1872
the bonded indebtedness of the State increased
enormously.[1]

[1] The figures relating to the expenditures and debts of the

In Georgia the appropriations for the pay and mileage of members and officers of one of the earliest legislatures of the reconstructed government amounted to $979,000, or more than four times as much as it had been the rule to appropriate for the same purpose by former legislatures. The State owned a railroad from which it received a net revenue in 1867 of $300,000. In 1870 all the gross receipts were consumed in the " operation " of the road, and a deficit still remained of more than $500,000, which had to be met out of the treasury.[1] From 1868 to 1874 the indebtedness of the State increased more than $6,000,000.

The chief result of the work of the first legislature of North Carolina under reconstruction was the issue of $14,000,000 of the bonds of the State in aid of railroads, none of which was ever constructed, and $11,000,000 more were authorized, but were not issued because the régime was set aside.

The debt of Alabama, including bonds which were issued or indorsed on account of railroads, was increased from $8,356,000 in 1868 to $25,503,000 in 1874.

Southern States, I have taken mainly from *The Last Quarter Century in the United States*, by E. Benjamin Andrews, and *Why the Solid South*, by Hilary A. Herbert.

[1] *Reconstruction in Georgia*, by Hon. H. G. Turner; *Why the Solid South*, pp. 134–137.

In South Carolina the legislators soon tired
of the simplicity with which their predecessors
had been content. They reveled in plate-glass
mirrors and Gothic chairs, and then stole them.
The furniture of the hall of the House, which
has since been furnished for $3000, cost over
$50,000 in a single session. In four years the
sum of $200,000 was expended for furniture, and
at the end of that time a diligent search failed
to disclose more than $18,000 worth, even esti-
mating it at the original cost. In a single session of the legislature the sum of $350,000 was
appropriated for " supplies, sundries, and inci-
dentals," of which $125,000 went for maintain-
ing a restaurant in the Capitol, where liquors
and other refreshments were furnished to members and their friends at the public expense.
In the year preceding the war the taxes did not
exceed $400,000. In 1871 they reached the
sum of $2,000,000, although the tax valuation
was but little more than one third as great as in
the first named year. Millions of the bonds of
the State were disposed of at a small fraction
of their full value. In four years the public
debt was increased by over $13,000,000, and it
represented little but extravagance and theft.
Real estate, by reason of its immovable character, could not, like personal property, be the
subject of larceny, but the confiscation through

taxation, to which it was subject, made its exemption from being stolen of little practical consequence. In 1874 2900 pieces of real estate in Charleston County were forfeited for taxes, and nearly half a million acres of land were sold for unpaid taxes or forfeited to the State.

Not only were state debts piled up, but municipal and county debts greatly increased also. Valuable franchises were lavishly granted. The doors of penal institutions were opened. In two years a single governor granted 457 pardons, and at the end of his term the number of convicts remaining in the penitentiary had dwindled to one third that number. Everywhere it was the same story — incompetency, bribery, robbery; and the governmental machine was chiefly employed as an agency of plunder. South Carolina enjoyed the evil distinction of leading in this hideous carnival, as she had led in the secession movement; but in all the States where the newly enfranchised freedmen formed a large proportion of the population, corruption and profligacy were the rule, and in some of them society was rapidly approaching the point of dissolution. Mr. Lecky did not color the picture too darkly when he characterized this régime as " a grotesque parody of government, a hideous orgy of anarchy, violence, unrestrained corruption, undisguised, ostentatious, insulting robbery, such as the world had scarcely ever seen." [1]

Nor did the loss of property measure the damage which resulted. The misgovernment soon reached the point where it invited revolution. Conspicuous as is the Anglo-Saxon for his devotion to law, he strives for it not as an end, but as an instrumentality in securing his well-being and bringing about progress and civilization. When Southern white men saw the forms of law undeniably employed for the destruction of social order and the disorganization of society; when that which they regarded as a chief agency of civilization was used to tear it down, they employed violent and unlawful methods to overturn the régime, and forcibly took possession of the state governments. Their power, however, which was sufficient for usurpation, was not sufficient to change the laws, some of which were national and beyond their control, and the demoralizing spectacle was witnessed for some years of a system of government finding a continuing basis in illegality and fraud. The same violence, too, which gave them control of the local governments gave them a political power in federal elections, and tainted the Presidency, the Congress, the national laws, and their administration, with the poisonous influences of

[1] *Democracy and Liberty*, 1-98.

the fraud.   It was by no means the least of the evil consequences of this system that law-abiding men in distant States were compelled to submit to violence as a factor in the enactment of the laws by which they were to be governed.

But the immediate effect of a policy does not alone constitute the true measure of its wisdom. The working of the experiment should not be received unreservedly and without caution, tried as it was in States lying prostrate under revolution piled upon revolution.   That some bad results followed the policy of reconstruction does not necessarily convict those who adopted it of unwise action.   As well might one judge of an amputation by pointing only to the fever, the suffering, and the maimed and crippled condition, as if the previous state of the patient had been perfect, and the alternatives were not the loss of a life or the loss of a limb.   The wisdom which passes judgment upon a situation a third of a century afterwards has an obvious advantage over the wisdom which is compelled to deal with it.   We of to-day also lose sight of many of the difficulties with which the problem was surrounded, and which have disappeared in the distance.   The choice, which Stevens and the statesmen associated with him were compelled to make, did not lie between the course actually adopted and an ideal condition of things.   In the light in which they acted, they were compelled to deal with as grave a national situation as ever existed. It was beyond the power of any surgery at once to deliver society, well and whole, from the condition in which its errors and crimes had placed it.

It may be admitted that great evils would inevitably result from conferring the suffrage upon large numbers of men who had just emerged from slavery, and who came of a race which had never been schooled in self-government. The real question is whether greater evils would not have come from adopting any other course. Those four million black men were in our country through no fault of their own. They had been held as unwilling slaves. It was not possible to evade the problem by their wholesale deportation. They were newly endowed with freedom as a result not of the enlightenment of their masters nor of any peaceful course, but of one of the bloodiest and most expensive of wars. What would have been the condition of those helpless beings left without the full rights of citizenship and at the mercy of legislation imposed by those who had ceased to own them only because they had been compelled to do so?

Proof was not wanting that, under such conditions, the freedom of the black man would have been in serious danger. If, before Congress had taken any action, and when the provisional governments were on their good behavior, such anti-negro laws were enacted as those to which I have alluded, what could have been expected if the President's policy had been approved and made permanent, and the States had been readmitted on the basis which he had proposed? Was there not ground for the fear that freedom would soon become but little better than a mere name? Even after Congress had acted by a two-thirds vote, and had been sustained at the polls by an enormous majority of the Northern people, the fourteenth amendment to the Constitution, which did not involve negro suffrage, was contemptuously rejected by the Southern States. The action of the Southern people was probably what that of the Northern people would have been under the same circumstances. It was doubtless entirely natural. But would it not also have been entirely natural that they should be willing to secure by law as much as possible of what they had lost by war, including their right to the labor of the black men whom they had claimed to own? It was necessary also that the remedy should be rigidly prescribed by legislation, for no assistance in the way of a discreet or friendly administration could be expected from the President, who was uncompromisingly opposed to any plan of reorganization except his own.

Whatever path might be followed was sure to be surrounded with some peril. Congress took that course which appeared at the time to be attended with the slightest danger to liberty. The undefended rights of freedmen were indeed weak. Armed with the ballot they would be none too strong. Having exterminated slavery at such a tremendous cost, Congress adopted that policy which, under the conditions then existing, promised the least risk to liberty. But it was most unfortunate that Johnson should have taken the place of Lincoln at a time when there was a more pressing demand for a man of sagacious statesmanship and great popular strength at the White House than at any time since the adoption of the Constitution. Lincoln had the wisdom to advise, and would probably have had the authority to secure, a system of gradual enfranchisement, which would have been safer for the country and infinitely juster to the black man, upon whom would not have been cruelly cast, suddenly and without any previous preparation, the heavy and exacting responsibilities of citizenship.

CHAPTER XVII

WIT AND OTHER CHARACTERISTICS

STEVENS possessed a remarkably strong sense of humor under the influence of a correct taste. He relied little upon mere extravagance, and rarely dealt those " sledge-hammer blows," so characteristic of what Sydney Smith terms " wut," which dispense with the necessity of the more delicate surgical operation generally required, according to the same authority, to get a joke through a Scotchman's head. His wit was light, usually genial, and in quality like the autumn sunshine. It was also unfailing. When it suited his purpose, however, he could make it bitter, cynical and even brutal in tone. He never indulged in elaborately constructed scholastic jokes, which smell painfully of the lamp, and which one requites with laughter largely from a sense of duty, as a tribute to the dignity of labor. Indeed he had no time to study up his witticisms even if he had possessed the inclination, for he was almost constantly upon his feet in the House or engaged with his overworked committees.

Page after page of the record of debates, while
he was a member of the House, is lighted up by
his sparkling answers to objections, and by his
free, offhand, and sometimes trifling playfulness.
He himself was a great part of what he said, and
his wit was so unstudied and so exactly apt to
the occasion that some use of the imagination is
occasionally necessary to reproduce the circumstances in which he spoke in order to understand
the merriment which the record shows. Mr.
Morrill, who was intimately associated with him
for many years in the House, speaks of his
" running undertone commentary," usually lost
by the reporters, upon the business of the House,
and of the fun which he created and which was
" lost in the whirl of business." " Never indeed," he added, " was wit of all varieties, coarse
and fine, exhibited in more bewildering profu-
sion. He daily wasted in this private and semi-
grotesque distribution of mirth, sense, and satire, often indiscriminately among friends and
foes, a capital sufficient, could it have been preserved, to rival almost any of the acknowledged
masters among the colloquial wits of this or
possibly of any age." [1]

He was fond of telling stories to his fellow
members. Many are the anecdotes that are told
of him, some of them very likely of doubtful

[1] Senate Proceedings. *Congressional Globe*, Dec. 18, 1868.

authenticity, but many also characteristic and doubtless genuine. It may not be inappropriate to give a few specimens of his humor, selected somewhat at random from the "Congressional Globe," or as I have received them from his associates in the House.

Stevens and Cameron were far from being warm friends. Even the State of Pennsylvania was not quite large enough for two such positive characters to associate peacefully together in the leadership of the same political party. Stevens was informed that Lincoln was intending to appoint Cameron to an important office, and he called upon the President to enter a remonstrance. What he said about Cameron was far from flattering as well also as far from definite. "You don't mean to say," said Lincoln, "that Cameron would steal?" "No," said Stevens, "I don't think he would steal a red-hot stove." This was too good for Lincoln to keep, and he told it to Cameron. The latter, not unnaturally, failed to show a keen appreciation of the humor of the remark, and soon afterwards a member of the House, who sat near Stevens, observed Cameron come into the hall in high dudgeon and enter into a very animated conversation with Stevens. Cameron said that he had been greatly injured and that Stevens should retract what he had said. Stevens endeavored to pacify him, and finally consented to do what Cameron asked of him. He called upon Mr. Lincoln, and this was the manner in which he made amends. " Mr. Lincoln," said Stevens, " why did you tell Cameron what I said to you ? " " I thought," said Lincoln, " that it was a good joke, and I did n't think it would make him mad." " Well," replied Stevens, " he is very mad and made me promise to retract. I will now do so. I believe I told you that I did n't think he would steal a red-hot stove. I now take that back."

During a debate in the House a member who was speaking kept walking continually up and down the aisle, and back and forth across the area, under the excitement of his effort, as members are sometimes prone to do. After watching this pedestrian performance for some time Stevens checked it by calling out to the member by name, " Do you expect to get mileage for that speech ? "

In April, 1862, a fierce attack, in which Mr. Blair, of Missouri, was prominent, was made in the House upon General Fremont for certain alleged transactions in connection with his command. It was enough for Stevens to know that Fremont was a warm friend of the slave, and he ardently defended him in a speech which affords a very good illustration of his offhand congres-

sional manner. He made a lawyer-like reply to
Blair, and after accusing him of overlooking
some material testimony in his eagerness to
blacken General Fremont, added: " Sir, such
things in a pettifogger would be detestable, but
in a member of this House they are respectable.
[Much laughter.] " Mr. Blair hereupon asked:
" What was the gentleman's remark? I did not
hear it." Stevens: " I said that in a member
of the House they were respectable, and I hope
the gentleman takes no offense at that. [Laugh-
ter.] " [1]

Later in the same speech Stevens discussed
the charge that one Sacchi, a member of Fremont's staff, had made a contract to provide
horses that were never furnished, and he proceeded to show from the testimony that Sacchi
had had nothing to do with the contract. Mr.
Conkling asked permission to interrupt Stevens
with a remark, which was freely granted, and
he then took the floor, not as might have been
supposed to say a word about horses, but to
indulge in a lofty flight in which he said that
Sacchi had been " decorated for heroic action
upon the battlefields of Italy," that he " came
here following the Star of Freedom as the shep-
herds followed the Star of Bethlehem," that he
came, " in the language of another, ' to crusade

[1] *Congressional Globe*, April 21, 1862.

for freedom in freedom's holy land.'" This was
too fine for Stevens, although it was upon his
side of the case, and amid much laughter he
punctured this magnificence and summoned the
House back to the earth again by saying dryly,
" It is enough for me to know that he is not the
man who made the horse contract at all." [1]

Upon one occasion a member who affected
great humility and a low estimate of the value
of his own views, which however he was willing
to inflict upon the House at all times, had urged
Stevens to yield him time to make a speech
upon a certain measure. When Stevens had
finished his own speech he said, apparently hit-
ting off what the member in question might
be expected to say of himself, " I now yield to
Mr. ——, who will make a few feeble remarks."

Mr. Brooks, of New York, the Democratic
leader, had made a most carefully prepared partisan speech which ransacked history, and Stevens was expected to reply. Stevens referred
to the gentleman's " elaborate speech, so full of
literary and historical allusions which in super-
ficial scholars might look like pedantry, but in
the learned gentleman are but the natural and
graceful overflow of a well-stored mind." He
would not say Brooks had lied, but he did say,
" there is nothing to the contrary but the remark

[1] *Congressional Globe*, April 21, 1862.

of the gentleman from New York, which, I beg leave to say, is not now evidence in a court of justice." As to the anti-Lincoln movement which Brooks had discovered in the Republican party, Stevens said that it would not call forth from the President " anything more than a pertinent joke." To the proposition to run McClellan for the presidency, he said that the Democrats could not be " in earnest in attempting to run him, as they know that he cannot raise a trot. He never did, when a forward movement was in question."

He had banter also for his friends. Mr. Washburne of Illinois, a leading Republican member, refused to support a bill in which Stevens was interested, and persistently fought it upon every occasion. Stevens spoke of him as displaying " that kind of pertinacity which I so much admire when directed to a laudable object, but which sometimes degenerates into obstinacy when he is wrong ; of course I do not mean in the gentleman from Illinois, but in others."

Sometimes his personal references were far less oblique, as will be seen from the following, which I give in the words of Mr. Dawes. " Mr. Maynard, of Tennessee, afterwards minister to Turkey and postmaster-general, although a native of Massachusetts and a scholar of culture as well as an exceedingly amiable gentle-

man, yet so resembled an Indian that most
people believed him to be at least half a one.
One intensely hot day in July a melting sun
was pouring in upon our heads through the
glass ceiling, while Mr. Stevens, in nankin trou-
sers and shirt-sleeves, was conducting the Indian
appropriation bill through the House and was
well-nigh worn out with the heat and fatigue.
Mr. Maynard had been all day persistently putting him questions and opposing features of his
bill, when some member, expressing great sympathy for Mr. Stevens, moved an adjournment
that he might have an opportunity to rest.   But
Mr. Stevens, turning just enough towards the
swarthy Tennessee member, remonstrated, saying : 'Mr. Speaker, I can get along well enough
with the Indians, but these half-breeds trouble
me 'most to death.' "[1]

Mr. Henry Winter Davis of Maryland was a
brilliant orator, but did not possess the fibre
necessary to endure the blows which inevitably
come to one who takes a prominent part in politics.   An instance of this was seen in his somewhat petulant request to be relieved from service
as chairman of the House Committee on Foreign
Affairs.   Stevens mildly interposed in the debate and said : " If the chairman of a committee

[1] MSS. Dawes' Dartmouth College Lecture on " Stevens as
a Leader in a Great Crisis."

is to consider himself personally offended when the House votes down propositions which he brings forward, some of us would have been out of employment long ago. Why, sir, when my friend here (Mr. Washburne) introduced his proposition to tax the stock of whiskey on hand, and rode triumphantly through this House upon the bead of the liquor, while I was completely submerged, I did not ask to be excused ; it was a gentle ducking, from which I expected to recover, hoping to come out renovated by the bath."

Quotations of this character from Stevens's speeches in Congress could be multiplied indefinitely. As he grew older his gayety of spirit increased, and no infirmity could restrain its expression. During the last months of his life his health was so slender that he had frequently to be carried about upon a chair. The solemn procession of the House each day from its hall to the Senate chamber, following the managers, among whom Stevens was carried, was one of the striking ceremonies of the impeachment. One day he said to the two stalwart fellows who bore him, " Who will carry me, boys, when you are dead and gone ? "

In appearance he was tall and commanding, and, although somewhat slender, he had an athletic frame. His favorite exercise during most

of his life was horseback-riding, and he spent
much of his leisure in the saddle. He was also
fond of attending horse-races. He was an excellent swimmer, and often swam across " Joe's
Pond," as he called it, which he said was one
and a half miles wide and " cold as a spring."
He declared that he could swim the Bosphorus
as easily as Byron did. He resembled Byron
in another particular, for he had a club foot;
but, unlike Byron, he did not seek to conceal
his deformity. This appears to have only
slightly affected his walking, — "a little lame,"
Mr. Morrill called him, — and he assisted himself with a cane. He had a large mouth, thin
upper lip, prominent aquiline nose, and massive
head. " No stranger," said Mr. Dawes, " would
pass him on the street without turning for a
second look at an unmistakably great character.
On great occasions, when his untamable spirit
had got the mastery of him, he no longer looked
like a man, at least like any other man I ever
saw." [1]

While usually cold and unemotional in his
later years, he was terribly in earnest upon the
great public questions with which he dealt. He
did not pursue reform because it was fashionable, nor because it gave him an opportunity

[1] Dartmouth College Lecture on "Stevens as a Leader in a
Great Crisis."

to abuse somebody, although upon occasion few enjoyed that privilege more keenly.

He was very fond of general literature, with the exception of fiction, and his miscellaneous library may be taken as illustrating his taste. It was rich in history and the classics, but contained few novels. He delighted especially in legal study, and his law library was one of the best in his State. During his last visit to Lancaster he looked about him upon the shelves laden with his law-books, and said sadly, "It's a pity that there is no one to keep this going."

In his prime he was impassioned in manner, and in his carefully prepared speeches he exhibited a directness and energy combined with a terse felicity of expression for which it is difficult to find his match among American orators. Nobody, said Mr. Sumner, could express more in fewer words, or give "to language a sharper bite." He aimed to express his idea in the fewest possible words, and never affected a rotundity of style. After the beginning of the war, the demands upon him were so great that he had little time for constructing elaborate orations, and his speaking was usually called forth by the occasion and was exactly adapted to it. Under these circumstances, his self-command and the form of his speech were remarkable. He was always striking and forcible, and occasionally he rose to the heights of spontaneous eloquence, all the more effective because unstudied.

During the period of his leadership in the House he had many personal encounters in debate, and with strong and much younger men, like Butler, Conkling, Schenck, Garfield, and Blaine; and the latter, who was so well fitted to speak, says that he was "a man who had the courage to meet any opponent, and who was never overmatched in intellectual conflict." Mr. Dawes aptly termed him "a great intellectual gladiator." [1]

He exhibited a remarkable aptitude for business when he attended to it, but he displayed a noble disdain of his private interests when his attention was required by public affairs. This course, and a willingness to assume obligations for others, appear to have reduced him, at least twice in his life, to a condition of insolvency; but he manfully discharged his obligations without taking advantage of any bankrupt law. "I feel that my creditors," he said, "are entitled, among my other worldly goods, to my labor until I am dead. If my debts are not paid then, the bankrupt law of another world will cancel them." [2]

[1] *Twenty Years of Congress*, vol. i. p. 326.
[2] Interview with the Washington correspondent of *New York Tribune*, printed August 14, 1868.

During their invasion of Pennsylvania in 1863 the Confederates burned his iron-works near Chambersburg. This reduced him to poverty a third time. His friends proposed to raise the large sum necessary to make good his loss, but, learning of the movement, he discouraged it and refused in advance to accept the money. Notwithstanding this reverse so late in life, he left a considerable fortune at his death. He lived in an unpretentious manner in a severely plain house in Lancaster. In Washington he lived with equal simplicity at a short distance from the Capitol. He never married.

It is not difficult to detect the secret of Stevens's success as a parliamentary leader. His ability to cope with any antagonist; his wit, which was employed unsparingly upon his timid supporters as well as upon his foes; his invincible courage; the facility with which he would sometimes make use of the enemy when his friends deserted him; and his resolute adherence to the important lines of his great policies, established him in the position of leadership beyond the reach of all competition. Mr. Blaine in his eulogy upon President Garfield accords Stevens a place among the three great parliamentary leaders in our history, naming him with Clay and Douglas. Clay surpassed Stevens in some important qualities, and notably in the power to devise the remedies to enable the country to pass peacefully through a great crisis. This however is rather an attribute of the statesman; but if the foremost place as a parliamentary leader is to be given to either, it must be accorded to that one who, during those years from 1860 to 1868, crowded thick as they were with events unsurpassed in magnitude, unequaled in difficulty, never took a backward step, never even faltered, who embodied upon the floor of the House the genius of war and the genius of victory, and who exercised the power of command with undiminished authority until he died.

CHAPTER XVIII

THE IMPEACHMENT

THE difference between the President and Congress had become so serious, and party spirit ran so high, that the threats to impeach him culminated in the presentation of three resolutions on the same day during the last session of the thirty-ninth Congress. But there was at that time no ground for impeachment which could appear to be sound, save to the most partisan imagination. It is only necessary to read the resolutions to see that the charges were mere sound and fury. There was, however, even at that early day, a large number of members who were in earnest in support of the impeachment proposition. No definite action was taken during that Congress.

The fortieth Congress would not have assembled, in the usual course of affairs, until December, 1867, unless called together by the President in extraordinary session. But since Congress had broken with him, and assumed as far as possible the government of the country, it

did not propose to permit him to exercise such
powers as he possessed under the Constitution
and such others as he might choose to assume,
without some restraint upon him. It showed its
distrust in a striking manner by passing a statute
under which the fortieth Congress assembled on
the fourth day of March, 1867, immediately upon
the expiration of the thirty-ninth. By taking
successive recesses, this session was prolonged
until the time of the December session.

During the short sittings before the first regular session, Stevens continued to devote his attention to the work of reconstruction and kindred measures, and it is needless to say that
he adhered rigidly to the lines which he had
long before laid down. He introduced a bill to
enforce the confiscation act, and to forfeit all
the public lands of the Confederate States to
the United States, as a measure in the nature
of war indemnity, to provide homes for former
slaves, and a fund out of which loyal claimants
might be paid for damages to their property by
the operations of the war. His elaborate speech
of March 19, 1867, in support of this bill, is not
wholly agreeable reading; but it was entirely
consistent with the principles he had advocated
during the rebellion. He sarcastically gave the
credit of the bill to Andrew Johnson, of whom
he claimed to have been a disciple, and in order

to mark the inconsistency of "the man at the other end of the Avenue," as he termed the President, he quoted from one of the numerous speeches which Johnson had made, urging the punishment and impoverishment of traitors and the division and sale of their plantations. The President, he declared, favored confiscation while he was "clothed and in his right mind," but "Seward entered into him, and ever since they have been running down steep places into the sea." He did not believe in bloody penalties, he said, but he strongly believed in the justice of confiscating the estates of the leading rebels as a punishment for their crimes, and to aid in repairing the ravages of the war. He made a strong case out of history and the authorities for the legality of the proceeding, but he signally failed to sustain it as a matter of sound policy.

The speech displayed a good deal of the lawyer, but little of the statesman. The war had been ended for two years, and the people of the South had paid the severest penalties. The enforcement of confiscation would not have paid even in the narrow financial sense. On the other hand, it would have produced a bitterness of feeling likely to survive for generations. Surely, if we were ever again to live as one nation, the time for such measures had long

gone by. It is probable that Stevens had in
view the ultimate payment of the great pecuniary losses inflicted upon Pennsylvania by Lee's
army, and that his demonstration was not without the purpose of securing the passage of a bill
having that object. He concluded this speech
with a eulogy upon Lincoln, whom he had
usually supported, but whom his biting wit had
not always spared. He denied that Lincoln
would have put in force the Johnson policy of
reconstruction ; but, if he was intending to do
so, "that overruling Providence that so well
guided him did not permit such a calamity to
befall him," but "allowed him to acquire a most
enviable reputation, and then, before there was
a single spot upon it, 'he sailed into the fiery
sunset and left sweet music in Cathay.'"

The breach between the President and Congress constantly widened as the session wore on.
Bills were passed strengthening the laws upon
reconstruction, and they were defiantly vetoed.
The efficiency of these measures was also much
impaired by hostile administration. The veto
of one of the supplementary reconstruction acts
was made the occasion for a good deal of violent
denunciation of the President, and for threats
of his impeachment. Stevens was very willing
to impeach him, but believed in the futility of
the proceedings. " I have taken some pains,"

he said during the debate of July 19, 1867, "to look into the position of this House and of the Senate, and am quite sure that there is power enough, first, to prevent the voting of the impeachment here; and, secondly, if impeachment were voted, to prevent conviction elsewhere." He was quite right in his estimate. The impeachment proceedings then pending were decisively beaten in the House at the beginning of the following session, and even when the case was so greatly strengthened by the removal of Stanton it was not sustained by the Senate.

What more effectually produced irritation in the minds of members than differences upon great policies was the course of the President with reference to the patronage. The distribution of offices was a dearly-prized function of the member of Congress, and the majority of the representatives little relished the wholesale removal of their political friends and the filling of vacancies by their foes. They could throw the broad mantle of charity over any little difference with the President upon the measures necessary to restore the Union, but when he assumed to appoint a postmaster who agreed politically with him, instead of with the member in whose district the office was located, outraged prerogative was apt to assert itself. In the case of the

average member, a collector came nearer home
than the Constitution. The tenure-of-office act
was designed to check the President in creating
and filling vacancies in office. It reversed the
practice established by the first Congress and
followed without interruption from that time;
and it cannot fairly be regarded in any other
light than as a formidable encroachment by Congress upon the constitutional powers of the
executive department. It was intended only for
a particular emergency; and after Andrew Johnson had ceased to be a political issue, Congress
embraced the first opportunity to recur to the
long-sanctioned usage, and repealed the most
obnoxious features of the measure. But none
the less it supplied the ultimate pretext for the
impeachment.

The resolution, based upon the vague charges
which had been pending during nearly the whole
year of 1867, came up for final action in December, and was rejected by a vote of nearly
two to one. Stevens voted for the impeachment
notwithstanding his belief in its futility. Johnson was safe, and would have continued so had
he confined himself to the stubborn use of the
veto, and to the other methods by which he had
endeavored to thwart the will of Congress. But
he chose the more dangerous course, and defiantly joined issue with Congress upon the tenure-

of-office act. The act required the consent of
the Senate to removals from office, but provided
that the members of the Cabinet should hold
office " during the term of the President by
whom they may have been appointed, and for
one month thereafter, subject to removal by and
with the advice and consent of the Senate."
There was also a provision for suspension from
office during a recess of the Senate. If the
Senate should subsequently concur and consent
to the removal of the officer, the President might
cause him to be removed; but if the Senate
should refuse to give its consent, the suspended
officer should be reinstated. During the summer of 1867, the President requested Mr. Stanton to resign his office as Secretary of War.
There had for a long time been an absence of
those friendly feelings between Johnson and
Stanton that should exist between the President and one of his advisers, and the harmony
of the administration required that the antagonism should come to an end. It is difficult to
point to the exact time of the estrangement of
the President from his Secretary. The fundamental cause of the controversy between the executive and Congress had been the plan of
reconstruction first applied to North Carolina,
and afterwards to the other Confederate States.
Stanton, himself a leader of men, apparently

deserved to be credited with the preparation of this plan.[1]

Responsible as Stanton was for the adoption of the reconstruction policy of the President, he succeeded in remaining loyal to him until that policy began to take on symptoms of unpopularity. But at last, when Congress showed itself hostile, and was supported in the election of 1866, the Secretary bowed to the popular will and took the congressional side. Three of his associates had resigned because they could not at the same time remain loyal to their own ideas of public duty and to the President, who was their executive chief. Stanton's opposition did not assume that shape. He antagonized the President, consorted with his political enemies, but remained at his council board, and steadfastly clung to office. Johnson did not fail to make known his desire for Stanton's retirement; but the latter was obdurate to all hints, and finally, when the President requested him to resign, he flatly and with little courtesy declined to do so. He was then suspended from his office, and General Grant temporarily took his place.

As required by the tenure-of-office act, the President sent to the Senate, at its next session,

[1] See speech of James S. Wilson in House of Representatives, December 6, 1867, also *Messages and Papers of the Presidents*, vol. vi. pp. 588, 589.

a statement of the reasons for his action. That body declined to sanction the removal, and Stanton was thereupon restored to his office. This point marked the high-water mark of the encroachments of Congress upon the presidential power. Had Johnson submitted, the degradation of his office would have been complete. The duty prescribed by the Constitution, that the President should take care that the laws were faithfully executed, would have been an idle injunction, and one impossible to be performed, if the necessary agents selected by him to execute the laws should be responsible, not to him, but to the Senate. There could have been no head nor unity to the administration of the government, if each of the members of the Cabinet should be at liberty to pursue his own peculiar policy, while the constitutional executive should be powerless to intervene, and could only supplicate the Senate for leave to dismiss an obnoxious and hostile adviser. The delightful harmony which would naturally result from this system was well illustrated by the very first case in which it was applied. In one of the messages which Stanton sent to the House of Representatives, after he had been reinstated in the War Office, he said : " After the action of the Senate on his alleged reason for my suspension from the office of Secretary of War, I resumed the duties of that office as required by the act of Congress, and have continued to discharge them without any personal or written communication with the President. No orders have been issued from this department in the name of the President with my knowledge."

After his restoration, Stanton refrained from attending the Cabinet meetings. He conducted himself as if he were the superior officer of the President. This system would have afforded the spectacle of seven little Presidents sitting about the Cabinet table, if they saw fit to attend, with the Chief Magistrate of the Constitution present for ornamental purposes, and of little more practical consequence than is the Vice-President in the Senate. Johnson would have been signally wanting in courage as well as patriotism — two qualities which he undeniably possessed in a degree only surpassed by his egotism — if he had tamely submitted. He played the part of a patriot. He did what Grant or Jackson or any other of our great Presidents would doubtless have done under similar circumstances, and on February 21, 1868, he issued an order summarily removing Stanton from the position of Secretary of War.

Stanton immediately sent a "message" to the House of Representatives, communicating the President's order. It was at once referred to the Committee on Reconstruction. The President's enemies were not slow in taking advantage of the excitement which his apparent defiance and disregard of the tenure-of-office act aroused. On the very next day, which was the birthday of Washington, Stevens reported the matter back to the House, with a resolution declaring " that Andrew Johnson, President of the United States, be impeached of high crimes and misdemeanors in office." When he took the floor, merely to present the report, the excitement was extraordinary, and the Speaker cautioned the members of the House as well as the crowded galleries against demonstrations of approval or disapproval, and announced that he had called upon the police to aid the officers of the House in preserving order. In the heated debate which followed, it was seen that the President had no defenders in the Republican party.[1] Wilson, who had so boldly and effectively opposed impeachment on the grounds upon which it was urged in December, now supported the resolution. The discussion lacked no element of excitement which partisanship could

[1] The prevailing opinion in the Republican party was doubtless expressed in a telegram, which was read in the debate, from the Governor of Illinois, in which he said : " His treason must be checked. . . . The peace of the country is not to be trifled with by this presumptuous demagogue. . . . Millions of loyal hearts are panting to stand by the stars and stripes."

impart to it. The President was stigmatized as a traitor, demagogue, and criminal. He was denounced as a usurper, and, with hardly an ideal consistency, by some of the very gentlemen who had been industriously voting for two years to strip his office of its constitutional powers.

The debate was closed on February 24 by Stevens, in a speech which was a bitter attack upon the President, and hardly less so upon General Grant. He declared that " the high crimes and misdemeanors," which the Constitution made the grounds of impeachment, did not mean indictable crimes only. Impeachment was " a purely political proceeding," — a remedy " for malfeasance in office, and to prevent the continuance thereof." " The people desire no victim," said he, " and they will endure no usurper." Johnson, he said, had taken an oath faithfully to execute the laws, and he could not plead exemption from its obligation " on account of his condition at the time it was administered to him." He had violated this oath when he first removed Stanton and appointed General Grant. The testimony of both Johnson and Grant made this clear. The only question at issue was, whether Grant was a party to the conspiracy, and upon that point Stevens confessed to indifference. The resolution passed by a vote of 126 to 47, and for the first time since the foundation of the government the representatives of the people had invoked the great remedy of impeachment against the Chief Executive of the nation.

Upon the motion of Mr. Stevens, a committee of two was appointed to appear at the bar of the Senate and impeach the President. He was made chairman of this committee. He was the first to throw down the gauntlet when, at the December session of 1865, he had forestalled the President's message upon reconstruction by making, in advance of its reception, his famous motion with reference to the senators and representatives from the Southern States. In the long and bitter struggle with the Executive, Stevens had been the acknowledged congressional leader. When the President singled him out for attack, he instinctively recognized in him his own most dangerous foe. It was most fitting, therefore, that the first declaration of impeachment made to the Senate should be made in the name of the House of Representatives by Thaddeus Stevens.

On February 25, he and his associate upon the committee went before the Senate. His health was at the time hopelessly broken; but he gathered strength from the transcendent occasion, and the hushed and expectant audience drank in every syllable of his great message. He had framed it tersely, with the art of a great lawyer, and every word flew straight to its mark. He spoke it with a solemnity and force that thrilled the listener. "I doubt," said Sumner, "if words were ever delivered with more effect. . . . Who can forget his steady, solemn utterance of this great arraignment? The words were few, but they will sound through the ages."[1] He was conscious that he was performing a great public act, which had never before been performed in our history, and his manner no less than his words fitly betokened it. "Mr. President," said Stevens, "in obedience to the order of the House of Representatives, we appear before you, and in the name of the House of Representatives and of all the people of the United States, we do impeach Andrew Johnson, President of the United States, of high crimes and misdemeanors in office; and we further inform the Senate that the House of Representa-

[1] The *Globe*, December 18, 1868. The conclusion of Sumner's speech, which was a eulogy upon Stevens, is well worth quoting. "Already he takes his place among illustrious names, which are the common property of mankind. I see him now, as I have so often seen him during life. His venerable form moves slowly and with uncertain steps; but the gathered strength of years is in his countenance and the light of victory on his path. Politician, calculator, time-server, stand aside! A hero statesman passes to his reward."

tives will in due time exhibit particular articles of impeachment against him, and make good the same; and in their name we demand that the Senate take order for the appearance of the said Andrew Johnson to answer said impeachment."

Stevens was chosen a member of the committee to prepare articles of impeachment, and also one of the managers to present the case to the Senate. He would probably have been selected as the leading manager, but his physical condition rendered him absolutely unable to discharge the duties of that position. The sickness was upon him from which he had so often rallied, but it was now destined to increase until he died. He was not able to perform the ordinary work of a representative, much less to take charge of the most important trial of the century. His mind, however, shone brightly, although fitfully, and his dauntless will would not let him yield. When he was too weak to walk, he was carried into the Senate chamber; and when he was too weak to talk, his fellow-managers would read his words.

Among the managers were some able lawyers. Next to Stevens, who would have been overmatched by no lawyer on either side, the ablest advocate among them was Butler, who, although not profound in his knowledge of law, had few equals, and probably no superior, at the bar in readiness, ingenuity, and the ability to overwhelm an antagonist with ridicule and abuse. The trial, however, did not prove an advantageous field for the display of his peculiar talents. Boutwell was a sound lawyer, a man of great industry, and probably contributed more towards making the impeachment successful than any other of the managers. Wilson, also, added strength to the prosecution; but the remaining managers, although able men, did not deserve to take high rank as lawyers.

The advantage in legal talent lay decidedly with the President. Every one of his five counsel was an experienced and able advocate, but the two men who stood out conspicuously among them were Benjamin R. Curtis and William M. Evarts. Curtis was a profound lawyer, who had served with distinction on the Supreme Bench of the United States, and in his youth had taken almost the highest rank at a bar of which Daniel Webster and Rufus Choate were the leaders. There was at that time no more accomplished advocate at the American bar than Evarts. He displayed remarkable sagacity in the management of a trial, was ready and eloquent, and in a bantering wit he reminded one strongly of Stevens when the latter was in his more genial moods. The charges contained in the articles might pass in the superheated atmosphere, and amid the clamor, of a partisan House, but they had now to endure the scrutiny of great and hostile counsel.

Such an array as appeared for the President had little difficulty in laying bare the substance of the articles, and in showing how much of them had legal merit, and how much was suited merely to a "political proceeding." Indeed, the trial had not proceeded far before the practical wisdom of Stevens's "political proceeding" theory was made manifest by the necessities of his case. If the Senate was a court, bound by those salutary rules of law which govern in judicial tribunals, if the "high crimes and misdemeanors," of which the President must be proven guilty, were to be fit companions of the treason and bribery mentioned with them in the Constitution, then there was very little substance in the charges of the House.

The article based upon the buffoonery contained in some of the President's speeches, and his undignified attacks upon members of Congress, was easily ridiculed out of court by Mr. Evarts; for he had ready to his hand the report of the debates of the House of Representatives, which showed how Mr. Manager Butler and Mr. Manager Bingham had abused each other in the presence of the House with a directness and vigor which, by comparison, made the President's efforts at scurrility sink into insignificance.

The only charge that seemed to possess legal merit grew out of the removal of Stanton and the alleged violation of the tenure-of-office act, and the struggle soon centred upon the articles in which that was involved. That charge, as a basis of impeachment, failed to survive the great legal argument with which for two days Curtis held the attention of the Senate. His extraordinary speech was none the less effective because it was made for the severe practical purpose of influencing the judgment of the judges, and because, after he had presented his reasons, he took his seat without invoking the past or posterity, or making any elaborate effort at a peroration.

The President had removed Stanton according to the construction placed upon the Constitution by the first Congress, of which one third of the framers of that instrument were members. That construction had been followed without deviation for nearly ninety years, and until Congress in its struggle with Johnson attempted to reverse it by the passage of the tenure-of-office act. It has since, too, been reëstablished; for so soon as the presidency of Johnson ended, the act was substantially repealed, so far as it was involved in the controversy.[1] In determining what were his constitutional duties, the President would have been justified in following the construction established by Washington and Madison, and sanctioned by uninterrupted usage during our whole history, rather than the construction imposed by his enemies for the purpose of curtailing his powers. But his defense stood upon even safer ground. As the guardian and trustee of the powers of his office, the preservation of which was vital to the whole nation, could he have done less than regard the constitutionality of the act as doubtful, and, by making a test case, have the question submitted for decision to the Supreme Court? Yet the performance of this obvious duty was charged against him as a "high crime and misdemeanor," for which he deserved removal from office.

But admitting that the President was bound to accept the tenure-of-office act as constitutional and to obey its provisions, it was far from clear that he had violated it. Cabinet officers were exempted from the general terms of the act, and it was provided as to them that they should hold "during the term of the President by whom they

---

[1] "As matter of fact, a Republican Congress, largely composed of the same members who had enacted the law, indirectly confessed two years later that it could not be maintained." Blaine's *Twenty Years of Congress*, vol. ii. p. 274.

may have been appointed, and for one month
thereafter, subject to removal by and with the
advice and consent of the Senate." The counsel for the President strongly took the position
that Stanton did not come under the provisions
of the act, and he could be removed by Johnson.
He had been appointed by Lincoln during his first
term, and if Lincoln were living he could remove
this Secretary during his second term. But the
case was even stronger with regard to Johnson,
who could reasonably claim that he was serving a
term of his own, during which Stanton had never
been appointed, and could therefore be removed
at pleasure. Was the President, then, to be impeached because he put this rational construction upon the law, — a construction, too, identical
with that which supporters of the law in Congress had put upon it, as shown by the debates
at the time of its passage?

I have referred somewhat in detail to the essential point in the controversy, because the article in which it was stated with the greatest force
was apparently drawn by Stevens himself.[1] Although he had prudently emphasized the political feature of impeachment, in view of the scar-

[1] See Stevens's speech, *Supplement to Congressional Globe*,
2d session, 40th Congress, p. 320. Hon. George S. Boutwell
also informed me that the most important article was drawn
by Stevens. The statement appears in newspapers of that day.

city of sounder material in his case, he devoted
his energies to proving that the President had
committed a high misdemeanor. When the
original articles had been reported to the House,
he urged the insertion of a new article. On the
charges as they then stood, he declared that the
President's lawyers would secure his acquittal,
unless " they are greener than I was in any case
I ever undertook before the court of quarter
sessions." An additional article was subsequently adopted. Upon that article Stevens
made the only public contribution to the trial
which he was able to make.

He prepared his speech with great care, but
it was not so strong or sustained an argument
as he was in the habit of making. Its vigor was
undoubtedly somewhat lessened by the condition
of his health; yet it was the most lawyer-like
argument made on his side of the cause, and was
utterly lacking in the cheap political buncombe
with which some of the managers disfigured
their addresses. After standing for a few minutes his strength gave out, and he was forced to
resume his chair. He spoke for nearly half an
hour from his seat, when his voice became inau-
dible, and the reading of his speech was concluded by General Butler. He argued that
Johnson was serving as President in Lincoln's
term, and that therefore Stanton's case came

strictly within the terms of the proviso of the act, as Stanton had been appointed by Lincoln. If Stanton was not covered by the proviso, then he came under the general scope of the act. In either alternative it would require the consent of the Senate to remove him.

This speech, so painfully made, represents the only part which Stevens took in the actual trial of the case. He had come to believe that the President would be convicted. "He will be condemned," Stevens predicted, "and his sentence inflicted without turmoil, tumult, or bloodshed, and the nation will continue its accustomed course of freedom and prosperity." This prediction appeared well founded. In a total membership of fifty-four senators, there were only eight Democrats, and, after adding to them those senators who usually supported the President, the Republicans outnumbered the combination by nearly four to one. Only two thirds were necessary to convict. In the partisan tempest that was then raging, it did not seem possible that a number of the constant Republican senators, within one as great as the entire Democratic membership, would be willing to step outside of their party ranks and vote for acquittal.

The test came upon the strongest article, which was the one advocated by Stevens. The friends of impeachment secured a vote ordering the eleventh article to be read first. When the vote was taken, it was found that the President was supported by seven Republican senators. Thirty-five senators declared for conviction, and nineteen for acquittal;[1] and by the narrowest possible margin the President had escaped conviction. A vote was taken upon two other articles, but it was found that the prosecution had mustered its full strength upon the eleventh article, and the Senate, sitting as a court of impeachment, adjourned without day.

There can be little doubt as to the wisdom of the verdict. Had the extreme political theory of the proceeding prevailed, which was most strongly advocated by Charles Sumner, the balance established by the Constitution would have been completely destroyed. When a majority of the House and two thirds of the Senate happened at any time to differ politically from the President, it would be in their power absolutely to control the government of the country, and the functions of the President as an independent officer would be obliterated. It was a fortunate circumstance that the Senate contained great lawyers like Trumbull and Fessenden, who were wise enough to judge rightly, and great enough

[1] Although few in number the Democratic minority was far from deficient in ability. Its most distinguished member, Mr. Reverdy Johnson, easily took rank among the three or four ablest senators.

to cast aside partisanship upon a question of such transcendent importance, and consult the interests instead of the passions of the people.

The impeachment of Andrew Johnson is inevitably contrasted with the impeachment of Warren Hastings, and the contrast is certainly great. The celebrated English trial was almost wholly spectacular, and was a fit subject for the fine writing Macaulay bestowed upon it half a century afterwards. The production of so imposing a spectacle appears to have absorbed all the energies of the British constitution, and to have paralyzed for the time the Anglo-Saxon talent for the administration of justice. Each trial partook much of the times, and the form of government, under which it occurred. The one was apparently conducted for ceremonial purposes, the other for practical effect. The charges against Hastings were concealed under five hundred pages of verbiage; those against the American President covered less than two pages of the "Congressional Globe." The trial of the former began in 1788 and ended in 1795. During this interval one third of the one hundred and sixty lords who attended the opening of the case had died; and when the tribunal finally met to record the judgment of posterity upon the evidence, the number of judges who retained sufficient interest to vote upon the

charges had dwindled to twenty-nine. In the American trial, less than sixty days elapsed from the time when the case of the House was opened until the Senate dissolved as a court of impeachment. During that period the interest had gone on increasing not merely in the Senate chamber, but in every portion of the country whose chief ruler was on trial, and at the end every one of the judges recorded his verdict.

The trial of Hastings was made memorable by the great parliamentary orators who represented the Commons. But its spectacular character is not wanting here. The eloquence of Burke, Sheridan, and Fox would undoubtedly decorate any historic occasion, but not one of them ever took high rank as a lawyer. They were admirably fitted to set in motion the smelling-bottles in the gallery, as Macaulay records, and to cause some hysterical lady to be carried out in a fit; but they were not the men one would choose to conduct a case that was to be governed by the rules of evidence received in the law courts. For a good deal of their speaking, too, we must take the account that tradition gives us. Modern methods of reporting were then unknown. But the lawyers who conducted the Johnson trial were not permitted to write out the polished periods of their speeches, a year after they had been delivered, in order to

thrill posterity. What was said was taken down
each day by stenographers, and appeared in cold
type the next morning; and the report presents
to us the accurate picture of great lawyers contending in a great cause, and bringing to bear
upon the minds of the judges, according to the
rules of law, every consideration that could pro-
perly influence their verdict. The impeachment
of Hastings enriched literature, and will stand
as a splendid historical pageant; but it signally
failed in its great and essential purpose. The
proceeding against Johnson was severely and
successfully devoted to the one object which gave
it an excuse for being, the trial of a President
charged with high crimes and misdemeanors.
The American impeachment trial was majestic
in its simplicity; it was eloquent in its direct
purpose; it was too great for the tinsel and
trappings of ceremony; and in the example
which it gave to mankind of the peaceful attempt to remove the chief ruler of the greatest
of republics, and of quiet and orderly submission to the result, it was wholly in line with
those other wonderful practical contributions
which that nation has made to the progress of
the world.

CHAPTER XIX

LAST DAYS

STEVENS was profoundly disappointed at the acquittal of the President, and for a time he appears to have taken a sombre view of the future of the country. But he soon regained his accustomed gayety of spirit. He attended the sessions of the House when he was able to do so, and, although his health was constantly growing feebler and his strength was nearly exhausted, he took a considerable part in the routine proceedings. On July 7, but little more than a month before his death, he introduced five additional articles of impeachment, apparently for the chief purpose of enabling him to review, in one of the longest speeches of his later years, the law of impeachments, and to express his dissatisfaction with the Senate and the rulings of the chief justice.

On July 16, he introduced a resolution looking to the acquirement of a naval station and depot in the West Indies. He supported it with a brief speech, in the course of which he paid a striking tribute to the sovereigns of Russia. "I look upon the rulers," said he, "who have held the destinies of that great nation since the time of Peter the Great as the most remarkable race of sovereigns that ever sat upon a throne. The later members of that dynasty, for wisdom and justice, are quite equal to any of their predecessors. They had a very difficult nation to construct into" an empire composed of Cossacks, Calmucks, and many millions of serfs. The Czar had accomplished a great revolution without civil war, and "with patience, courage, and uncommon wisdom" he had "made every man within his empire free."

On July 27, Congress took a recess until September. Stevens was too weak and worn to stand the trip to Lancaster, and he remained in Washington, with the hope of gaining strength for the journey. His vitality had been so great that it had more than once enabled him, after a little rest, to rally from the weakness which his tremendous labors in Congress had brought upon him. At last, however, the hopes of himself and his friends were destined not to be realized. His cheerfulness remained with him, and his courage, which no misfortune could daunt. "I am going to die, like Nicanor, in harness," he said to a friend within a few months of his death; "I mean to die hurrahing." This was a

favorite expression with him, and the meaning
which he gave to it was very likely original with
himself. He intended to keep up the fight until
the last. " You have changed my medicine ? "
he said to the physician a few days before he
died. " Yes," replied the doctor. " Well," replied Stevens grimly, and with a smile, "this is
a square fight." He had about him, to care for
his wants, his two nephews, one of whom bore
his name, a few family friends, and two Sisters
of Charity, who had watched over him in his
former illness. On the afternoon of Tuesday,
August 11, he was very weak. He could talk
but little, but that little was almost wholly upon
public matters. He said that Seward had done
" very well recently in relation to our foreign
affairs. His purchase of Alaska was the big-
gest thing in his life, and, if he could have purchased Samana, it would have been the crowning
event of his whole career." He expressed the
opinion that Evarts, who was then the attorney-
general, was " not only a sound lawyer but a
statesman," and that he would advise Johnson
" so to administer the laws as to render unnecessary a meeting of Congress in September. If
he does, I shall feel prouder than ever that I
urged his confirmation." He talked with his
nephew, who had just arrived from Pennsylvania, about his iron furnace and also gave him

some very clear instructions about a lawsuit in which he was engaged.

Two colored clergymen called, and asked leave to see Stevens and pray with him. He ordered them to be admitted; and when they had come to his bedside, he turned and held out his hand to one of them. They sang a hymn and prayed. During the prayer he responded twice, but could not be understood. Soon afterwards the Sisters of Charity prayed, and he seemed deeply affected. The doctor told him that he was dying. He made a motion with his head, but no other reply. One of the Sisters asked leave to baptize him, and it was granted, but whether by Stevens or his nephew is not clear. She performed the ceremony with a glass of water, a portion of which she poured upon his forehead. It was then within ten minutes of midnight, and the end was to come before the beginning of the new day. He lay motionless for a few minutes, then opened his eyes, took one look, placidly closed them, and, without a struggle, the great commoner had ceased to breathe.

Stevens died on Tuesday, August 11, 1868. The Republican primaries in Lancaster County for the nomination of the member of Congress had been called for the Saturday of that week. No candidates dared to show themselves while the body of the representative whom the people loved was yet unburied. Although they knew that he was no more, a common impulse inspired them; and when the votes were counted, it was found that all had been cast for Thaddeus Stevens.

His body was buried in a humble cemetery in the city of his home. His choice of the spot grew out of his unswerving devotion to the cause which lay close to his heart during every moment of his life. Upon the monument which has been reared may be read the following inscription, prepared by himself: " I repose in this quiet and secluded spot, not from any natural preference for solitude, but, finding other cemeteries limited as to race by charter rules, I have chosen this, that I might illustrate in my death the principles which I advocated through a long life, [the] Equality of Man before his Creator."

His epitaph well indicates his chief distinction. A truer democrat never breathed. Equality was the animating principle of his life. He deemed no man so poor or friendless as to be beneath the equal protection of the laws, and none so powerful as to rise above their sway. Privilege never had a more powerful nor a more consistent foe.

INDEX

ABOLITIONISTS, convention to oppose, meets at Harrisburg, 48–51; value of their work, 133; their narrrowness, arrogance, and violence, 133; really fail to impress North, 133, 134.

Adams, Charles Francis, proposes constitutional amendment to prevent abolition of slavery, 122.

Adams, John Quincy, his conspicuousness in House of Representatives, 66.

Adams, Professor, at Dartmouth College, 13.

Alabama, contract labor laws in, against negroes, 252; carpet-bag government in, 301.

Alexander II. of Russia, eulogized by Stevens, 350.

Allen, Charles, in House in 1849, 69; supports Stevens for speaker, 86.

Anderson, Thomas L., in Congress in 1859, ridiculed by Stevens, 99.

Anti-Masonic party, its origin, 29; organized in New York and Pennsylvania, 29, 30; its failure as a national party, 30; attempts to crush Masons in Pennsylvania legislature, 31–33, 34, 46; carries Pennsylvania for Ritner in 1835, 46.

Ashley, John M., proposes thirteenth amendment, 225.

Ashmun, George, in House, in 1849, 69.

BANK OF UNITED STATES, chartered by Pennsylvania, 47; its branches

prohibited in Democratic States, 47.

Bar, conditions of success at, in 1820, 26.

Black, Jeremiah S., forces Buchanan to alter his policy in 1861, 118, 119; made secretary of state, 119; on Stevens's legal ability, 202.

Bingham, John A., on Committee on Reconstruction, 259; wishes to join amnesty with reconstruction, 290; abuses Butler in debate, 339.

Blair, Francis P., his theory of status of Confederate States controverted by Stevens, 236; attacks Fremont, 312; retort of Stevens to, 313.

Border States, save Republican party in 1862, 221.

Boutwell, George S., on Committee on Reconstruction, 259; a manager of Johnson impeachment, 338.

Breckenridge, John C., candidate of slavery extensionists in 1860, 113.

Brooks, James, raises question of status of reconstructed States, 257; retorts of Stevens to, 258, 314, 315.

Buchanan, James, advises Stevens in 1827 to support Jackson, 28; his unfitness to meet the crisis in 1861, 116; his message on secession, 116, 117; forced to alter his policy, 118; sends message threatening resistance to secession, 119; attacked by Stevens, 124–126.

Blaine, James G., on Stevens's rhe-

torical accuracy, 16 ; on his unquestioned leadership of the
House in 1861, 138 ; urges combination of reconstruction with amnesty, 290 ; aids Stevens to force
through Reconstruction Act, 292 ;
on Stevens's ability in debate,
320, 321.

Butler, Benjamin F., a manager of
Johnson impeachment, 337; abuses
Bingham in debate, 339 ; reads
Stevens's speech, 343.

CALIFORNIA, settlement and organization of, 72, 73 ; asks admission
as a free State, 73.

Cameron, Simon, supported by Stevens in Republican National Convention of 1860, 112 ; withdraws,
then reënters contest for seat in
Lincoln's cabinet, 136 ; witty remark of Stevens upon, 311, 312.

Cass, Lewis, resigns from Buchanan's cabinet, 118.

Champneys, Benjamin, displaced by
Stevens from leadership of Lancaster bar, 59.

Chase, Salmon P., reduces Lincoln's
estimates of war expenses, 141;
struggles to avoid a deficit, 142 ;
his error in not recommending
taxation, 143 ; estimate of his
character and ability as a financier, 143, 144 ; attempts to borrow in 1861, 153 ; aided by banks,
154 ; urged by banks not to damage their coin reserves, 155 ; insists
on paying government creditors
in specie, 156 ; reports failure of
revenue law, 158 ; wishes to escape responsibility of legal-tender
issue, 170 ; urges national banking system, 174 ; expects a short
war, 175 ; does not at first recommend taxation, 175 ; slow to recognize its necessity, 176 ; hesitates
to ask for increased taxes, 177 ;
recommends law restricting gold
transactions, 208.

Chiriqui Improvement Company,

corrupt appropriation for, defeated by Stevens, 107-109.

Clay, Henry, asks Stevens's support in 1844, 62 ; introduces Compromise measures of 1850, 74 ; attacked by Stevens, 84 ; compared
with Stevens as a parliamentary
leader, 322.

Clemens, Jeremiah, retort of Stevens to, 103.

Cobb, Howell, in House in 1849, 69 ;
Democratic candidate for speaker,
70, 71 ; declares secession irrevocable, 129.

Colfax, Schuyler, opposes direct tax
upon land, 147.

Compromise of 1850, introduced by
Clay, 74, 75 ; opposed by all sides,
75 ; defeated in form of Omnibus
bill, 85 ; finally passed, 85, 86 ; its
effect, 86.

Conkling, Roscoe, opposes tax on
land, 147 ; opposes issue of legal-
tender notes, 160 ; his financial
scheme condemned by Stevens,
165 ; introduces resolutions of inquiry as to responsibility for defeat at Ball's Bluff, 192, 193 ; introduces resolution to aid States
in compensated emancipation, 216;
on Committee on Reconstruction,
259 ; sarcasm of Stevens upon,
314.

Constitution, in relation to fugitive
slaves, 20, 74 ; tends to prevent
development of statesmen, 69 ; in
relation to slavery, 76-85 ; attitude of Republican party toward,
104 ; Buchanan's theory of secession under, 117 ; proposals to
amend, to prevent secession, 121-
123 ; its relation to legal tender,
163-165 ; strained by North during civil war, 187 ; considered as
set aside in South, by Stevens,
188, 191, 200-202, 229 ; in case of
West Virginia, 188-191 ; in regard
to military power of President,
193 ; in relation to suspension of
habeas corpus, 194, 195 ; in rela-

tion to draft, 196; amended by abolition of slavery, 226; question of its relation to reconstruction, 229-240, 261, 262, 266; amendments to, proposed, 260; fourteenth amendment to, introduced by Stevens, 271, 272; fourteenth amendment of, rendered inefficacious to guarantee negro suffrage, 295, 296; necessarily neglected in reconstruction, 297, 298; in relation to tenure-of-office act, 328, 331, 332, 340-342; in relation to impeachment, 334, 339, 345.

Corwin, Thomas, suggests a compromise in 1860 preventing abolition in the district of Columbia, 121; derided by Stevens, 126.

Crittenden, J. J., introduces resolution declaring object of war, 148.

Curtis, Benjamin R., counsel for Johnson in impeachment case, 338; his argument, 340.

DARTMOUTH COLLEGE, its early prosperity, 13; its faculty, 13, 14; course of study at, 14, 15; Stevens's connection with, 15, 16.

Dawes, H. L., describes Stevens's speech on slavery in 1861, 127, 128; on legal fictions in creation of West Virginia, 189; on Stevens's personal appearance, 318; on his ability as a debater, 320.

Davis, Henry Winter, introduces Congressional plan of reconstruction, 234; his sensitiveness ridiculed by Stevens, 316, 317.

Davis, Jefferson, elected President of Confederate States, 129, 130.

Democratic party, in Pennsylvania, urges governor not to prevent repeal of free-school act, 36; in other States, prohibits branches of United States Bank, 47; controls Pennsylvania constitutional convention, 47; its contest with Whigs for control of Pennsylvania legislature, 51-53; attacks state

arsenal, 52; defied by Stevens as rebels, 53; defeats Whigs in "Buckshot War," 53; expels Stevens from House, 54; in Congress in 1850, opposes admission of California, 75; considered destroyed by Stevens, 87; elects Pierce in 1852, 88; defied by Stevens, 103, 104; broken up by quarrel of Douglas and Buchanan, 110, 111; feeble in Congress after 1861, 138; denounced by Stevens for hindering war, 196, 197; denounces war as for abolition, 218, 219; makes great gains in Congress, 220; hopes to defeat Lincoln for reëlection, 224; badly beaten in election of 1864, 226; demands admission of members from reconstructed States, 256, 257; accused by Stevens of forging Johnson's speeches, 268; beaten in elections of 1866, 284.

Douglas, Stephen A., opposes Buchanan's Kansas policy, 110, 113; hated by South, 111; his power as a speaker, 111; his party opposes extension of slavery, 113.

Dred Scott decision, its effect, 102.

Dwight, Timothy, on entrance requirements for Yale College, 14.

ELECTION of 1860, its significance, a triumph of slavery restriction, 113, 114.

England, question of its neutrality discussed by Stevens, 184, 185.

Evarts, William M., counsel for Johnson in impeachment case, 338; ridicules articles of impeachment, 339; praised by Stevens, 351.

FARRAGUT, ADMIRAL DAVID G., accompanies Johnson "round the circle," 281.

Fessenden, William P., reports plan of reconstruction to Senate, 273; votes against impeachment of Johnson, 345.

Financial history, deficit after panic of 1857, 104 ; tariff act of 1860, 105, 106 ; war estimates of Lincoln and Chase, 139–141 ; difficulties of increasing revenue, 141 ; amount of new revenue necessary to carry on war and meet deficit, 142, 143 ; position of Chase in history of treasury, 143, 144 ; passage of loan bill, 144 ; preparation and passage of revenue bill, 145–148 ; details of taxation, 146, 147 ; decline of government credit, 153 ; loan of 1861 aided by patriotic bankers, 153–155 ; refusal of Chase to permit banks to safeguard their coin reserves, 155, 156 ; resulting suspension by banks in December, 156 ; error of Chase in thus hastening collapse of banks, 157 ; failure of revenue law to meet expectations, 158 ; estimates for 1863, 158, 159 ; first issue of legal-tender notes, 160–167 ; renewed issue called for, 167 ; Stevens's criticism of Senate amendments to legal-tender act, 168 ; discussion of wisdom of issue of legal tender, 169, 170 ; their issue a result of necessity, 171 ; their evil effects seen since the war, 172, 173 ; summary of loans passed, 174 ; national banks and their success, 174, 175 ; reluctance of Chase to recommend taxation, 175 ; opposition in Congress to any increase in taxes, 175, 176 ; policy of Chase to tax for merely ordinary expenditures and interest on debt, 176, 177 ; adoption by Congress of extensive internal taxes, 178 ; details of Stevens's system, 178–180 ; in spite of legal tender, management of war finances a success, 180, 181 ; expenses denounced by Stevens as excessive, 186 ; payment of interest in coin opposed by Stevens, 204–206 ; laws restricting operations in gold, 208.

Florida, vagrant and labor contract laws in, after war, 252, 253 ; carpet-bag government in, 300.

Free - soilers, prevent election of Winthrop as speaker of House, 70, 71 ; vote for Stevens, 71, 86 ; their policy defended, 71, 72.

Fremont, John C., attacked by Blair, 312 ; defended by Stevens, 313.

Fugitive slaves, question of their recapture under the Constitution, 20, 21, 74 ; zeal of Stevens in defending, 26 ; irritation over, between South and North, 74 ; proposed law concerning, denounced by Stevens, 75 ; law to enforce return of, passed, 86.

GEORGIA, follows South Carolina in secession, 115 ; " carpet-bag " government in, 301.

Gerry, Elbridge, of Maine, in House in 1849, 69.

Giddings, Joshua R., in House in 1849, 70 ; supports Stevens for speaker, 86.

Gilbert, Amos, describes Stevens's law studies, 21.

Gorsuch, Edward, killed in attempting to recapture fugitive slave, 90.

Grant, General Ulysses S., takes Vicksburg, 224 ; on Johnson's tour in 1860, 281 ; appointed Secretary of War by Johnson, 330 ; denounced by Stevens, 334.

Greeley, Horace, on Chase's integrity, 143.

Grow, Galusha A., Republican candidate for speaker of House, 97 ; chosen speaker in 1861, 138.

HALLECK, GENERAL H. W., his order sending back fugitive slaves attacked by Stevens, 216.

Hanway, Castner, defended by Stevens in fugitive-slave case, 90, 91.

Harris, Isham G., in House in 1849, 70.

Harrison, William H., said to have

offered Stevens a seat in his cabinet, 57; nominated by Stevens's influence, 57.

Hastings, Warren, his impeachment contrasted with that of Johnson, 346–348.

Hibbard, Harry, in House in 1849, 69.

Hood, Alexander, on Stevens's indebtedness, 58.

House of Commons, better fitted to develop statesmanship than Congress, 68, 69; its superiority in settling contested election cases, 106.

House of Representatives, its character and organization in 1849, 67; fails to develop statesmanship as compared with House of Commons, 68, 69; membership of, in 1849, 69; struggle for organization of, 70, 71; passes compromise of 1850, 85; organized peaceably in 1850, 86; retirement of Stevens from, 89; return of Stevens to, 94–96; contest over organization of, 96–104; violent scenes in, 97, 98, 101; its management of contested election cases, 106, 107; fails to pass resolution of Stevens suggesting that Buchanan prepare to defend Sumter, 119, 120; appoints special committee on state of country, 120, 121; committee of, discusses compromise measures, 121–123; violent scenes in, during Stevens's speech against compromise, 127, 128; passes constitutional amendment to prevent abolition of slavery, 129; organizes quickly in 1861, 138; led by Stevens, 138; receives Lincoln's war message with enthusiasm, 140; passes loan and appropriation bills, 144, 145; debates direct tax on land, 147, 148; passes revenue bill, 147; passes Crittenden resolution, 148; later lays it on table, 149; rejects confiscation bill,

later passes it, 150; debate in, on legal-tender issue, 160–167; passes legal-tender act, 167; passes series of loan acts, 174, 175; passes national banking act, 174; unwilling to impose taxes, 176; later passes elaborate tax laws, 178–180; debates resolution calling on secretary of war to investigate responsibility for defeat at Ball's Bluff, 192–194; debates and passes bill indemnifying President for suspending writ of habeas corpus, 194, 195; passes conscription act, 195, 198; passes confiscation act, 199; passes Pacific Railroad bills, 203; led by Stevens to reject sham military improvements of rivers, 204; passes, and fifteen days later repeals, act restricting operations in gold, 208; complete leadership of Stevens in, 208, 209; passes resolution offering to aid in compensated emancipation, 216; passes bill to abolish slavery in District, 217; passes bill to prohibit in Territories, 217; passes bill to arm negroes, 223; fails to pass thirteenth amendment, 225; later yields to popular will, 226; defeats Vallandigham's resolutions on object of war, 230; excludes members from reconstructed States, 256–258; votes to appoint a joint committee on reconstruction, 258; debates in, on reconstruction, 261–270; fails to pass Freedmen's Bureau bill over veto, 270; passes second freedmen's bill and other bills over veto, 271; becomes more radical, 286; considers bill to repeal statute of limitations concerning treason, 287; considers reconstruction bill, 288–291; forces Senate to yield, 291; passes bill over veto, 292; threatens to impeach Johnson, 323; passes statute obliging next Congress to assemble March 4, 1867, 324 ; considers bill to enforce confiscation act, 324, 325 ; rejects plan to impeach Johnson, 327, 328 ; passes tenure-of-office act, 328 ; passes resolution to impeach Johnson, 332–335 ; appoints a committee to impeach, 335 ; last days of Stevens in, 349, 350.

House of Representatives of Pennsylvania, career of Stevens in, 31–56 ; appoints committee to investigate Masonry, 32 ; rejects bill to suppress Masonry, 34 ; passes bill for free public schools, 35 ; driven by popular excitement for repeal of law, 37 ; Stevens's speech in, for free schools, 38–45 ; votes against repeal, 40 ; carried by anti-Masons, 46 ; fails to investigate Masonry, 46 ; charters Bank of United States, 47 ; contest over organization of, between Whigs and Democrats, 51–54 ; captured by Democrats, 54 ; refusal of Stevens to attend, 53, 54 ; expels Stevens, 54 ; later expels Democratic leader, 55 ; later career of Stevens in, 56.

Houston, Samuel, proposes extension of Missouri Compromise line, 121.

Hunter, General David, praised by Stevens for arming negroes, 215.

ILLINOIS, carried by Democrats in 1862, 220.

Impeachment of Andrew Johnson, 323–348 ; steps leading up to, 332–337 ; articles of, 337–339 ; managers of, 337, 338 ; Johnson's counsel for defense, 338, 339 ; trial, 339–345 ; centre of effort on tenure-of-office question, 340–342 ; speech of Stevens upon, 343, 344 ; vote upon, 344, 345 ; acquittal of Johnson, 345 ; contrasted with impeachment of Warren Hastings, 346–348.

Indiana, carried by Democrats in 1862, 220.

Iowa, carried by Republicans in 1862, 221.

JACKSON, ANDREW, attacked by Stevens, 31.

Johnson, Andrew, in House in 1849, 70 ; continues Lincoln's plan of reconstruction, 241 ; probably persuaded by cabinet, 241, 242 ; becomes President, his character, 244 ; his egotism and vindictiveness, 245, 246 ; issues amnesty and reconstruction proclamation, 246, 247 ; his temporary popularity, 249 ; protected at first by Lincoln's prestige, 258 ; attacked by Stevens, 261–263 ; denounces committee on reconstruction, 265 ; satirically eulogized by Stevens, 267–269 ; his inconsistencies shown up by Stevens, 269, 270 ; vetoes Freedmen's Bureau bill, 270 ; vetoes other bills, which are passed nevertheless, 271 ; his tour " swinging round the circle," 280, 281 ; his violent language, 281 ; sarcastic speech of Stevens upon, 282–284 ; becomes a nullity in government, 284 ; his message of December, 1866, 285 ; tries to kill reconstruction act by delaying veto, 291 ; early threatened with impeachment, 323 ; quoted by Stevens as authority for confiscation, 324, 325 ; failure of first attempt to impeach, 326, 327 ; enrages Congressmen by his use of patronage, 327 ; defies tenure-of-office act, 328 ; asks Stanton to resign, 329 ; removes him and substitutes Grant, 330 ; ignored by Stanton, 332 ; again removes him, 332 ; resolution to impeach, introduced by Stevens, 333 ; bitterly denounced, 334 ; impeached before Senate, 335, 337 ; his defence by Evarts and Curtis, 339–342 ; Stevens's argument against, 343, 344; acquitted, 344, 345.

Johnson, Reverdy, on impeachment, 345.

KANSAS, attempt of South to gain control of, 102; carried by Republicans in 1862, 221.

King, Preston, in House in 1849, 69.

Know - Nothing party, controls House in 1854, 96.

LECKY, W. E. H., on carpet-bag government, 303.

Legal-tender notes, Stevens's argument for, 160–167. See Financial History.

Lincoln, Abraham, his skill as leader of Republicans, 111; nominated for president, 112; significance of his election by a minority vote, 112, 113; his caution, 136; selects his cabinet out of all elements of party, 136; obliged to act by fall of Fort Sumter, 137; begins war for the Union, 138; his war message asking for money and men, 139, 140; attacked by Vallandigham, 144; declares Southern ports blockaded, 185; criticised for slowness by Stevens, 186; his action called unconstitutional, 192; indemnified by Congress for suspending habeas corpus, 194, 195; reluctant to approve confiscation act, 199; asked to cancel order prohibiting negroes to enter Union lines, 216; asks Congress to offer to aid States in compensated emancipation, 216; his plan sneered at by Stevens, 216; finally sees necessity of emancipation, 217, 218; issues proclamation, 218, 222; continues to hope for compensation, 222; reëlected, 226; suggests reconstruction, 231; issues amnesty proclamation, 232; his plan opposed by Stevens, 233; vetoes reconstruction bill, 237;

his plan criticised, 237; signs resolution excluding reconstructed States from presidential election, 239; prepares to carry his plan through, 239–241; his ideas followed by Johnson, 241, 242; his cabinet brings Johnson to follow him, 241; would have avoided a rupture with Congress had he lived, 242, 243, 308; his influence at first makes Congress unwilling to quarrel with Johnson, 258; anecdotes concerning, 311, 315; eulogized by Stevens, 326.

Louisiana, reconstruction in, 233; senators and representatives from, excluded from Congress, 234; question of its status, 234.

Lovejoy, Owen, introduces bill prohibiting slavery in Territories, 217.

McCLELLAN, GENERAL GEORGE B., his incompetence described by Stevens, 197, 198; candidate for presidency, 226; sarcasm of Stevens upon, 315.

McClure, Alexander K., on relations of Harrison with Stevens, 57; describes Stevens's legal ability, 92.

McCulloch, Hugh, on Johnson's reconstruction policy as continuing Lincoln's, 241.

McElwee, Thomas B., proposes committee of Pennsylvania to investigate Stevens's conduct, 54; expelled from legislature, 55.

McLean, John T., preferred by Stevens for president, 112.

Mann, Horace, in House in 1849, 69; supports Stevens for speaker, 86.

Maryland, Stevens's bar examination in, 21–23.

Maynard, Horace, question of validity of his election to House, 257; joke of Stevens upon, as a "half-breed," 315, 316.

Minnesota, carried by Republicans in 1862, 221.

Mississippi, passes apprentice and

contract laws for negroes, 250, 251.

Missouri Compromise repealed by South, 101.

Moore, Professor, at Dartmouth College, 13.

Morgan, William, murdered by Masons, 29.

Morrill, Justin S., opposes issue of legal-tender notes, 160; on Committee on Reconstruction, 259.

NEW ENGLAND, remains Republican in 1862, 221.

New Mexico, its admission as a slave State proposed in 1861 to pacify the South, 126, 129.

New York, carried by Democrats in 1862, 220.

North, its subserviency to South denounced by Stevens, 83, 84, 98; stirred to anger by repeal of Missouri Compromise, 102; rebuked by Buchanan for having forced South to secede, 116; defended by Stevens, 125; its timidity in 1861, 130; not led by abolitionists, 133, 134; swayed by sentiments of Union taught by Webster and Clay, 134, 135; rises at news of Fort Sumter, 137, 138; ceases to volunteer, 195; alters attitude toward slavery during war, 212; begins to consider its abolition necessary to end war, 212; disaffection in, over emancipation and draft, 223, 224; disgusted at anti-negro laws of South, 254, 255.

North Carolina, reconstruction of, under Johnson, 246, 247; "carpet-bag" government in, 301.

OHIO, carried by Democrats in 1862, 220.

PATTON, GOVERNOR, vetoes Alabama anti-negro laws, 252.

Pennsylvania, reasons for Stevens's removal to, 20; organization of anti-Masons in, 29, 30; Stevens's political career in, 31–65; public school system of, 34; objection of its inhabitants to taxation for schools, 35, 36; agitation in, against free schools, 36; carried by anti-Masons, 46; charters Bank of United States, 47; constitutional convention, 47, 48; limits suffrage to whites, 48; anti-abolition convention in, 49; "Buckshot war" in, over organization of House, 51–54; reputation of Stevens in, 56, 91; Democrats gain in, during 1862, 220; renominates Stevens after his death, 352, 353.

Pennsylvania College, gets state aid through Stevens, 33.

Phelps, Abner, an anti-Mason in 1832, 30.

Phillips, Wendell, denounced by Johnson, 265, 281.

Pierce, Franklin, attacked by Stevens, 87; promises to maintain compromise, 101.

Pierpont, Francis H., governor of reconstructed Virginia, 269.

Protection, Stevens's arguments for, 105.

RAYMOND, HENRY J., defends Johnson's reconstruction policy, 264; sneered at by Stevens, 266.

Reed, John M., in Castner Hanway suit, 91.

Reconstruction, begun in Louisiana, 231; plan of, outlined by Lincoln, 231–233; President's plan of, displeases Congress, 233; congressional plan of, formed and passed, 234–237; vetoed by Lincoln, 237; superiority of congressional plan over Lincoln's, 238; controversy over, postponed until after Lincoln's death, 238, 239; its probable course, had Lincoln lived, 239–243; identity of Lincoln's and Johnson's plans for, 240–242; Johnson's plan of, promulgated, 246–248; working of Johnson's plan, 249-255; joint committee on, appointed by Congress, 258, 259; Stevens's conquered-province theory of, 261, 262, 266, 267, 269; report of committee on, 273–275; Stevens's theory of, adopted by Congress, 273–275, 294; negro suffrage advocated as part of, by Stevens, 276, 277, 286; and by the North, 278, 279; message of Johnson upon in 1866, 285; joint committee on, renewed, 285; bill for, reported to House, 288; debate upon, 290, 291; vetoed by Johnson, 291; passed over veto, 292; alterations in bill for, as passed, 292–294; efficacy of, damaged by representation clause, 294, 295; discussion of process of, 296–308; necessity of thoroughness in, 297, 298; effectiveness of military government under, 298, 299; carpet-bag government under, 299–305; violent overturn of negro rule after, 304; justified by necessity, 305–308; by impossibility of leaving negroes to mercy of whites, 306, 307; rendered harsh by fact of Johnson's presidency, 308; further acts to carry out, passed over veto, 326.

Republican party, attempt of Stevens and others to form, in 1855, 93; organized in 1856, 94; its struggle for control of House in 1859, 96–101; succeeds after eight weeks, 104; its national convention of 1860, 112; elects Lincoln by a minority vote, 112, 113; attempt of Lincoln to unite, by cabinet appointments, 136, 137; supports Crittenden resolution, 148; saved by Border States in 1862, 220, 221; committed to emancipation, 223; reasons for its nomination of Johnson, 244; leadership of, by Stevens, in reconstruction period, 259; successful in elections of 1866, 284; irritated at Johnson's control of offices, 327, 328.

Ritner, Joseph, anti-Masonic candidate for governor of Pennsylvania, 30; renominated and elected, 46; appoints Stevens on Canal Commission, 50; defeated for reëlection, 51; issues proclamation calling Democrats an "infuriated mob," 52.

Sacchi, ———, anecdote of his defense by Conkling and Stevens, 313.

Schenck, Robert C., in House in 1849, 70.

Schools, public, in Pennsylvania, controversy over, 34–45; Stevens's great speech in behalf of, 38–45.

Schwarz, John, eulogy of Stevens upon, 95.

Scott, General Winfield, praised by Stevens, 87, 88; defeated for presidency, 88.

Secession, Stevens's argument upon, 125, 126.

Senate, of United States, empowered by tenure-of-office act to prevent removals from office, 329; refuses to ratify removal of Stanton by Johnson, 331; appearance of Stevens before, to impeach Johnson, 335–337; more than two thirds Republican, 344; fails to convict Johnson, 345.

Seward, William H., an anti-Mason in 1830, 30; unsuited to be a Republican candidate, 112; his influence upon Johnson, 246; accompanies Johnson on tour, 281; held responsible by Stevens for Johnson's change of attitude toward rebels, 325.

Shellabarger, Samuel, replies to Raymond's speech defending Johnson, 264.

Sherman, John, Republican candidate for speaker in 1859, 97; his high rank as financier, 144.

Shurtleff, Professor, at Dartmouth College, 13.

Sickles, Daniel E., vetoes South Carolina black code after the war, 251, 252.

Slavery, causes of struggle over, in Territories, 72; speeches of Stevens against, 76-78, 80-85, 127, 128; passage of constitutional amendment to preserve, 129; with outbreak of war, ceases to be main political issue, 130, 131; steps by which it became necessary to South, 132; in course of war, becomes again a political issue, 212; its abolition urged by Stevens, 212; abolished in District of Columbia and in Territories, 217; abolished by thirteenth amendment, 225, 226; could have been abolished only by a convulsion, 226-228.

Slaves, of secessionists, proposal of Stevens to emancipate, 213-215; arming of, advocated by Stevens, 215, 222, 223; compensated emancipation of, urged by President, 216, 222; emancipated by Lincoln's proclamation, 217, 218, 222.

Smith, Dr. George, describes effect of Stevens's speech on free schools in Pennsylvania legislature, 39.

South, wishes to profit from Mexican war, 72; exasperated by Castner Hanway case, 90; members of Congress from, exasperated by Stevens, 98, 99; its bad faith in carrying repeal of Missouri Compromise, 102; responsible for reëntrance of slavery into national politics, 110; sees that election of 1860 means its own ultimate decline, 113, 114; urged by Buchanan not to secede, 117; encouraged by Buchanan's message, 118; refuses to consider compromise offers, 124, 129; forms Southern Confederacy, 129, 130; not responsible for existence of slavery, 131; at first disposed to abandon it, 131; later bound to it economically, 132; necessity of blockading, during war, 182, 183; proposal of Stevens to repeal laws creating ports of entry in, 183-185; constitutional status of, according to Stevens, 191, 192; confiscates property of alien enemies, 198, 199; resolution of Stevens to confiscate slaves of, 213; rapid reconstruction of, under Johnson, 249; in hands of rebels, 249; passes laws to reduce negroes to servitude, 250-253; turns North against it by anti-negro laws, 254, 255; proposal of Stevens to rule, through negro vote, 262, 263; rejects fourteenth amendment, 272, 285, 286; turbulent condition of, 289; carpet-bag government in, 299-305; turns to violence to escape negro rule, 304, 305; would have oppressed negroes but for reconstruction, 307; proposal of Stevens to punish leading rebels by confiscation, 323-326.

South Carolina, leads in secession, 115; sends "ambassadors" to ask surrender of Fort Sumter, 118; when reconstructed, passes laws oppressing negroes, 251, 252; carpet-bag government in, 302-304.

Speed, James, resigns from Johnson's cabinet, 278.

Stanton, Edwin M., declines to order inquiry upon responsibility for Ball's Bluff, 193; presents Lincoln's reconstruction plan to Johnson, 241; remains in Johnson's cabinet, 277; requested by Johnson to resign, 329; remains in office to antagonize Johnson, 330; refuses to resign and is removed, 330; his removal not allowed by the Senate, 331; sends message to House, 331; ignores Johnson, and is again removed, 331, 332.

Stephens, Alexander H., in House in 1849, 70.

Stevens, Joshua, father of Thaddeus Stevens, 1 ; his career, 2, 3.

Stevens, Sally, mother of Thaddeus Stevens, 1 ; determines to send Thaddeus to college, 7, 10 ; her courage during pestilence, 8 ; indebtedness of Thaddeus to her, 8.

Stevens, Thaddeus, birth and ancestry, 1, 2 ; learns shoemaking, 2 ; boyhood, 6, 7 ; his ambition kindled by visit to Boston, 7 ; aids his mother in visiting the sick, 8 ; his gratitude to his mother, 8, 9 ; education and school life, 11, 12 ; studies at Dartmouth, 12–16 ; gains literary accuracy, 16 ; at University of Vermont, 16, 17 ; writes a tragedy, 17 ; anecdote of his killing a cow, 17, 18 ; studies law, 19 ; moves to Pennsylvania and teaches school, 19, 20 ; gains a hatred of slavery, 20, 21 ; admitted to Maryland bar, 21–23 ; begins practice at Gettysburg, 24 ; first success in murder case, 25, 26 ; gains an important practice, 26 ; aids fugitive slaves, 26 ; his early political views, 28.

In Pennsylvania Legislature. Joins anti-Masons, 29 ; at national convention, 30 ; slow to admit decline of party, 30, 31 ; elected to Pennsylvania House of Representatives, 31 ; attacks Jackson, 31 ; attacks Masonry, 31–33 ; secures aid for Pennsylvania College, 33 ; reëlected to legislature, 32 ; determines to oppose repeal of free-school bill, 37, 38 ; his great speech against repeal, 38–45 ; turns opinion of legislature, 40 ; thanked by Governor Wolf, 41 ; becomes a leader in the State, 45 ; again reëlected, attacks Masonry, 46 ; introduces bill to charter United States Bank, 47.

In Constitutional Convention. Elected to constitutional convention, 47 ; leads radicals, 47 ; opposes Democratic majority, 47, 48 ; his bitterness in debate, 48 ; opposes discrimination on account of color, 48 ; refuses to sign Constitution, 48 ; upsets a pro-slavery convention at Harrisburg, 49 ; his personalities, 49, 50.

In Legislature. His speech in favor of endowing colleges, 50 ; appointed on Canal Commission, 50 ; said to have used public money to aid Whigs, 51 ; leads Whigs in separate organization of legislature, 52 ; obliged to escape through a window, 52 ; calls the Democrats rebels, 53 ; refuses to submit to Democratic victory, 53 ; at constituents' request, attends legislature, 54 ; refuses to appear before committee to investigate his conduct, 54 ; expelled from House, 54 ; announces himself a candidate for reëlection, 55 ; assails legality of legislature, 55 ; reëlected, 55, 56 ; speech in favor of right of petition, 56 ; favors banks, 56 ; summary of his career thus far, 56 ; greatest debater in the State, 56 ; supports Harrison for president, 56 ; mentioned for a cabinet position, 57 ; involved in financial disaster, 58 ; retires from politics to retrieve himself, 58 ; practices law successfully at Lancaster, 58, 59 ; gains leadership of bar, 59 ; his legal methods, 59, 60 ; continues to defend fugitive slaves, 60 ; opposed by Whig machine in Lancaster, 60, 61; tries to divide Whigs in 1843 on Masonic issue, 61 ; ignored by party, retires from politics, 61, 62 ; his aid begged by Clay in 1844, 62 ; outdoes Webster at a campaign meeting, 62, 63 ; gains increasing legal fame, 64 ; nominated for Congress in spite of the " machine," 64, 65 ; elected, 65.

In House of Representatives.

Advantage of his previous training, 66, 67 ; leads radical Whigs, 70 ; candidate of Free - soilers for speaker, 71 ; attacks proposed Fugitive Slave Law, 75 ; attacks slavery, but admits binding force of constitutional guards, 76–78 ; on economic weakness of slavery, 77, 78 ; urges prevention of slavery extension, 78 ; on Judiciary Committee, 79 ; speech on California, 79 ; again attacks slavery, 79–84 ; on fugitive slaves, 82–85 ; condemns Webster and Clay, 84 ; votes against concessions to South, 85 ; in next Congress receives votes of radicals for speaker, 86 ; speech upon the tariff, 86, 87 ; campaign speech upon Pierce's candidacy, 87 ; praises Scott, 88 ; his last speech, 89 ; retires to private life, 89 ; resumes practice of law, 89 ; Hanway treason case, 90, 91 ; increases his practice, 91 ; his ability and methods described, 92, 93 ; disapproves of compromises of Whig party, 93 ; attends meeting to form Republican party, 93 ; delegate to Republican convention, 94 ; reëlected to Congress, 94 ; his career reviewed to this point, 94, 95 ; feels burden of age, 95, 96 ; taunts Southern members who threaten secession, 98 ; his humorous remarks, 99, 100 ; enjoys the radical feeling of Northern members, 102, 103 ; attacked by Southern members, 103 ; his replies, 103, 104 ; on Committee of Ways and Means, 104 ; tries to prove English policy protective, 105 ; condemns partisan decisions of contested election cases, 106 ; his later partisanship, 107 ; attacks grant to Chiriqui Improvement Company, 108 ; attacks Granada scheme, 109 ; in Republican convention, favors McLean for president, 112 ; votes for Lincoln, 112 ;

presents resolution calling upon President to report on defense of Southern forts, 119 ; votes against compromise propositions, 123 ; his speech against yielding to South, 124–127 ; condemns Buchanan, 125 ; on secession, 126, 127 ; effect of his speech, 127, 128 ; keen to see real situation, 128 ; candidate for a position in Lincoln's cabinet, 136 ; assumes leadership of House, 138 ; at head of Committee on Ways and Means, 139 ; reports first bill for a loan, 144 ; introduces appropriations for army and navy, 145 ; introduces revenue bills, 146 ; defends the land tax, 147 ; withholds vote on Crittenden resolution, 148 ; later, moves to lay it on table, 148 ; supports confiscation bill to free slaves, 149 ; on real object of the war, 149 ; predicts emancipation, 150 ; reports bill for issue of legal tender, 160 ; his speech in its behalf, 160–167 ; argues its necessity, 161–163 ; on its constitutionality, 163, 164 ; and expediency, 164 ; later admits depreciation and inflation, 167 ; opposes payments on bonds in coin, 168 ; his course necessary, 172 ; introduces other financial measures, 174, 178 ; proposes to repeal bill creating Southern ports of entry, 183 ; condemns blockade, 184 ; on England's policy, 184, 185 ; objections to his measure, 186 ; criticises Lincoln's slowness, 186 ; condemns extravagance of administration, 186, 187 ; considers Constitution as set aside in the South, 188, 191 ; ridicules theory of consent of Virginia to admission of West Virginia, 190, 191 ; condemns Lincoln's attitude toward seceded States, 192 ; condemns Lincoln's claim to uncontrolled command over army, 193 ; introduces bill to indemnify President for suspen-

sion of habeas corpus, 194, 195 ;
accuses Democrats of rendering
draft necessary, 196 ; his retort
to Vallandigham, 197 ; comments
on McClellan's ability, 198 ; denies that seceding States are in
Union, 200 ; on belligerent status
of rebels, 201, 202 ; too radical
for his party, 202, 203 ; urges severe punishment of South, 203 ;
favors construction of Pacific railroads, 203 ; opposes useless improvement of Illinois River, 204 ;
urges payment of principal of
debt in coin, 204–206 ; becomes
advocate of paper money, 207 ;
his unquestioned leadership in
House, 208, 209 ; on Crittenden
resolutions, 211 ; favors arming
slaves, 212 ; urges action against
slavery, 213 ; on advantages of
emancipation, 214, 215 ; despises
Lincoln's plan for compensated
emancipation, 216, 217 ; moves
abolition in District of Columbia,
217 ; supports emancipation in Territories, 217 ; urges enlistment of
negroes, 222, 223 ; proposes constitutional amendment abolishing
slavery, 225 ; considers rights of
seceding States destroyed, 229,
230 ; votes against admission of
Louisiana delegates, 231 ; opposes
Lincoln's plan of reconstruction,
233 ; opposes congressional plan
of reconstruction, 235–237 ; votes
reluctantly to nominate Johnson
for vice-president, 244 ; prepares
to oppose Johnson's plan of reconstruction, 257, 258 ; moves
for a committee of inquiry, 258 ;
shows skill by delaying attack,
259 ; his work on Committee on
Appropriations, 260 ; suggests
fourteenth amendment, 260 ; his
constitutional theory of reconstruction, 261, 262 ; proposes to
delay admission of Southern Congressmen until Constitution is
amended, 262 ; urges negro suf-

frage to aid Republicans, 263 ;
condemns results of presidential
reconstruction, 263 ; proposes to
reduce representation of South
if negroes cannot vote, 264 ; attacked by Johnson, 265 ; his scorn-
ful answer to Raymond, 266 ; denies secession to be more than de
facto, 266, 267 ; makes a mock
defense of Johnson, 267–269 ;
ridicules fictions of Johnson's
reconstruction plan, 269, 270 ;
reports fourteenth amendment,
271 ; proposes to admit any State
ratifying fourteenth amendment,
272 ; presents report of Committee
on Reconstruction, 273–275 ; advocates giving negroes suffrage,
275–277 ; suffers from ill-health,
280 ; denounced by Johnson, 281 ;
his sarcastic remarks on Johnson's
tour, 282–284 ; reports reconstruction bill, 285 ; his opinions
inflexible, 286 ; urges courage,
287 ; opposes bill to punish traitors, 287 ; urges immediate establishment of military governments
in South, 288 ; opposes Blaine's
amendment offering amnesty, 290 ;
forces bill through House, 292 ;
not responsible for representation
clause in fourteenth amendment,
294 ; proposes apportionment according to legal voters, 295 ; does
right in discarding legal techni-
calities, 296, 297 ; not a parchment
worshiper, 298 ; his wit and humor, 309–311 ; anecdotes concerning, 311–317 ; his joke upon Cameron, 311, 312 ; defends Fremont
at Blair's expense, 312, 313 ; punc-
tures Conkling's grandiloquence,
313, 314 ; sarcasms upon Brooks
of New York, 314, 315 ; upon
Maynard, 316 ; upon Davis, 316,
317 ; personal appearance, 317,
318 ; fondness for riding, 318: for
study, 319 ; his manner in speaking, 319, 320 ; unsuccessful in
private business, 320 ; his iron-

works burned by Confederates, 321; refuses help offered by friends, 321; reasons for his parliamentary success, 321; compared to Clay, 322; introduces bill to confiscate public lands in Confederate States, 324, 325; his proposition unwise, 325; remark upon Lincoln, 326; considers impeachment impracticable, 326, 327; votes for it, 328; moves impeachment after Johnson's defiance of tenure-of-office act, 333; attacks Johnson bitterly in speech, 334; indifferent as to Grant, 334; chairman of committee to impeach, 335; delivers message to Senate, 335–337; on committee to prepare articles of impeachment, 337; prevented by illness from managing case, 337; responsible for main strength of impeachment, 343; unable to deliver all of his speech, 343, 344, expects Johnson's condemnation, 344; disappointed at defeat of impeachment, 349; continues to participate in business of House, 349; reviews case, 349; praises czar of Russia, 350; remains in Washington during recess to regain strength, 350; remains cheerful to the end, 351; on purchase of Alaska, 351; last moments and death, 352; renominated by Republicans of his district, 353; final estimate of his character, 353.

Personal Traits. Ambition, 7, 19, 37, 61, 94, 136; business ability, 58, 320; cheerfulness, 350; courage, 24, 38, 89, 127, 147; education, 9, 16, 22; generosity, 18, 26, 89; legal ability, 25, 27, 58–60, 64, 91–94; literary tastes, 319; leadership, 138, 145, 208, 259, 286; oratory, 16, 39–44, 63, 79, 85, 160, 319, 336; parliamentary ability, 67, 94, 320–322; partisanship, 47, 48, 51–55, 56, 87, 88, 106, 107,

196; personal appearance, 38, 39, 317, 318; radicalism, 102, 128, 286; sarcasm, 41, 48, 85, 98, 108, 109, 137, 145, 198, 258, 266, 309–317, 325, 334; vindictiveness, 149, 287, 288, 325, 326; wit, 49, 50, 79, 100, 268, 269, 282–284, 309–317.

Political Opinions. Alexander II., 350; anti-Masonry, 29, 31–33, 46, 61; blockade, 183–185; compromise of 1850, 85; compromises of 1860, 121–124, 126; confiscation act, 149, 200, 324; Constitution, 76, 80, 104, 127, 163, 164, 187, 191–194, 200–203, 230, 236, 260, 261, 267, 274, 297, 298; Copperheads, 196, 197; Crittenden resolution, 148, 211, 229; direct tax, 147; education, public, 33, 37, 39–44, 50; emancipation, 212–217; fourteenth amendment, 271, 272, 295; fugitive slaves, 26, 60, 75, 83–85, 89–91; habeas corpus, suspension of, 195; impeachment of Johnson, 326, 332, 336, 337, 343, 344, 349; legal tender, 160–168; negro soldiers, 223; negro suffrage, 260, 263, 264, 276, 277, 295; Pacific railroads, 203; reconstruction, 233, 235, 258, 262, 263, 269, 270, 273–275, 286, 287, 290; secession, 125, 126; slavery, 21, 26, 60, 76–78, 80–82, 127, 149; specie payment, suspension of, 204–208; tariff, 86, 87, 105, 106; war of 1861, 148, 186; West Virginia, 190, 191, 269.

Sumner, Charles, his indictment of slavery surpassed by Stevens, 128; dislikes issue of legal-tender notes, but supports bill authorizing it, 170; denounced by Johnson, 265; on Stevens's terseness, 319; on Johnson's impeachment, 345.

TARIFF, speeches of Stevens upon, 86, 87, 105; effect of act of 1857, 104; passage of act increasing duties, 105, 106.

Taylor, Miles, proposes constitutional amendment in 1861 to prevent negro suffrage, 121.

Ticknor, George, describes President Wheelock of Dartmouth, 13, 14; his difficulty in finding German books, 15.

Toombs, Robert, in House in 1849, 70; his violence, 97.

Trumbull, Lyman, votes against impeachment of Johnson, 345.

UNIVERSITY OF VERMONT, studies of Stevens at, 16-18.

"VAGRANT" acts against negroes, 249-255.

Vallandigham, Clement L., attacks Lincoln, 144, 196; denounces the draft, 196; accused of treason by Stevens, 196, 197; denounces war as for abolition, 218; offers resolutions reaffirming Crittenden's theory of the war, 230.

Vermont, scenery and climate of, 3, 4; democracy of social life in, 5-7; independent spirit of, 6; early education in, 9; carried by anti-Masons, 30.

Virginia, its decay under slavery described by Stevens, 77, 78; said by legal fiction to have consented to formation of West Virginia, 189, 269, 270.

WADE, BENJAMIN F., begs Johnson to be lenient to rebels, 246.

Walker, Amasa, anti-Mason in 1832, 30.

War of Rebellion, financial burdens of, 139-148; its purpose stated by Lincoln, 139, 140; declared to be for Union and not abolition, 148; begins with Southern victories, 152; general finances of, 153-173; blockade in, 183-186; management of, condemned by Stevens, 187.

Washburne, E. B., on Committee on Reconstruction, 259; humor of Stevens at expense of, 315.

Watterson, Henry, classes Stevens and Clay with Pitt and Mirabeau, 322.

Webster, Daniel, imitates Dr. Wheelock, 14; surpassed by Stevens on the stump, 63; his course upon compromise denounced by Stevens, 84; influence of his advocacy of Union, 135.

West Virginia, inhabitants of, set up a state government, 189; applies for admission, 189; constitutional difficulties, 189; legal fiction of Virginia's consent ridiculed by Stevens, 189-191, 269, 270.

Wheelock, John, president of Dartmouth College, 13; described by George Ticknor, 14.

Whig party, its origin, 31; carries Pennsylvania, 46; aided by Stevens as canal commissioner, 51; defeated in election, 51; contests legislature with Democrats, 51-53; defeated in "Buckshot war," 53; supported by Stevens in campaign of 1840, 57; leaders of, in Pennsylvania, antagonize Stevens, 61; persuades Stevens to work in campaign of 1844, 62; members of, join Democrats to pass Compromise of 1850, 85; defeated in 1852, 88; despaired of by Stevens, 93; disappears in 1859, 96.

Wilmot, David, in House in 1849, 69.

Wilson, James F., introduces amendment abolishing slavery, 225; supports impeachment resolution, 333; a manager for the House, 338.

Winthrop, Robert C., in House in 1849, 69; Whig candidate for speaker, 70, 71; defeated by Free-soilers, 71.

Wirt, William, nominated for president by anti-Masons, 30.

Wolf, Governor, thanks Stevens for his speech on free schools, 41; remarks of Stevens upon, 42; refuses to testify before committee of legislature on Masonry, 46.

𝔒𝔥𝔢 𝔑𝔦𝔳𝔢𝔯𝔰𝔦𝔡𝔢 ℜ𝔯𝔢𝔰𝔰

CAMBRIDGE, MASSACHUSETTS, U. S. A.

ELECTROTYPED AND PRINTED BY

H. O. HOUGHTON AND CO.